Praise for THE STRUGGLE TO BE STRONG
and A LEADER'S GUIDE TO THE STRUGGLE TO BE STRONG

"Thought-provoking, easy to read, and often inspiring."

—*School Library Journal*

"*The Struggle to Be Strong* gives voice to youth courageously finding their way. It is an inspiring and provocative work. It comes as a ray of hope at a time when too many youth are pushed out and pushed away.

"What a gem [the] *Leader's Guide* is. Steeped in the science of resiliency, this fine work offers practical strategies for helping beat the odds. I recommend it highly—to both youth and adults."

—**Peter L. Benson, Ph.D.**
　President, Search Institute
　Author of *What Kids Need to Succeed* and *All Kids Are Our Kids*

"The moving stories in *The Struggle to Be Strong* and the accompanying *Leader's Guide* are very important resources for all working to improve the lives of young people. The teens' own words stress the importance of resilience, building on inner strengths, asking tough questions, being one's self, connecting with people who matter, taking charge, using imagination and humor, and doing the right thing. We adults should act on their valuable insights."

—**Marian Wright Edelman**
　President, Children's Defense Fund
　Author of *The Measure of Our Success: A Letter to My Children and Yours*

"This slim but mighty volume is a beacon of hope and good sense for young people and their counselors."

—**Martin E.P. Seligman, Ph.D.**
　Author of *Learned Optimism* and *The Optimistic Child*

"Where does the ability to be strong in the face of adversity come from? The many teen authors of this book wrestle with this question. Their answer? From the inside. It's all about resilience."

—*Youthworker*

"A unique and empowering guide for anyone concerned with youth development. *A Leader's Guide to The Struggle to Be Strong* presents a creative and insightful connection of thirty stories written by teens about their own struggles to the seven resiliencies developed by Sybil and Steven Wolin. This is a masterpiece of strengths-based practice! It is refreshing and truly empowering to find a book that uses kids' struggles and pride to help other kids identify their unique resiliencies. . . . The concrete session plans offer suggestions for group leader preparation and practical suggestions for using the thirty stories in *The Struggle to Be Strong*. An excellent and one-of-a-kind resource for changing hearts and minds! I will immediately give a personal copy to my teachers and group leaders."

—**Erik K. Laursen, Ph.D.**
　Director, United Methodist Family Services Residential Treatment Center
　President, Strength Based Services International

"Explores a world that is the other side of the Taste Berries and Chicken Soup for the Soul series."

—*KLIATT*

"The authors of this guide have touched the heart of human relationships. . . . Those of us who have the privilege of entering the struggle with young folk as they wrestle for resilience and strength are given a dynamic and efficacious structure in which to work. Their work offers hope because its foundation is right and its method is doable."

—The Right Reverend Jane Holmes Dixon
    Suffragan Bishop of the Episcopal Diocese of Washington

"When I feel like whining about my hard life, I instead page through *The Struggle to Be Strong*. After a few paragraphs, I've usually gotten some much-needed perspective from Danielle, Jamel, Craig, or one of the book's other young writers."

—Ronnie Polaneczky
    The Philadelphia News

"*The Struggle to Be Strong* is wonderful—and so needed, as my experience is that adults are talking about youth resilience with other adults, but not nearly enough with kids themselves. This book is the best: Kids to kids."

—Nan Henderson, M.S.W.
    President, Resiliency In Action, Inc.
    Author of *Resiliency in Schools: Making It Happen for Students and Educators*

A Leader's Guide to

THE STRUGGLE TO BE STRONG

How to Foster Resilience in Teens

Sybil Wolin, Ph.D., of Project Resilience
Al Desetta, M.A., and Keith Hefner of Youth Communication

Edited by Bonnie Zucker Goldsmith

free spirit
PUBLiSHiNG®
Works for kids®

ISBN 1-57542-080-5

Resilience in Practice and Youth Communication are registered trademarks of Project Resilience and Youth Communication, respectively.

Some of the information and suggestions in "Guidelines for Group Leadership: Providing a Safe Place," pages 6–10, and the reproducible sheet "Discussion Group Evaluation," page 149, are adapted from *Talk with Teens about Feelings, Family, Relationships, and the Future* by Jean Sunde Peterson (Minneapolis: Free Spirit Publishing, 1995) and are used with permission. Some material in "Handling Sensitive Issues," pages 7–8, is adapted from *A Teacher's Guide to Starting with "I"* by Andrea Estepa (New York: Persea Books, 1997) and is used with permission.

Cover and interior design: Dao Nguyen
Index: Randl Ockey

10 9 8 7 6 5 4 3 2
Printed in the United States of America

Free Spirit Publishing Inc.
217 Fifth Avenue North, Suite 200
Minneapolis, MN 55401-1299
(612) 338-2068
help4kids@freespirit.com
www.freespirit.com

To all adults who have supported youth
in their struggles to be strong.

ACKNOWLEDGMENTS

This leader's guide would not exist without the hard work, talent, and courage of the teens whose stories appear in *The Struggle to Be Strong.* We are moved and inspired by all of them.

Sybil Wolin would like to thank Steven Wolin for his love, help, and partnership in the study of resilience; Jessica Wolin and Benjamin Wolin for their sincere interest in her work; Paul Mahon for his sense of humor and wise counsel; and Jeffrey Jay for his insights about suffering and healing.

Al Desetta would like to thank Leah Weinman for her many insightful contributions to this project, and especially for her help in developing the journal writing exercises and other lessons.

Keith Hefner would like to thank the Hyde School, which helps teens (and their parents) in the struggle to be strong, and Diana Autin for her love and support.

Many foundations, corporations, and others support Youth Communication's work to train teens to tell their stories. One anonymous donor in particular has supported our work to promote resilience. We deeply appreciate her support and insight.

Over the past two years, the work that created *The Struggle to Be Strong* was also supported by the Child Welfare Fund, The DeWitt-Wallace Reader's Digest Foundation, J.P. Morgan, The New York Community Trust, the New York Foundation, The Pinkerton Foundation, the Scherman Foundation, the WKBJ Partnership Foundation, the Ackman Family Fund, the Altman Foundation, the Annie Casey Foundation, the Stella and Charles Guttmann Foundation, the Bay Foundation, Bertelsman Music Group, the Booth Ferris Foundation, the Boyd Foundation, the Catalog for Giving, the Charles Hayden Foundation, Chase Manhattan Bank, Citibank, the Colin Higgins Foundation, Dress Barn, the Fund for the City of New York, the Yip Harburg Foundation, the Heckscher Foundation for Children, the Henry van Ameringen Foundation, the Kenworthy-Swift Foundation, Keyspan Energy, the Joseph E. Seagram and Sons, Inc. Fund, the Merchants & Traders Bank, Manhattan Borough Presidents Ruth Messinger and Virginia Fields, the Metzger-Price Fund, Morgan Stanley, the Samuel I. Newhouse Foundation, the City of New York's Department of Youth & Community Development, the New York Times Company Foundation, the Open Society Institute, the Paul Rapoport Foundation, the Public Welfare Foundation, the Rita and Stanley Kaplan Foundation, New York State Senator Tom Duane, the Stella and Charles Guttmann Foundation, Time Warner, and the Valentine Perry Snyder Fund.

Several people read the manuscript and made important contributions: Chris Henrikson at the DreamYard Drama Project in Los Angeles; Anthony Conelli, former director of Forsyth Satellite High School in New York and currently director of the Students at the Center Project; high school teacher Alison Koffler; Peter Kleinbard, program officer at The DeWitt-Wallace Reader's Digest Foundation; and Tom Brown, the administrative director at Youth Communication.

We would like to thank Youth Communication teacher developer Sean Chambers for the ideas and practical advice he contributed in the early stages of this project. Youth Communication teen writers Cheryl Davis and Phillip Hodge gave many helpful comments on the manuscript.

Finally, we would like to express our thanks to the staff at Free Spirit for their editorial guidance and support during this project: Judy Galbraith, Marjorie Lisovskis, and freelance editor Bonnie Goldsmith.

CONTENTS

FOREWORD x

ABOUT THIS BOOK 1

RESILIENCE: A STRENGTHS-BASED
APPROACH 2

GUIDELINES FOR GROUP LEADERSHIP:
PROVIDING A SAFE PLACE 6

HOW THE SESSION PLANS WORK 11

GETTING STARTED 19

THE SESSIONS 21

INSIGHT
(Asking Tough Questions) 23

I Don't Know What the
Word Mommy Means
Youniqiue Symone 24

Beauty Is More Than Skin Deep
Danielle Wilson 28

Controlling My Temper
Christopher A. Bogle 32

The Answer Was Me
Eliott Castro 36

Color Me Different
Jamal K. Greene 40

INDEPENDENCE
(Being Your Own Person) 45

I Was a Beauty School Sucker
Tonya Leslie 46

My Weight Is No Burden
Charlene Johnson 50

Losing My Friends to Weed
Jamel A. Salter 54

Out, Without a Doubt
Craig J. Jaffe 58

I'm Black, He's Puerto Rican . . .
So What?
Artiqua S. Steed 63

RELATIONSHIPS
(Connecting with People
Who Matter) 67

All Talk and No Action
Elizabeth Thompson 68

She's My Sister (Not Foster)
Tamara Ballard 72

Bonding Through Cooking
Aurora Breville 75

A Love Too Strong
Tamecka Crawford 79

Learning to Forgive
Christopher A. Bogle 83

INITIATIVE
(Taking Charge) 89

It Takes Work to Flirt
Danny Gong 90

My Struggle with Weed
Craig J. Jaffe 94

College Can Be Hell
Tamecka Crawford 97

Poetry Brought Out the Performer
in Me
Shaniqua Sockwell 100

How I Graduated
Angi Baptiste 104

**CREATIVITY
(Using Imagination)** 109

How Writing Helps Me
Terry-Ann Da Costa 110

Why I Live in a Fantasy World
Cassandra Thadal 114

Walking Out the Anger
Tamara Ballard 117

**HUMOR
(Finding What's Funny)** 121

My Hair Is Blue—But I'm Not a Freak!
Lenny Jones. 122

How to Survive Shopping
with Mom
Chris Kanarick. 125

**MORALITY
(Doing the Right Thing)** 129

A Mother to My Mother's Children
Charlene Johnson 130

No One Spoke Up for Irma
Ana Angélica Pines 134

I'm a Seventeen-Year-Old
Therapist
Quantwilla L. Johnson. 138

Soldier Girl
Max Morán 142

How I Made Peace with the Past
Paula Byrd. 145

DISCUSSION GROUP EVALUATION 149

ABOUT YOUTH COMMUNICATION. 150

ABOUT PROJECT RESILIENCE 152

FOR FURTHER READING 154

INDEX 156

ABOUT THE AUTHORS. 162

FOREWORD
by Karen Johnson Pittman

A Leader's Guide to The Struggle to Be Strong is the best book I know that gives adults specific, practical methods for encouraging youth to identify their strengths and to develop resilience. Its beauty is that it can be used by all adults—educators, youth workers, social workers, counselors—who work with youth.

Resilience is one of those buzzwords sometimes associated with achieving dazzling success in difficult circumstances. While this image may be heartwarming, it puts resilience out of reach for most youth. This book presents resilience as an active process of finding one's personal strength to work through pain, setbacks, and challenges. It promotes a concept of resilience that is relevant and useful to all youth as they struggle to persist in the face of the inevitable challenges of their teenage years.

The Struggle to Be Strong links thirty true stories written by teens in the Youth Communication writing program in New York City with seven resiliencies identified by Drs. Sybil and Steven Wolin of Project Resilience in Washington, D.C. The resiliencies—insight, independence, relationships, initiative, creativity, humor, and morality—are important skills and behaviors that can be named, discussed, and learned by all young people.

In my years of working to understand the foundations of successful work with young people, I have learned that one of the most powerful strategies to prevent "problem behaviors" is to provide teens with the skills necessary for adulthood. By offering practical ways of helping young people acknowledge their resilience and build on their strengths, *A Leader's Guide to The Struggle to Be Strong* will help you support teens in their efforts to achieve pride and purpose. The wisdom contained in this volume will make a huge contribution toward helping young people become better prepared and more actively engaged when challenges come their way.

Karen Johnson Pittman is senior vice president of the International Youth Foundation and executive director of its new operating arm, IYF–US, which brings insights and international lessons about youth development into key U.S. discussions. For almost thirty years, Karen has been involved in promoting youth development through research, policy, practice, public speaking, and advocacy. Sociologist, columnist, prolific author, and mother of three, Karen continues to be amazed and inspired by young people's struggles and successes.

ABOUT THIS BOOK

This leader's guide is designed to be used with the anthology, *The Struggle to Be Strong: True Stories by Teens About Overcoming Tough Times*. It explains how you can use the stories in the anthology to build young people's resilience, which we define as persistence in the face of adversity. It provides discussion, writing, role plays, and other group activities to help teens deepen their understanding of how the young authors in *The Struggle to Be Strong* meet the challenges facing them. In the process of reading the stories and participating in the activities suggested here, teens can discover and build on their capacity to face difficult situations and struggle through them.

In these pages, you'll also find introductory material on resilience as a strengths-based approach to working with teens. You'll find suggestions for leading groups through the stories in the anthology and step-by-step instructions for conducting activities for each story. Also included are suggestions for further reading.

This guide is intended for adults who work with teens in many capacities, as teachers, social workers, youth group leaders, clinicians, prevention specialists, counselors, independent living coordinators, and others. It may be especially useful for adults working with groups of teens who face particularly difficult problems and challenges, such as drug abuse, incarceration, foster care, bereavement, and early pregnancy. It can also be used in the regular classroom, as part of the curriculum in social studies, life skills, or language arts. *All* teens can benefit from reading and discussing the stories in *The Struggle to Be Strong*.

When you work with your group, you'll want to have several copies of the anthology on hand. Ideally, each teen will have his or her own copy.

The Struggle to Be Strong and this guide are based on research conducted by Dr. Sybil Wolin and Dr. Steven Wolin at Project Resilience in Washington, D.C., and on work with teens at the Youth Communication youth development program in New York City.

Youth Communication teaches writing, journalism, and leadership skills to teens. The young people trained by Youth Communication, most of whom are New York City public high school students, become writers for two teen-written magazines, *New Youth Connections* and *Foster Care Youth United*. The thirty true stories in *The Struggle to Be Strong* were originally published in these two magazines. (For more about Youth Communication, see pages 150–151.)

Project Resilience advances a balanced view of the effects of hardship on young people, one that includes both the pain and damage that hardship can cause and the strength that can be forged under pressure. Project Resilience conducts research, writes educational materials, and provides training for use in education, treatment, and prevention settings. (For more about Project Resilience, see pages 152–153.)

RESILIENCE
A STRENGTHS-BASED APPROACH

Working with teens can be intensely challenging, particularly when many classrooms and youth groups include kids who have gone through trauma or hardship. As a committed teacher or youth worker, you may sometimes feel overwhelmed by the problems you see.

This guide offers suggestions to help you focus your energy where you can be most effective. You probably have little or no immediate control over the environments or personal challenges of the kids you work with—you can't change their neighborhoods, their families, or their personalities. But you can foster the resilience young people need to persist in the face of challenges. This guide and *The Struggle to Be Strong* can help you find a satisfying and productive middle ground between giving up on teens' problems and feeling like you have to solve them.

In many of the stories, the writers grapple with typical coming-of-age issues, such as dating, body image, friendships, and peer pressure. In others, the writers describe serious adversity, such as disrupted families, abuse, or the death of a parent. Some recall the tangible success of graduating from high school or kicking a drug habit. Others explain their continuing struggle to overcome the obstacles in their way; their ability to persevere is their success.

These are important issues—friendship, loss, self-image, peer pressure—for people of any age. When young people reflect on these issues as described by their peers, they may discover strengths they didn't know they had. They may be motivated to make changes in their own lives.

Resilience, then, is the theme that unites the stories in *The Struggle to Be Strong.* As you and the teens in your group work with these stories, you help them discover and develop their own resilience. Together, the stories in the anthology and the activities in this guide are a powerful, strengths-based way to engage and inspire the young people you work with.

SEVEN RESILIENCIES

Hardship and suffering are inescapable facts of life. Everyone suffers disappointments, losses, rejections, and setbacks. Everyone experiences the death of loved ones. Fortunately, more people respond to hardship with resilience—persistence in the face of adversity—than with collapse.

Resilience isn't a new or rare concept. Everyone is resilient to one degree or another. It's part of being human. What is relatively new is the attempt to pinpoint aspects of resilience that enable some people to survive adversity better than others, and to translate resilience theory into a strengths-based teaching approach.

In this recent work, the precise meaning of resilience is slippery and widely debated. Some define resilience as "success against the odds." Others call it a trait, a capacity, or an approach. In this guide, resilience is defined as persistence in the face of adversity, persistence made possible by specific behaviors that can be named, discussed, and learned.

The stories in *The Struggle to Be Strong* are organized into sections that correspond to seven resiliencies. Think of these resiliencies as a kind of mental map to help you know where to look for strengths in the young people you work with. The seven resiliencies, defined as behaviors, are:

- Insight—asking tough questions

- Independence—being your own person

- Relationships—connecting with people who matter

- Initiative—taking charge

- Creativity—using imagination

- Humor—finding what's funny

- Morality—doing the right thing

Insight

Insight is the habit of asking tough questions and giving honest answers. People with insight see themselves and their circumstances clearly and realistically. They don't avoid difficult or painful truths. They take responsibility for themselves, instead of blaming others for their troubles. Insight is a resilience because it helps people see things as they really are, not as they wish things would be.

Independence

Independence is being one's own person by keeping a safe physical, psychological, or emotional distance from the pressures of family, friends, and circumstances. People with independence stand back and make conscious, thoughtful decisions based on what's best for them—even when that means breaking or limiting connections with important people in their lives. Independence is a resilience because it helps people feel safe knowing they can rely on themselves.

Relationships

Relationships are intimate and fulfilling ties to people who matter. These connections are based on sharing, mutual respect, and openness. People who form lasting relationships learn to balance giving and taking, helping and being helped. They take the risk of trusting others. Relationships are a resilience because they provide a sense of belonging, give opportunities for self-expression, and offer support, understanding, friendship, and sometimes love.

Initiative

Initiative is taking charge and tackling difficulties head-on. People with initiative don't see themselves as helpless victims; rather, they see their problems as challenges they can overcome. They plan, set goals, and take action. Initiative is a resilience because it helps people make a difference in their lives.

Creativity

Creativity is using one's imagination to express oneself and to handle hurt feelings and difficult experiences. People with creativity use their imagination as a safe haven from feelings that seem overwhelming. They channel their feelings in positive, satisfying ways: through art, invention, performance, daydreaming, and so forth. Creativity is a resilience because it helps people manage difficult feelings.

Humor

Humor is finding what's funny in situations that seem sad, tragic, stressful, or embarrassing. People with humor avoid taking themselves and their problems too seriously. They have perspective, seeing their personal troubles in a larger context. Humor is a resilience because it helps people release tension and relieve pain.

Morality

Morality is doing the right thing, even if it's not easy or natural. People with morality see what others need and try to give it to them, even when that means sacrificing their own best or short-term interests. They connect with other people by remembering and doing what's decent and fair. Morality is a resilience because it creates an inner sense of goodness and keeps people from becoming cynical or giving up on the world.

For a handy summary of the seven resiliencies, see pages 160–162 in the anthology.

RESILIENCE AS PARADOX

Each of the seven resiliencies can be found in people who have struggled with hardship. No one emerges from tough circumstances unhurt, but few people are completely destroyed by them. The stories in *The Struggle to Be Strong* show the paradox of vulnerability and strength in the same person at the same time. For instance, Pamela Byrd, in "How I Made Peace with the Past," is angry at her mother and wounded by her rejection. She is also forgiving and compassionate toward her mother. In "Why I Live in a Fantasy World," Cassandra Thadal worries that she spends too much time daydreaming and fantasizing. She also takes great pleasure in her imagination and uses it to help solve her problems.

Seeing resilience as a paradox will enable you to look for strengths in even the most troubled young people and to encourage them to search for examples of their own competence. Your understanding that everyone has strengths communicates an optimism that can "rub off" on teens and be a starting point for constructive change. The seven resiliencies are strong, self-protective behaviors that can serve as a framework for identifying the strengths (or potential strengths) in the young people you work with, no matter what their problems or circumstances.

You show that you take those strengths seriously by giving them names and explaining what they involve and how they help. Referring to these seven resiliencies—talking about strengths—in your group sessions will encourage teens to begin building on what they've got. Reflecting on the components of insight, independence, relationships, initiative, creativity, humor, and morality allows teens to see themselves less as victims by enabling them to reframe painful events in their past to include the persistence and strengths they used to survive.

Reframing

Reframing is viewing an old story from a new perspective. Teens or adults, we all tell ourselves stories about our lives. The stories are never simply collections of facts. They're subjective. We choose what to omit, what to include, and what to make central. Because our life stories are subjective, we can reframe them. The purpose of reframing is to transform destructive stories into constructive ones. Reframing gives people a new way to look at their past. For instance, a story about abuse could be told this way:

"I was helpless as a child. I was a victim of my father's abuse. He damaged me forever. Now I can't do anything right or ever trust anyone again."

Telling the story this way causes considerable pain and can get in the way of a productive life. But there's another way to frame the same story:

"As a child, I was abused. But I was shrewd and used my wits to escape the worst that my father dished out. I've always had the ability to watch out for myself. Today, that skill is one of my greatest strengths."

Telling the story this way centers the plot on the person's pride, bravery, resourcefulness, and determination.

You can use the stories in *The Struggle to Be Strong* not only to help teens see the power of their own stories, but also to emphasize the difference between destructive stories and constructive ones. Use the names of the seven resiliencies to identify and describe the strengths shown by the teen writers and to encourage your group to search for similar strengths in themselves. Point out how people who may once have seen themselves as "bad," "helpless," or "damaged" were really quite capable and resilient. By doing so, you invite teens to see themselves in a new light, and to reframe their own stories in a way that helps them realize the best in themselves.

RESILIENCE AS REALITY, NOT FAIRY TALE

All around us, resilience is confused with dramatic success. Too often, the media feature "superkids"— young adults who grew up in unspeakable circumstances and have defied the odds by achieving dazzling success. These stories make resilience seem like an almost magical process in which problems are simply conquered, once and for all. Typically, the stories downplay the struggle and ignore the pain that may linger, even in successful adulthood.

These kinds of stories are caricatures. They may comfort people who are far removed from the difficult situations facing young people, but they don't help teens who are faced with real challenges. The stories of "superkids" can also demoralize teachers and youth workers, whose successes with teens are not nearly so stunning or complete.

Defining resilience as persistence in the face of adversity avoids the pitfall of associating resilience strictly with success. For many young people, "success" in school, work, and personal life may be a distant dream. They need resilience if they are to eventually achieve that dream, and they need models to show them why and how they should continue to struggle toward it. They need to know that we appreciate what they're going through and respect them for their efforts, whether or not they achieve success as measured by others.

As mentioned earlier, defining resilience as behavioral (that is, something one can learn) and paradoxical (something that includes both pain and pride) allows you as leader to focus on young people's struggles while still honoring their victories. Sometimes success in these stories is obvious, even dramatic—some of the teen writers graduate from high school despite great obstacles, give up a drug or alcohol habit, or read their poetry to an audience for the first time. But for others, success is less clear-cut: to succeed means to maintain hope, courage, and the determination to persevere.

Look, for instance, at Tamecka Crawford, the author of "A Love Too Strong." Tamecka's trust has been betrayed again and again by the adults in her life. She responds by withdrawing from people. Convinced that a social worker in her group home has taken a special interest in her, Tamecka takes the risk of dropping her guard and forming a relationship. When the social worker is transferred, Tamecka is devastated. But she wrestles down her pain and by the end of the story seems ready to risk forming a relationship again. Your students can discuss what strengths Tamecka will need in the future to form satisfying relationships.

What stands out in Tamecka's story and in most of the other stories in The Struggle to Be Strong is the writers' complex and messy struggle—the efforts these kids make to keep going and how they work to bring self-defeating feelings under control. Because the stories are real in this way—because they reflect the conflicts, contradictions, and hard work of resilience—they can help you reach teens whose lives are filled with challenges and to work with them to build their strengths.

GUIDELINES FOR GROUP LEADERSHIP
PROVIDING A SAFE PLACE

One consistent finding in resilience research is that caring adults are critically important in helping young people get through difficult times. The research shows that teens who have overcome hardship rarely describe a savior who solves their problems or rescues them. Rather, they say adults help by conveying that teens matter, validating their strengths, acknowledging their struggles, and showing them reasons to be hopeful.[1]

Discussing the stories in *The Struggle to Be Strong* is a powerful way to convey to teens that they matter. Because the stories are by teens, each honors the competence, experience, and talent of teens. The stories say that teens know things worth hearing. The stories touch on issues that concern teens deeply but that often estrange them from adults, such as family relationships and disruption, peer pressure, sexuality, the use of alcohol and other drugs, racial identity. By facilitating discussion of these issues, you show your group that you're authentically interested in them and that you're open to hearing what they have to say, even on sensitive topics.

OTHER PEOPLE'S STORIES: A SAFE STARTING POINT

The stories in *The Struggle to Be Strong*—because they are other people's stories—allow for the personal distance teens need to consider important issues and relate them to their own lives. The stories hit close to home, but not too close. The teens who wrote them are, in effect, confiding personal aspects of their lives to your group. They're acknowledging their problems, but they've cast those problems in a narrative form that took a lot of thought and time.

These teen authors have considered not only their problems but also how they've dealt with the problems, how they felt, and how various experiences changed them. The stories share complicated reflections that involve actions, memories, feelings, reactions, and the power of hindsight. Talking about these stories is a way for your group members to explore issues in their own lives at a safe distance.

For example, when you discuss Jamel A. Salter's story, "Losing My Friends to Weed," discussion can range widely over Jamel's choices and behavior without making teens feel pressured to reveal their own experiences with drugs or peer conflicts. When you consider Artiqua S. Steed's story, "I'm Black, He's Puerto Rican . . . So What?" teens can reflect on the pressures Artiqua felt to break off an important relationship without necessarily confiding their own views about interracial dating.

The stories can also be a bridge between you and your group members because they offer a way for you to listen to their deepest concerns. When you show teens that you're willing to listen to them, you may be amazed (or even somewhat unnerved) at what they'll share with you. You'll find students coping with intense peer pressure, or pressure from parents who are trying to live through their kids' achievements. You'll find young people who long for parents to pay attention to them, or who are in abusive relationships. You'll find teens burdened by secrets, such as family members with drinking or mental health problems.

In more distressed neighborhoods, you'll typically find higher frequencies of abuse, of families that have spun out of control due to unemployment, drugs, or ill health. You'll find more kids who are in foster care or not living with parents. In many communities you'll find kids who are struggling with language and immigration issues.

In many classrooms and youth programs, the conditions troubling teens are an unacknowledged backdrop to the "real work" of education, enrichment, recreation, and so on. For young people,

---

[1]See, for example, Emmy E. Werner and Ruth S. Smith, *Vulnerable But Invincible: A Longitudinal Study of Resilient Children and Youth* (New York: McGraw-Hill, 1982; New York: Adams, Banister, Cox, 1989); and Gina O'Connell Higgins, *Resilient Adults: Overcoming a Cruel Past* (San Francisco: Jossey-Bass, 1994).

however, these issues are not a backdrop—they are front and center. Teens think about them all the time. They hamper academic work. They disrupt effective participation in group activities.

The stories in *The Struggle to Be Strong* provide a way for you to engage the teens you work with in issues that are central to their lives. They give you a window into what teens are thinking and feeling, and they can help teens open up.

You can tap the full potential of *The Struggle to Be Strong* by providing a safe place where the stories can be discussed. Your group will feel safe if you:

- establish group guidelines

- offer respect

- acknowledge pain, but talk about strengths.

ESTABLISH GROUP GUIDELINES

Clear group guidelines provide a set of shared understandings about the way group sessions will be run. They let your group know what to expect from you and from each other. By giving sessions structure and predictability, guidelines help group members feel safe. As a result, teens will be more willing to participate and to benefit from the stories and related activities.

You, your school, or your agency may already have guidelines in place for class or group discussions. If so, before beginning work on the first story, make sure everyone understands them and agrees with them. If not, you might want to discuss these general guidelines with your group:

- Group members listen to and respect each other.

- Everyone is welcome to share thoughts and feelings, but no one has to share.

- Everyone in the group should feel valued and accepted. All points of view are welcome. There are no "wrong" answers.

Confidentiality

Confidentiality can be important in establishing a safe environment for learning and discussion. You may want to ask teens not to share information outside the group. However, depending on your setting, expectations about maintaining confidentiality can vary. As a leader, you should know where you stand on this issue and what's realistic to expect in your environment. In a classroom setting, confidentiality rules can be almost impossible to enforce, while in more intimate, "quasi-therapeutic" settings, such as family groups, support groups, or 12-step programs, they're more likely to be heeded. In general, you'll find that teens will know how much to reveal about themselves during discussion and in writing.

Be aware that reading and discussing personal stories by their peers raises the likelihood that teens in your group will reveal significant issues in their lives. For the most part, frank and open discussion of these realities can help spur personal growth and change. If you have concerns about maintaining confidentiality in your group, consult your colleagues or supervisor for advice.

Handling Sensitive Issues

Several of the stories in *The Struggle to Be Strong* deal with sensitive emotional issues such as drug abuse, parental neglect, and depression. Your group may reveal very personal connections to these issues in writing and during discussions. At times, a discussion may veer into an area that's too emotional, private, or sensitive for your group to handle. Don't hesitate to stop such a discussion and return to the topic another day, or to talk in private with the teen or teens involved.

You'll need to decide the degree to which you want to encourage teens to talk or write about sensitive subjects, such as sexuality or drug use. You can then tailor discussion questions and writing activities accordingly. Whatever approach you take, consider asking group members if they have any questions or concerns about confidentiality or privacy (for example, there may be information they're comfortable sharing with you but wouldn't want their families or classmates to know about). Also, tell them any concerns you have about information you wouldn't feel comfortable keeping to yourself or that you're legally obligated to report. If there are any subjects you feel are inappropriate for an assignment, you should make that clear. Finally, assure students that sharing their writing with classmates is entirely voluntary.

Keep in mind that the purpose of these group sessions is not to force members to reveal private thoughts and experiences, but to reflect on the meaning and personal relevance of stories by teens who've overcome tough times. As mentioned, the stories provide a safe arena for teens to engage important issues without revealing specifics of their own lives. When students do choose to be personally revealing, the benefits of such candor usually far outweigh any negative consequences. While you need to be aware of problematic situations that may develop, be aware also of the many positive interactions that can evolve from frank, open engagement of issues central to the lives of teens today.

Know When to Seek Outside Help

From time to time, reading and discussing personal stories about sensitive issues may prompt teens in your group to reveal private information about their lives. If a teen's disclosure troubles you, tell your principal or supervisor. You may also need to seek help from a counselor, social worker, or therapist.

If a teen reveals that he or she is living in an abusive situation, you have an obligation to report what you've heard. Regulations governing the reporting of child abuse differ from state to state. Many states have specific guidelines identifying certain professionals as "mandatory reporters." Check with your principal or the head of your agency to determine the proper course of action and your responsibilities if such a situation should arise.

Do

- use the stories to connect with teens
- establish group guidelines
- know where you stand on confidentiality
- decide how you'll handle sensitive issues
- know when to ask for help

Don't

- pressure teens to talk about their lives
- pursue a discussion if it goes into overly sensitive areas

OFFER RESPECT

Being respected makes teens feel safe. Your respect lets them know that you see them as important and valuable. According to Bonnie Benard, who writes widely on the topic of resilience, respect figures heavily in "turnaround relationships" that help teens to change course and improve their lives.[2] There are specific ways of talking to and acting toward teens that leaders can use to convey respect.

Show interest in what teens think. One of your major roles is to be a sounding board for the range of views these stories will raise. You don't need to have all the answers. Listening and responding respectfully assures teens of your interest and concern.

Some teens may be eager contributors to discussion. Others won't respond at first—they're waiting to see if you're serious, if you can be trusted. They'll watch you, and they'll watch each other. By listening to what they say, not getting sidetracked by what you want them to say, and watching their body language and facial expressions, you'll get a sense of how to encourage participation.

After they've looked you over and sized you up, a few brave souls will begin to show interest. They'll engage tentatively in discussion, volunteering more about themselves. They'll talk to you alone when the group session or class is over. They may take advantage of the privacy that writing offers to be more open about their lives and concerns.

Wait for teens to talk. As you lead your group through discussions and activities, be sure to listen to what members have to say. Don't rush to closure or be too hasty in moving along to another topic. Let teens react to the stories, or even tell their own stories. Ask questions to clarify what you don't understand. When group members see that you're interested in them and respect their

---

[2]Bonnie Benard, "How to Be a Turnaround Teacher," in *Reaching Today's Youth, The Community Circle of Caring Journal* 2:3 (spring 1998), 31–35.

reactions to what they've read—and that your goal is to understand them and help them develop their own personal strengths—they'll keep talking.

Emphasize choice, freedom, and personal responsibility. It can be difficult at times to withhold judgment about what you hear. You may worry that refraining from criticizing behavior or telling teens what they should be doing is condoning what shouldn't be condoned, such as smoking marijuana or misusing alcohol.

However, being critical, passing judgment, and resorting to your adult authority can destroy the feeling of respect that teens need to participate and benefit fully from group meetings. When you work with the stories in *The Struggle to Be Strong,* you're not being irresponsible when you refrain from judging. (This isn't the same as staying uninvolved if you suspect something is happening to a student that you must report to a colleague or outside professional. See "Handling Sensitive Issues" and "Know When to Seek Outside Help," pages 7–8.) While the stories show how difficult being a teen can be, each one is infused with positive values— forgiveness, devotion, self-control, responsibility, the importance of education, and much more. Each young writer has clear strengths and the determination to work through problems. Without sacrificing your role as leader, you can safely let these stories speak for themselves. Each conveys positive values that young people need to hear about—in a language they'll understand and accept.

Do

- show interest in what teens think
- wait for teens to talk
- emphasize choice, freedom, and personal responsibility

Don't

- fish for answers you want to hear
- take sides
- rush to closure
- judge or criticize

ACKNOWLEDGE PAIN, BUT TALK ABOUT STRENGTHS

Teens who have faced even minor adversity often want you to know how bad they feel. Sometimes they reveal their hurt by treating others as unjustly as they've been treated. Sometimes it just shows on their faces, or in symptoms like depression, an inability to concentrate and learn, or anxiety. Sometimes, if you have a trusting relationship with them, teens will tell you about their hurts directly.

No matter how group members let you know they're feeling bad, you'll help them most by fostering their resilience through acknowledging their pain, crediting the efforts they're making to prevail, and conveying your expectation that they can make it despite the obstacles in their path. Teens don't want our pity, our diagnostic label, or our analysis of how they've gone wrong. More often than not, they don't even want our advice.

As you work with *The Struggle to Be Strong,* you'll see the need, sometimes, to walk a fine line—to acknowledge the hard times and painful feelings experienced by group members while focusing equally on their strengths and their accomplishments. The suggestions in this guide will help you find the right balance.

Focus on each story's underlying theme of resilience. The stories present enough variations on the themes of personal challenges and adversity to touch everyone in your group. However, one of your main jobs as group leader is to remind teens that pain and setbacks are only part of each story. The other part, the underlying theme, is about strength and perseverance. When you point out the strengths of the teen writers, you help group members recognize their own strengths and see ways to act on them.

Use the names of the resiliencies. If you ask teens what their strengths are, they're likely to respond as many adults would, with a blank look or an embarrassed shrug of the shoulders. Some may even suspect that your question is a prelude to a speech about what they should be doing.

The resiliencies provide a framework for you to show group members what they, and other teens like them, are doing. The names of the seven resiliencies are common, everyday words. The definitions are written in a language that is natural and meaningful for teens. Use the names and definitions as you work with the stories. They'll give you the vocabulary you need to point out the strengths of the teen writers and to help your group members see and talk about their own strengths.

For example, when they read Chris Kanarick's story, "How to Survive Shopping with Mom," they'll see how humor can get people through embarrassing situations. When they read "Color Me Different," they'll see how insight, or asking tough questions, helps Jamal K. Greene deal with being unfairly stereotyped; they may work up the courage to ask some tough questions of their own. When they read "How Writing Helps Me," they'll see how Terry-Ann Da Costa's sense of loss diminishes as she uses her creativity to express herself and help others. They may be encouraged to think of times when creativity helped them.

Emphasize possibilities and opportunities for personal growth. The stories are paradoxical, mingling strengths with vulnerabilities, victories with setbacks. Resist getting sidetracked by the problems described; instead, encourage students to see how the authors find the possibility and opportunity for growth in their situations. When you do, group members may begin to connect the strengths they see in the stories with their own lives. They may even be pleasantly surprised or relieved to see that you're more interested in talking about what teens do right than in what's wrong with them.

Note each author's capacity to grow and learn from experience. Many of the teen writers describe the obstacles they've faced in their lives—and for some, those obstacles were considerable: living on the streets, living in foster care, facing peer pressure to abuse alcohol or drugs, having a sick or addicted parent. Each writer, however, shows the capacity to grow and learn from experiences, even bad or painful ones. Many advise their readers to look at their own problems as learning experiences that can make them stronger. Encourage group members not to dwell on the obstacles described but to focus on ways the writers gain strength and maturity from their experiences.

Do

- focus on each story's underlying theme of resilience
- name the resiliencies
- emphasize possibilities and opportunities
- note each author's capacity to grow and learn from experience

Don't

- lament the pain of the authors or group members
- get sidetracked by problems
- dwell on obstacles

HOW THE SESSION PLANS WORK

This guide presents activities for each of the stories in *The Struggle to Be Strong* in sequential order. However, the success of your sessions doesn't depend on starting with the first story and going sequentially through the thirtieth story. As mentioned earlier, the stories are grouped in sections, each section highlighting one of the seven resiliencies. After previewing the stories, you may decide that some are more relevant or appropriate for your particular group than others. You may also find that certain activities work better with your group. The anthology is flexible enough to accommodate your needs. (For stories on specific topics, see "Guide to Topics" on pages 171–173 of the anthology.)

Similarly, there are probably as many ways to use the stories in *The Struggle to Be Strong* as there are leaders. You have your own teaching style and strengths, and should feel free to lead group sessions in ways that suit you and meet the needs of the teens you're working with. Since many leaders appreciate ideas and approaches they can use immediately, without burdensome preparation, the sections that follow offer specific suggestions for working with the stories.

It's important that you have several copies of the anthology on hand for teens to use. Ideally, each group member will have his or her own copy and bring it to each session. Teens should come to each session with writing materials. You may want them to bring notebooks they can use as journals. If you'll be writing along with your group during the freewriting activities (see pages 14–15), you'll want to bring your own notebook or journal. You'll also find it useful to have a chalkboard or an easel. A few group activities include materials lists.

If, after your program is finished, you'd like group members to give you feedback about the group, use the "Discussion Group Evaluation" on page 149.

The chart on this page presents a typical sequence of preparation and group activities. Suggested activity times are based on a one-hour session; you'll need to adapt these to your specific circumstances. Times can be adjusted if, for example, journal writing or other writing activities are done at home. Another option is to take two sessions to cover a story, leaving more time for discussion, writing, and an additional role play.

You might want to refer to the chart as you read the descriptions of the activities in the following pages. Please note:

- Each set of story sessions begins with guidelines for a discussion of the particular resilience that the stories will illustrate.

- Each story session begins with a section of information and suggestions for leaders called "Preparing to Lead the Activities." These are followed by the various group activities.

- Each set of story sessions ends with a summary activity asking teens to reflect on and compare the stories in the section.

A Typical Session

This plan for leading the session on the first story in the Insight section, "I Don't Know What the Word Mommy Means" by Youniqiue Symone, shows a typical sequence of activities.[3]

PREPARING TO LEAD THE ACTIVITIES

Story Summary
A Moment of Reflection
How Insight Works in the Story
    Seeing Youniqiue's Insight
    Why Insight Is a Struggle for Youniqiue
Useful Concept Words

ACTIVITIES

1. **Freewriting: Finding Yourself in the Story** (10 minutes)
2. **Discussion: Understanding Events** (5 minutes)
3. **Discussion: Understanding Issues** (10 minutes)
    Youniqiue's Insight
    Connecting with the Issues
4. **Role Plays** (15 minutes)
5. **Writing Activities: Taking It Further** (10 minutes)
6. **In Your Journal: Making It Personal** (10 minutes)

---

[3]Please note that the number and type of group activities vary from story to story.

The Value of Writing

Reading and discussion may seem like natural choices to use with your group. However, writing may seem a less obvious or practical choice—even somewhat intimidating—if you don't customarily use it in your work with teens. When group members are reluctant writers or have limited skills, you may choose to focus most of your group time on discussion, role play, and other group activities. However, writing, even in modest amounts, can be an extremely effective tool for encouraging reflection in all teens, including those with limited writing ability or experience.

Research has shown that writing about important personal experiences and complex feelings is difficult, but ultimately very helpful when the writer links events and emotions.[4] During discussions, teens may simply vent their emotions or describe what happened to them. Writing allows them to reflect privately and helps them make deeper connections between their thoughts, feelings, and experiences.

Louise DeSalvo makes this point in her excellent analysis of the writing process, *Writing as a Way of Healing:* "Writing that describes traumatic or distressing events in detail *and* how we felt about these events then and feel about them now is the only kind of writing about trauma that clinically has been associated with improved health. . . . [S]imply writing about traumatic events or venting our feelings about trauma without *linking* the two does not result in significant health or emotional benefits. . . .

We must write in a way that links detailed descriptions of what happened with feelings—then and now—about what happened." [Emphasis in original.] In support of her point, DeSalvo cites research showing that "the more days people wrote, the more beneficial were the effects from writing. And these benefits occurred despite educational level: people with sixth-grade educations benefited as much as those with advanced degrees."[5]

Perhaps you've had the personal experience of keeping a diary or journal, or writing letters. If so, you know that writing can reveal things about yourself that weren't obvious before. Using writing to make sense of chaotic feelings can give them a form and order that allow you to have distance from them, and thus more control over them.

Writing can serve this function for the teens in your group. Activities are designed for students with a wide range of ability and interests. Responses need not be lengthy (or have perfect spelling or grammar); a few sentences can prompt valuable reflection. As necessary, assure teens that you're looking not for length but for their thoughtful engagement with the material.

For further suggestions on using writing, see "Freewriting: Finding Yourself in the Story," pages 14–15, "Writing Activities: Taking It Further," page 17, and "In Your Journal: Making It Personal," page 17.

---

[4]See, for example, the following work by James W. Pennebaker: "Confession, Inhibition, and Disease," in *Advances in Experimental Social Psychology,* Vol. 22, edited by Leonard Berkowitz (New York: Academic Press, 1989); *Opening Up: The Healing Power of Confiding in Others* (New York: Morrow, 1990); "Writing Your Wrongs," *American Health* 10, no. 1 (1991), 64–67; "Writing About Emotional Experiences as a Therapeutic Process," *Psychological Science* 8, no. 3 (1997), 162–66.

[5]Louise DeSalvo, *Writing as a Way of Healing: How Telling Our Stories Transforms Our Lives* (San Francisco: Harper, 1999), 25–26. DeSalvo cites the work of Pennebaker. See the preceding note.

LEADING YOUR GROUP

Following are descriptions of each preparation and activity section.

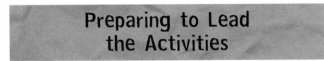

Preparing to Lead the Activities

Story Summary

Here you'll find the gist of the story so you can review the main points right before you discuss it with your group.

A Moment of Reflection

This section asks you to consider from your own perspective the questions group members will address during freewriting (see "Freewriting: Finding Yourself in the Story," pages 14–15). "A Moment of Reflection" helps you bridge the gap between you and your group, inviting you to remember your own challenges as a teen or to focus on a current dilemma or set of circumstances. The goal is to put you in a frame of mind that will make working with the stories a more satisfying experience. For example, when you reflect in advance on your own experiences with seeking independence, you're in a better position to explore that theme as it comes up in your group.

How the Resilience Works in the Story

Seeing the Writer's Resilience

This section provides a clear, concise description of how a particular resilience works for the writer of each story. As mentioned, many of the teen writers demonstrate more than one resilience, but each story highlights or features a particular resilience. For example, in "I Don't Know What the Word Mommy Means," as Youniqiue Symone strives to forge her own future, insight is her most crucial resilience, although independence and initiative also play roles. "Seeing Youniqiue's Insight" focuses on those parts of Youniqiue's story that emphasize insight.

Why the Resilience Is a Struggle for the Writer

This section goes to the heart of the stories in *The Struggle to Be Strong*, showing the obstacles that get in the way of each writer's resilience. The commentary emphasizes that resilience is not about overcoming problems once and for all, but learning to deal with them day by day. For the teens you work with, resilience is often a matter of winning small victories, rather than having a single dramatic success. This section highlights the writer's struggle so you can help group members identify with the person, rather than feel intimidated by a success that, at first glance, might seem beyond reach.

Useful Concept Words

Building a vocabulary of resilience is an essential part of *The Struggle to Be Strong*. In this section, you'll find a list of several "concept words" that are central to a story's themes, along with definitions for each word and sentences relating the words to the story. To assist students in understanding and discussing the story, you may want to write these words on the board and explain them when they're used in a discussion question or activity (where the words are shown in italics).

The seven resiliencies provide a vocabulary of strengths that teens can use to help understand how they themselves meet challenges. By devoting time to the concept words specific to each story, you offer group members an additional tool for describing thoughts, feelings, and situations. You also support their academic success. Since the words are presented in the context of a story teens can relate to, they're more likely to be retained than are words from a conventional vocabulary list.

(If teens are unfamiliar with any of the slang terms or other special language in the stories, direct them to the glossary on page 170 of the anthology.)

Activities

Discussion, writing exercises, and group activities are all intended to help teens develop a deeper understanding of each story. Most important, they're designed to help group members see the relevance of the resiliencies to their own lives. Feel free to pick and choose among these activities, adapting them to your own style and objectives. For example, many of the discussion questions can be used as writing assignments, and vice versa.

If, as suggested in this guide, you choose to discuss the stories before moving on to the other exercises, you'll find that the discussion will help teens participate fully in the writing, role play, and other group activities that follow. Group and writing activities, in turn, build on the discussion that precedes them. Similarly, freewriting (discussed next), when used as your first session activity, can enrich the discussions and activities that follow.

Freewriting: Finding Yourself in the Story

After teens have read the story, a few minutes of freewriting about their personal connection to the story's main theme can enrich the activities that follow. Freewriting tends to deepen reflection and stimulate discussion. It can make the difference between an aimless discussion and one in which teens are really engaged. Think of freewriting as a warm-up not only for discussion, but also for the various activities that follow.

In freewriting, teens are freed from customary rules in the interest of getting their thoughts and feelings down on paper. Correct grammar, spelling, and punctuation don't matter in freewriting. The only rule is to write without stopping. Writing nonstop frees up emotions and ideas. When teens are stuck, tell them to write, "I don't know what to say" over and over, until something occurs to them. Limit writing to a brief amount of time (usually 90 seconds per question, two minutes maximum), so there's no pressure to write at length. These techniques—deemphasizing correctness, writing without stopping, and writing for only a brief time—free teens to go straight to the heart of an issue and to tap directly into what they feel and think.

Expect all group members to participate in freewriting, but emphasize that doing so won't be hard and that they don't have to share what they write. Since the only requirement is for the writer to keep his or her pen moving, freewriting is easy for all teens, including unskilled or reluctant writers.

The format of each freewriting exercise is a statement beginning with "Think of a time when." This statement anchors the group in the freewriting theme by asking them to think about a particular incident or circumstance in their lives—one that is linked to a major theme of the story. Questions about the incident or circumstance follow. Pause after each question, allowing 90 seconds for writing (two minutes maximum).

Freewriting requires only writing materials, a watch or clock, and clear instructions. It's best if everyone has read the story first, because the purpose of freewriting is to encourage a personal connection with the story's themes. It's suggested that you write along with your group, perhaps in a journal you keep for these sessions. (The statement and questions are similar to those you considered in "A Moment of Reflection," described on page 13.) Whatever you jot down, even a few short sentences, can help highlight the emotional common ground between you and your group. If you'll be writing, have handy your own journal and tell students you'll be participating.

The first time you present this activity, explain the procedure. Say:

To connect with the themes of this story, we're going to do something called freewriting. Freewriting is just that: writing that lets us feel free to write whatever comes to mind. Here's how it works. First I'll read a statement for you to think about. Then I'll read several questions. These all have to do with the basic ideas of the story we're going to discuss—but from your own point of view. After each question, I'll pause to give you time to write your answers. Don't worry about spelling or grammar. Just write freely for 90 seconds without stopping. Let your ideas flow. If nothing at all comes to mind, write "I have nothing to say" until something occurs to you. Remember that this writing is private. It's up to you whether you choose to share it with the group.

After teens are done writing, allow time for volunteers to either read what they've written or to discuss their feelings about freewriting if they prefer not to reveal specifics. (Occasionally, you may want to read some of what you write to help build trust and encourage discussion.) If no one volunteers, ask them to think about what they've written as the group begins discussing the story. Teens are specifically asked to read over their freewriting silently before you ask certain questions from the "Understanding Issues" section (see below).

Even if you've never used writing in your work with teens, try freewriting. You may be pleasantly surprised by the results. Feel free to substitute your own topics as you become more comfortable with this technique.

Avoiding Roadblocks

While many of the stories in *The Struggle to Be Strong* present typical coming-of-age issues, others deal with more emotional and potentially controversial subjects: drug abuse, eating disorders, sexual identity. For those stories (and for stories in which the writer's behavior or actions could be misconstrued), you'll find a boxed note with guidelines on possible reactions from teens that could derail discussion. Suggestions are offered on ways to work around such "roadblocks"; for example, by focusing discussion on how the writer demonstrates a particular resilience or on other important themes in the story.

Discussion: Understanding Events

Basic comprehension of the story is essential before teens can reflect on themes and issues. The first set of suggested discussion questions focuses on concrete details of plot. (Reviewing these questions will also help teens who haven't read the story get an idea of what you're talking about.) Depending on your objectives, you can use these questions to help teens develop their reading comprehension.

Discussion: Understanding Issues

Questions here move group members to the underlying themes of the story and then to the relevance of those themes to their own lives. The first set engages teens in reflection on the writer's resilience, the behavior that allows him or her to overcome obstacles and make changes. The second set encourages teens to make connections between their own experiences, conflicts, and strengths and those of the writer. By helping them make these connections, you increase their capacity to recognize and build on their resilience.

You can adjust the emotional temperature of the discussion, depending on your own comfort level and situation and how the group is responding. Teens should not be expected to confide intimate experiences or private feelings during a group discussion. Questions are organized to allow a range of responses. (See "Handling Sensitive Issues," pages 7–8).

Role Plays

Most stories include one or two suggested role plays that can help teens more directly explore and experience the ideas in the stories. Role play helps them connect with the stories in ways that go beyond reading, discussion, and writing. Not every teen in your group will want to participate in the role plays, nor do they need to (unless participation is a requirement in your group). But in every group there will be teens who want to participate—who, in fact, especially enjoy this kind of activity. Observers contribute by participating in the suggested discussion following each role play. Notice that each role play section begins with an objective connecting the scenarios with the main ideas of the story.

Guidelines for Role Plays[6]

Objectives

"Doing" is a powerful learning tool. Role playing can make the stories and resiliencies come alive for teens. By introducing the ideas of dramatic conflict and dramatic need, role plays enable teens to connect emotionally with the conflicts and challenges faced by the writers. Participating in role plays encourages teens to think and act on their feet, loosen up creatively, and become comfortable with each other. Role plays also give them practice in listening carefully and working cooperatively.

Procedure

The first time your group tries a role play, explain the purpose of the activity: to help them better

---

[6]These guidelines are adapted from a drama curriculum used with teens at the DreamYard Drama Project in Los Angeles and are used with permission. Thanks to Chris Henrikson of DreamYard for sharing the curriculum and for his assistance in developing the role plays in this book. For more information on role plays or on using a drama curriculum with teens, contact DreamYard L.A., P.O. Box 3151, Santa Monica, CA 90404.

understand the story. Point out that you're not looking for great performers—merely for two and sometimes three volunteers to show what characters from the story would do and say in a certain situation. Tell them that each role play will last no more than five to ten minutes.

Also discuss the role of observers. Tell group members that they are to listen closely, refrain from talking, think about what they would say or do in the same situation, and be ready to discuss the role play when it's over.

Establish guidelines for role plays. For example:

• No physical contact between role players.

• Players should follow the role play description, but they're also free to introduce information that seems appropriate to the character and the scene.

For each role play:

1. Before beginning, review the basics of the story.

2. Read the scenario aloud. Allow time for questions or comments.

3. Ask for volunteers. If no one volunteers, you might offer to play one part yourself; this will usually induce someone to join you. In most groups, however, there are likely to be at least two people so drawn into the story's themes that they're eager to do the role play.

4. Once you have volunteers, quickly review with each person what his or her *dramatic need* is in the scene. The characters' needs (what they want, as most scenarios phrase it) establish a clear conflict that should drive the action of the role play. Players are to keep their character's need or want in mind as they act out the scene. What they say should be related to getting the need or want satisfied. For example:

• Youniqiue wants her mother to know how angry she is. Youniqiue's mother wants to avoid the confrontation.

• Eliott's friend drinks a lot but wants to convince Eliott that he or she doesn't have a problem with alcohol. Eliott wants to convince his friend that the drinking is out of control and that the friend should give it up.

Before a role play you might list each character's dramatic need on the board. Be sure players and observers are clear about the scene. Suggest that players refer to the board if they get stuck during the role play and don't know what to say.

Be prepared to stand back and let teens act out their roles and gain momentum. Provide prompts and guidance as necessary. If a role play seems stalled, you may want to intervene. Try these strategies:

• Ask the players to check the board and review their dramatic needs in the scene.

• Ask observers for suggestions.

• If a player seems out of ideas, ask an observer to take his or her place in the scene.

• If a role play gets out of hand because of silly or inappropriate remarks, note that such remarks are not in character.

Some scenarios concern sensitive situations. Remind group members that they're not playing themselves—they're playing and interpreting characters. No one should be made uncomfortable during a role play, so if you see that happening, end the activity.

Discussion

When the scene has played itself out, encourage teens to reflect on what they saw and how they interpreted it. Use the suggested questions that follow each role play, or substitute your own. You might also ask the players how they felt while playing their respective characters.

Follow-up

It's sometimes useful to ask for new volunteers to play the same scene again. This allows teens to compare the impact and meaning of the scene when it's played by different actors. You might also ask group members to describe in writing their reactions to the role plays or to compose new scenarios.

As time permits, encourage your group to create and perform new role plays on the resilience themes in the stories. These scenarios can be variations on the stories or come from teens' own experiences.

Group Activity

Some stories include a group activity instead of or in addition to role plays. Like role plays, these activities encourage teens to more directly explore and experience the ideas in the stories. Each group activity includes a specific objective and a step-by-step procedure. Each is followed by suggested discussion questions asking teens to consider what they learned from the activity and to explore the connection between the activity and the story.

Writing Activities: Taking It Further

All writing activities can be geared to the needs and level of your group. To encourage students to write, downplay grammar and spelling errors. Instead, look hard at the content of what they write, and don't be shy about asking them to strive to express their ideas as clearly as they possibly can. Once students believe that you care about their ideas, they'll probably be willing to listen to your suggestions about other aspects of their writing, if making such suggestions is part of your role.

Writing activities can be done individually, in small groups, or at home. The objective for each activity links the writing topic to themes and ideas from the story. The first activity for every story asks teens to describe the writer's resilience in their own words. They do this in the form of a letter written as though they were the story writer. Other writing activities challenge teens to explore the story's themes from a variety of perspectives and to make a personal connection to them.

Keep in mind that one paragraph is sufficient for most of the activities, making them appropriate for teens with limited writing ability. However, depending on your group and your objectives as a leader, topics can also be used for advanced writing assignments, such as essays, formal letters, opinion pieces, or reports. If you choose to evaluate writing activities, don't hesitate to hold group members to high standards of expression and thinking. Teens are usually grateful for that kind of attention and direction.

When activities are completed, you can invite volunteers to read their work to the group. You might also discuss how teens felt about the purpose and value of the writing.

See "The Value of Writing," page 12, for more information.

In Your Journal: Making It Personal

Writing in a journal provides teens the opportunity to reflect on their personal connection with the stories. Journals are a means of private enrichment—not essential, but valuable to teens' understanding. As always, you can adapt journal writing to fit the goals and needs of your group. You may want members to write in their journals after every story, only after particular stories, or whenever they choose to.

As with freewriting, you'll want to assure group members that their privacy will be respected. If your program or objectives require you to collect and evaluate journals, be sure teens understand this so they can decide how revealing to be in entries. Emphasize that you will be the only person reading the journals and tell students what you'll be looking for. Some leaders make journals optional and prefer that teens keep them private.

However you use journal writing, remember that it's not the length of the entries that makes them effective, but the degree to which teens become emotionally connected with the writing. One way of fostering that connection is to encourage teens to move beyond merely describing events or people in their lives; instead, challenge them to remember what they were *feeling* in reaction to those people and events.

Directing a Typical Group Session

Most group sessions, no matter how well-planned, take on a life of their own. As a leader you will often have to go with the flow, while also trying to guide and direct activities as best you can. Here are a few suggestions for how to give general direction.

First, before you start a session, read the story, take time for "A Moment of Reflection," and familiarize yourself with all the preliminary information, discussion questions, and activities. Plan to follow the suggested sequence, but be prepared to ask questions and assign activities at whatever point they seem appropriate.

Second, have your group read the story, either in class or at home, before the session. Third, use the freewriting exercise to help teens focus, before you begin the discussion. Fourth, begin discussion with the questions under the heading "Discussion: Understanding Events" to make sure teens have understood what happened in the story. However, expect that group members will go off on tangents, bringing in their own related experiences. That's fine—getting teens to talk about their experiences is one of the main objectives of reading the story. However (and here's the tricky part), you don't want them to stray *too far* from the story and just start venting about their own issues.

Challenge teens to relate their own experiences and feelings to those of the writer. For example, Christopher A. Bogle's story, "Controlling My Temper," may spark many accounts of situations in which group members lost their temper, thought they were treated unfairly by adults, and so forth. That's the first step. The next step is to move the discussion to the point where teens are comparing themselves with Christopher. Identifying situations where they, like Christopher, worked on controlling their tempers will help them see their own resilience. If they haven't been able to control their tempers as Christopher did, or if they're silent

on the subject, you can mention that seeing the benefits of what Christopher did is a way for them to develop their own resilience. Remind them that Christopher's achievement wasn't easy; point out what he did to help himself. To encourage group members' identification with the writer, move from "Discussion: Understanding Events" to "Discussion: Understanding Issues." Questions here focus on the writer's resilience and on teens' personal connections with the issues in the story.

You may at times want to stop the discussion and either move to role plays or assign one of the writing activities. This may be advisable when you feel a shift in the group's attention, when you want to change the pace of the session, or when time is limited.

You may find that the entire session unfolds from the group's reactions to the plot questions suggested in "Discussion: Understanding Events." If you expect members to go beyond literal answers to those questions and if you've previewed the questions under "Discussion: Understanding Issues" and the role play and writing activities, you'll be prepared both to go with the flow and also to channel it in a constructive direction.

GETTING STARTED

Once you know who will be in your group, schedule an introductory meeting. Following is a suggested agenda for such a meeting.

INTRODUCTORY MEETING

Welcome group members and introduce yourself, if necessary. If teens don't know each other, allow time for introductions. Suggest that members briefly tell something about themselves they'd like the group to know.

Then say:

This group will be discussing and working with stories from an anthology called *The Struggle to Be Strong*. These are true stories written by teens who've found the strength to get through tough times. We'll talk about the stories, do some group activities that will help us understand them better, and write about ways the stories connect with our own lives, feelings, and experiences.

You might also explain your role as leader, perhaps saying that you won't be a "teacher" in the usual sense of the word. Instead, the focus will be on teens themselves. You'll be their guide, listening carefully and contributing your own ideas when appropriate, but mostly helping them to connect with the themes of the stories. Emphasize that you will all learn from each other.

Talk with your group about logistics:

- meeting place and time

- materials they should bring—pen, paper, perhaps a journal

- any advance preparation—decide if you'll expect them to read the story before each session or whether you'll allow group time for reading

- procedure to follow if they must miss a session

At some point during this meeting, discuss group guidelines. As appropriate, distribute copies of your own guidelines. Go over what you expect from group members and ask if anyone has questions or needs clarification. You might post a copy of the guidelines in your meeting room.

Distribute copies of the anthology and ask teens to read the first story before the first session. (If you'll be allowing group time for reading, tell students.) Direct the group's attention to the "Think About It" questions following the story; suggest that teens reflect on—and possibly jot down ideas about—these questions before the session.

Next, if time permits, introduce the concept of resilience by conducting the following activity. (As necessary, review the explanation of freewriting on pages 14–15.)

Procedure

1. Ask everyone to take out writing materials. Explain that you'd like them to write freely for a short time in response to some questions you'll read. Assure them that spelling and grammar aren't important and that they won't be asked to turn their papers in or read them aloud. What they write will be kept private if they choose, but those who want to share will get time to read some of what they've written or talk about it.

   Note: Consider writing along with your group. It can be valuable for teens to see you participating and to know that the questions about going through tough times apply to you as well as to them—to adults as well as to teens.

2. Read the following, pausing 60–90 seconds after each question to allow time for writing and thinking:

   Think of a hard time you've gone through. What was the situation? Did your friends or family understand what you were going through? If not, what might have helped them understand? Did you get over those hard times? If so, what helped you? If not, what do you think would help you?

Tell group members when time is almost up. When time is up, let people finish their sentences.

3. Ask for volunteers willing to read what they wrote or to talk in more general terms about their responses to the topic. (For example, they might say they wrote about "a family problem.") You might also consider sharing what you wrote, particularly if no one volunteers to talk. Your openness can build trust and spur participation.

4. Explain that the writers in *The Struggle to Be Strong* have felt some of these same emotions and have gone through similar experiences. They write about issues like controlling a bad temper, being overweight, being shy, being abandoned, going against the crowd. But besides describing tough times, these writers also describe their *resilience.*

5. Write *resilience* on the board or on a flip chart. Next to the word, write this definition: *helping yourself through tough times.* Note again that besides describing their troubles, the writers in *The Struggle to Be Strong* also describe their resilience—their persistence; what they do to keep going, learning, and changing. Mention that by reading and discussing these stories, you hope group members will recognize their own strengths and see ways they can use their own resilience.

Optional: Read aloud or have volunteers read "A Message to You" and Veronica Chambers' introduction, "A Way Out of 'No Way Out,'" pages 1–5 in the anthology. Lenny Jones and Veronica Chambers discuss resilience in personal terms that teens will appreciate. (If you've run out of time, ask teens to do this reading at home.)

WE'D LIKE TO HEAR FROM YOU

Let us know how these stories and activities work for you. Write to us, send us an email, or contact us on the Web:

The Struggle to Be Strong
Free Spirit Publishing Inc.
217 Fifth Avenue North, Suite 200
Minneapolis, MN 55401-1299
Email: help4kids@freespirit.com
Web site: *www.freespirit.com*

We hope you'll find that reading and reflecting on true stories by resilient teens helps you recognize and build strengths in the young people you work with.

Sybil Wolin

Al Desetta

Keith Hefner

THE sEssIONs

INSIGHT
ASKING TOUGH QUESTIONS

Before discussing the stories in this section, ask the group to read the introductory material about insight in their anthology, pages 10 and 11. Allow time for questions and brief discussion. Be sure teens understand the following:

- **Insight** is asking tough questions and giving honest answers about yourself and the difficult situations you find yourself in.

- The opposite of **insight** is avoiding a painful truth.

- **Insight** is hard because the urge to blame others for your troubles, instead of looking honestly at your own role, is powerful.

- **Insight** helps you see things as they really are, not as you wish they would be.

As teens read each story, encourage them to look for ways the writer demonstrates insight. Also suggest that they reflect on—and possibly jot down ideas about—the questions that follow each story ("Think About It"). Refer them to the introductory section "'Think About It'—and Maybe Write About It," pages 7–8 in the anthology.

I DON'T KNOW WHAT THE WORD MOMMY MEANS
by Youniqiue Symone

Pages 12–15 in *The Struggle to Be Strong*

PREPARING TO LEAD THE ACTIVITIES

Story Summary

Youniqiue and her two sisters have been abandoned by their mother, who is a drug addict. They are raised by an unloving aunt and uncle. Each time their mother visits, Youniqiue's sisters pretend everything is okay. Youniqiue is the only member of her family who speaks honestly about her mother's neglect and abandonment. She sees that her mother is repeating a long family history of poor parenting and is unlikely to stop. So Youniqiue gives up trying to change her mother and instead takes action to change herself. She vows to break her family's destructive cycle and to put her children first when she becomes a mother.

A Moment of Reflection

To connect with the story's themes, consider from your own perspective the questions group members will address during freewriting: Think of a time when a problem was staring you in the face, but everyone around you was ignoring it or making excuses. What were you seeing that others were trying not to see? Did you speak up about the problem? If you did, how were you treated? If you didn't, how did it feel to keep silent?

How Insight Works in the Story

Seeing Youniqiue's Insight

We see Youniqiue's insight in the beginning of the story. She describes how easy it is to create an illusion: "If you looked at any of my baby pictures, you would see a little girl who seemed happy, loved, and cared for." Then she dispels the illusion that she had a happy childhood: "But the hardcore truth is, my mother didn't take care of us." Once Youniqiue drops the illusion that hers is a perfect family, she asks questions no one else in her family asks. She demands to know why her mother isn't part of her children's lives. Unlike her sisters, she acknowledges her bitter feelings: "I hated when my mother came around, period." However, Youniqiue also realizes that her mother is repeating a family history of irresponsible parenting. This insight helps her in two ways. It leads her to see an important truth: "my mother is not going to change because I want her to." It is also the foundation of an identity that's different from her family's. She will have children when she's ready to be a good parent. She wants to "break the cycle."

Why Insight Is a Struggle for Youniqiue

Children—even those who have been abused—want to believe their parents are good, competent, and caring. The alternative is almost unthinkable, since children rely on their parents for survival. Because of this natural inclination, Youniqiue at first wants to deny that her mother abandoned her: "For a while, when people asked me why I lived with my aunt, I would say my mother died when I was three." Eventually, however, she asks herself what's wrong with her mother and faces the truth. She "grows up," realizing that her mother isn't going to change. This insight is hard for Youniqiue, particularly because her family hates her outspokenness. But she is able to see beyond her anger at them. Against the odds, she is determined to break the family cycle.

Useful Concept Words

To assist teens in understanding and discussing this story, you may want to introduce some or all of the following concept words by making them part of discussions and activities. Write them on the board in advance and plan to explain each word when it appears in a suggested discussion question or activity (where the words are shown in italics). Here are the concept words, with definitions and sentences relating them to the story.

confront: *to come face-to-face with something or someone*

Unlike her sisters, Youniqiue **confronts** *her mother about her drug abuse.*

cycle: *something that happens again and again*

Youniqiue wants to break her family's destructive **cycle** *of bad parenting.*

deny: *to refuse to accept or acknowledge something*

Youniqiue's family **denies** *the truth about her mother's neglectful behavior.*

ACTIVITIES

1. Freewriting: Finding Yourself in the Story

After group members have finished reading the story, ask them to take out writing materials. If you'll be writing also, have handy your own journal and tell students you'll be participating. For a description of freewriting, see pages 14–15.

The following statement and questions are similar to those you considered earlier in "A Moment of Reflection." This time, you may want to write along with your group.

Think of a time when a problem was staring you in the face, but everyone around you was ignoring it or making excuses. What was the problem? Why didn't people want to face it? Did you speak up about the problem? If you did, how were you treated? If you didn't, how did it feel to keep silent?

After the freewriting, invite volunteers to share what they wrote. Allow time for brief discussion.

NOTE: Avoiding Roadblocks

Some group members may feel that Youniqiue is being too hard on her mother. Some may say, "I'd never give up on my mom." Encourage teens to discuss whether it is better to remain loyal to a parent who is addicted and has abandoned you, or to break off from that parent and get on with your life. Encourage the group to decide the question. Discuss the difference between respect that's deserved and respect that's undeserved. Ask the group:

Would it have been better if Youniqiue hadn't rebelled against her mother? How would she be a different person today if she hadn't?

2. Discussion: Understanding Events

To be sure group members have understood the story, ask questions such as:

- **How do Youniqiue's aunt and uncle treat her? Give examples.**

- **What are some ways Youniqiue rebels against her mother? How is her behavior toward her mother different from her sisters' behavior?**

- **Why does Youniqiue say that her mother "had a rough childhood"? Why does she think her mother had children at a young age?**

- **What is Youniqiue's mother doing now? What is Youniqiue herself doing?**

- **At the end of the story, what does Youniqiue say about the children she will someday have?**

3. Discussion: Understanding Issues

Youniqiue's Insight

Review with the group what insight is, why it's sometimes hard to come by, and how it can be helpful. Then, referring as necessary to "How

Insight Works in the Story" (page 24), ask questions such as:

- Youniqiue says her aunt and uncle abuse her. Do you agree? Explain your answer.

- Why do you think Youniqiue used to tell people that her mother had died? Why doesn't she tell people that now?

- What does Youniqiue mean when she says, "I grew up when I realized this: my mother is not going to change because I want her to"? What is the painful truth she *confronts*? Do you believe she has grown up? Why or why not?

- What is the family *cycle* that Youniqiue is determined to break? What actions does she take to help her succeed where others in her family have failed?

- Do you think it would have been better if Youniqiue hadn't *confronted* her mother? Why or why not? How would she be a different person if she hadn't rebelled?

Connecting with the Issues

Suggest that group members silently review what they wrote during freewriting. Then ask questions such as:

- Do you think growing up means letting go of dreams that won't come true, such as Youniqiue's dream of "one big, happy family"? Explain your answer.

- Do you think there are times when it's better not to confront a problem? Explain your answer.

- Have you ever been the only one to speak up about a problem? If so, what happened when you did?

- If you were Youniqiue, would you be able to forgive your mother? Why or why not?

4. Role Plays

For guidelines on role playing, see pages 15–16.

Objective: Group members will realize how difficult it is to confront uncomfortable truths about a family member and will practice ways of communicating such truths effectively.

Scenario A

Characters: Youniqiue, her mother

Procedure
Ask for volunteers to enact this scene:

Youniqiue wants her mother to know why she's angry and disappointed. Youniqiue's mother wants to avoid the confrontation.

Allow five to ten minutes for the role play. Afterward, discuss questions such as:

- What did you see happening in this scene?

- If you were Youniqiue, how would you feel about your mother's reaction to your feelings? If you were Youniqiue's mother, how would you feel about what your daughter said?

- How did this role play affect or change your understanding of Youniqiue's story?

Scenario B

Characters: Youniqiue, one of her sisters

Procedure
Ask for volunteers to enact this scene:

Youniqiue wants her sister to speak up about her true feelings when their mother visits. Youniqiue's sister wants to remain silent.

Allow five to ten minutes for the role play. Afterward, discuss questions such as:

- What did you see happening in this scene?

- If you were Youniqiue, how would you feel about what your sister said? If you were Youniqiue's sister, how would you feel about what Youniqiue said?

- How did this role play affect or change your understanding of Youniqiue's story?

5. Writing Activities: Taking It Further

Ask students to complete one or more of the following activities individually, in small groups, or at home. Modify the activities as needed to suit the writing ability of group members. When activities are completed, invite volunteers to read their work to the group. Discuss how teens felt about the purpose and value of the writing.

Activity A

Objective: Group members will describe Youniqiue's insight in their own words.

Pretend you're Youniqiue. Write a letter to your sister explaining what you have come to accept about your mother and your family.

Activity B

Objective: Group members will consider the story from Youniqiue's mother's point of view.

Pretend you're Youniqiue's mother. Write a letter to Youniqiue explaining how your past has influenced the mother you are (or aren't) today.

Activity C

Objective: Group members will describe how a friend or relative handled a difficult situation using insight.

Write about someone you know—a friend or relative—who got through a difficult time by facing, rather than avoiding, the situation. What tough questions did the person have to face? How did the person handle his or her troubles?

6. In Your Journal: Making It Personal

Encourage group members to reflect on the following topic in their journals:

Although the truth is very painful, Youniqiue is able to face it. She has insight and sees things as they are, not as she wishes they were or as others say they are. Think of a time in your life when, unlike Youniqiue, you were not completely honest with yourself about a situation in your family, at school, among friends, or at work. What was the situation, and why weren't you honest with yourself about it? What did you gain by _denying_ the truth? Although the truth may have been painful, what could you have gained by being honest with yourself?

PREPARING TO LEAD THE ACTIVITIES

Story Summary

When Danielle turns fourteen, she's no longer an average kid with pimples but has turned into a beauty. Soon she becomes totally absorbed in her appearance and makes insulting comments to boys she considers ugly. Then a friend confronts her about her conceited attitude. At first, Danielle gets angry, but then she realizes that her friend is right. Their conversation leads Danielle to reconsider how she treats others. She begins to accept compliments graciously and to pay more attention to activities she likes, such as creative writing. She helps a friend improve her appearance, advising her to "stay the nice person" she is. Danielle learns, "To be beautiful outside, you have to be beautiful inside, too."

A Moment of Reflection

To connect with the story's themes, consider from your own perspective the questions group members will address during freewriting: Think of a time when a friend told you something about yourself that you didn't want to hear. Why didn't you want to hear it? How did you react? How did the incident change your feelings about your friend and about yourself? How did you change?

How Insight Works in the Story

Seeing Danielle's Insight

We see Danielle's insight through her response to Rick's criticism. At first she's angry and defensive. But then she reflects on her behavior and asks herself a tough question—whether she has allowed her "stuck-up attitude" to take over her personality. Danielle answers honestly: "I started to realize I had let my looks take over my inner person." This kind of self-questioning and reflection is the essence of insight. From the moment Danielle is honest with herself, she becomes less self-absorbed. She stops insulting boys and accepts compliments graciously. She develops empathy for her friend Tasha and reaches out to help her, giving Tasha, rather than herself, credit for changing. Danielle also grows intellectually. No longer pre-occupied by her looks, she finds satisfaction in activities such as reading and writing. By the end of the story, Danielle's insight has changed her from a conceited, self-centered person into someone who understands the importance of inner beauty: "Looks ain't everything!"

Why Insight Is a Struggle for Danielle

By the time Rick confronts Danielle about her conceited attitude, she has let vanity take over her personality. She also has recent memories of feeling unattractive and being teased by boys. As a result, she's inclined to angrily dismiss what Rick says. Although it's a struggle to hold back her anger, Danielle controls herself, truly hears Rick's criticism, and acts on the uncomfortable truth she sees about herself to overcome her vanity.

Useful Concept Words

To assist teens in understanding and discussing this story, you may want to introduce some or all of the following concept words by making them part of discussions and activities. Write them on the board in advance and plan to explain each word when it appears in a suggested discussion question or activity (where the words are shown in italics). Here are the concept words, with definitions and sentences relating them to the story.

conceited: *holding too high an opinion of yourself*
Danielle is ***conceited*** *when all she thinks about is her beauty.*

humility: *the quality of being modest and respectful of others, rather than proud or stuck-up*

Danielle shows **humility** *when she gives Rick credit for helping her change her attitude.*

values: *what a person considers important*

Danielle's **values** *change after Rick talks with her.*

ACTIVITIES

1. Freewriting: Finding Yourself in the Story

After group members have finished reading the story, ask them to take out writing materials. If you'll be writing also, have handy your own journal and tell students that you'll be participating. For a description of freewriting, see pages 14–15.

The following statement and questions are similar to those you considered earlier in "A Moment of Reflection." This time, you may want to write along with your group.

Think of a time when a friend told you something about yourself that you didn't want to hear. What did the friend tell you? Why didn't you want to hear it? Did you get angry and dismiss what your friend said? Or did you listen and take steps to change? How did the incident change your feelings about your friend? How did it change the way you saw yourself? How did you change?

After the freewriting, invite volunteers to share what they wrote. Allow time for brief discussion.

NOTE: Avoiding Roadblocks

Group members may note that, despite her insight, Danielle still comes across as rather vain: "I've always had a perfect shape. . . ." If necessary, help them appreciate her personal growth by pointing out her fearless self-appraisal ("My stuck-up attitude had become my whole personality") and her humor ("Looks ain't everything!"). Ask the group:

Would it be easy or difficult for you to write about yourself as honestly as Danielle writes about herself? Why?

2. Discussion: Understanding Events

To be sure group members have understood the story, ask questions such as:

- **How did Danielle feel about herself before she turned fourteen? How do her feelings and behavior change from then on?**

- **How does Danielle feel about mirrors, car windows, and getting her picture taken?**

- **How does she treat boys? Give an example.**

- **What does Rick tell Danielle? What's her first reaction to what he says? What's her reaction after she thinks about it for a while? What does she begin to understand about herself?**

- **How does Danielle change her ideas about what's really important—her *values*? How does she change the way she behaves? How do her interests change?**

- **How does Danielle help Tasha?**

3. Discussion: Understanding Issues

Danielle's Insight

Review with group members what insight is, why it's sometimes hard to come by, and how it can be helpful. Then, referring as necessary to "How Insight Works in the Story" (page 28), ask questions such as:

- **Why do you think Danielle gets so angry with Rick?**

- **Danielle not only comes to accept that she has a "bad attitude," but also takes action to change. Why was it so hard for her to gain insight into her behavior? Why was it so hard for her to change?**

- **What does Danielle mean when she says, "I started to realize I had let my looks take over my inner person"?**

- How does Danielle's changed behavior with boys show her new understanding? How does helping Tasha show Danielle's new *humility*—modesty—about herself?

- What do you think might have happened to Danielle if she hadn't gained insight and changed her ways?

Connecting with the Issues

Suggest that group members silently review what they wrote during freewriting. Then ask questions such as:

- Have you known someone who seemed *conceited* or stuck-up, but who changed her or his *values,* as Danielle did? What happened?

- What's the difference between being stuck-up and feeling good about yourself? How can you tell the difference? Can you like the way you look without being *conceited*? Explain.

- Did anyone ever tell you something about yourself that was hard to hear? How did you feel about it? What did you do?

- Did you ever tell someone something that was hard for the person to hear? What happened?

4. Role Plays

For guidelines on role playing, see pages 15–16.

Objective: Group members will identify with Danielle's struggle to accept and act upon the uncomfortable truth that she is conceited.

Scenario A

Characters: Danielle, a male friend

Procedure
Ask for volunteers to enact this scene:

Danielle is still *conceited* about her looks. The boy wants the "old" (not conceited) Danielle back as his friend. Danielle doesn't think she's conceited and doesn't understand what the boy is talking about.

Allow five to ten minutes for the role play. Afterward, discuss questions such as:

- What did you see happening in this scene?

- If you were Danielle, how would you feel about what your friend said?

- How did this role play affect or change your understanding of Danielle's story?

Scenario B

Characters: Danielle, Tasha, a boy Danielle once insulted

Procedure
Ask for volunteers to enact this scene:

Danielle is helping Tasha shop. A boy she once insulted comes up to them. He wants to get back at Danielle by telling her what he thinks of her. Tasha wants to defend Danielle. Danielle wants to convince the boy that she's a different person now.

Allow five to ten minutes for the role play. Afterward, discuss questions such as:

- What did you see happening in this scene?

- If you were Danielle, how would you feel about what the boy said to you? If you were Tasha, how would you feel about Danielle during this scene? If you were the boy, would Danielle have convinced you that she's a different person now?

- How did this role play affect or change your understanding of Danielle's story?

5. Writing Activities: Taking It Further

Ask students to complete one or more of the following activities individually, in small groups, or at home. Modify the activities as needed to suit the writing ability of group members. When activities are completed, invite volunteers to read their work to the group. Discuss how teens felt about the purpose and value of the writing.

Activity A

Objective: Group members will explain Danielle's insight in their own words.

Pretend you're Danielle. Write a letter to Rick explaining how what he told you helped you understand yourself and changed you for the better.

Activity B

Objective: Group members will reflect on a common expression about the effects of facing the truth.

You may have heard these two common expressions: "The truth hurts" and "The truth will set you free." Choose one of them and write about it. What does the expression mean to you? Do you agree with it? Why or why not? How does this expression apply to Danielle's story?

Activity C

Objective: Group members will distinguish between "inner beauty" and outward appearance.

Through her insight, Danielle changes from a narrow focus on physical beauty to a broader appreciation of inner beauty. Write about what "inner beauty" means to you. How is inner beauty different from physical appearance? Next, make a list of what you like about your appearance. Then make a list of what you like about the "inner you." Which list is more important or valuable to you? Why? What is the connection between the two lists?

6. In Your Journal: Making It Personal

Encourage group members to reflect on the following topic in their journals:

As Danielle learns, having self-confidence without becoming *conceited* isn't easy. What areas of your life do you feel self-confident about? Why do you feel self-confident about them? In what areas do you lack self-confidence? Why do you think you aren't self-confident about them? What could you do to become more self-confident?

CONTROLLING MY TEMPER
by Christopher A. Bogle

Pages 21–24 in *The Struggle to Be Strong*

PREPARING TO LEAD THE ACTIVITIES

Story Summary

Christopher, who lives in a group home, has completed over twenty chores for the week and believes each one is worth two dollars. Robert, an adult staff member who is temporarily in charge of distributing allowances, refuses to pay what Christopher thinks he deserves. Robert also refuses to give Christopher a savings bond he wants to cash in to buy a jacket he needs. Robert and Christopher get into a verbal and physical confrontation that ends when a supervisor intervenes. Several weeks later, Eric, Christopher's cousin, comes to the group home and insists on speaking with Robert about the incident. Christopher worries that Eric will hit Robert, but instead, Eric and Robert talk calmly. Impressed, Christopher thinks about his own behavior and the importance of controlling his temper.

A Moment of Reflection

To connect with the story's themes, consider from your own perspective the questions group members will address during freewriting: Think of a time when you were treated unfairly by someone who had power over you, such as a parent, teacher, supervisor, or boss. How did you handle the situation? Did you get angry, or were you able to control your temper? If the situation happened again, would you change anything about your behavior?

How Insight Works in the Story

Seeing Christopher's Insight

When Robert treats Christopher unfairly, Christopher's angry feelings are intense. We see his insight when he stands back from his anger and asks himself some tough questions—Could he have handled himself better? How much of the situation was his fault and how much was Robert's? Does he have a problem controlling his temper? His answers are honest and reflect his regret over the incident: "If I had it to do over, I would never have gone inside the office and been disrespectful to Robert." While Christopher is tough on himself and accepts responsibility for his own behavior, he also notes that Robert shares blame in the matter. Impressed by the way Eric handled the situation, Christopher devises techniques for controlling his temper: talking to someone, avoiding situations he knows will make him angry, going for a walk, isolating himself until he calms down. He learns "you can solve problems without using violence."

Why Insight Is a Struggle for Christopher

It's difficult to ask tough questions about your own behavior after having been treated unfairly. It's a lot easier to blame the other person and nurse a grudge. Although Christopher feels his anger was justified, he's able to acknowledge his problem controlling his temper and take steps to change. But the process of changing isn't easy, and at the end of the story he admits that his struggle isn't over: "I still have a problem controlling my temper. . . ."

Useful Concept Words

To assist group members in understanding and discussing this story, you may want to introduce some or all of the following concept words by making them part of discussions and activities. Write them on the board in advance and plan to explain each word when it appears in a suggested discussion question or activity (where the words are shown

in italics). Here are the concept words, with definitions and sentences relating them to the story.

acknowledge: to admit; to recognize
Christopher acknowledges that he shouldn't have gone into Robert's office and been disrespectful to him.

anticipate: to realize beforehand; to see ahead; to expect
Now, Christopher is able to anticipate and avoid situations that he knows will make him angry.

disrespect: a lack of regard or consideration
Both Christopher and Robert feel they've been treated with disrespect.

reflect: to think things over; to reconsider
After seeing how Eric handles the talk with Robert, Christopher reflects on his own behavior.

ACTIVITIES

1. Freewriting: Finding Yourself in the Story

After group members have finished reading the story, ask them to take out writing materials. If you'll be writing also, have handy your own journal and tell students you'll be participating. For a description of freewriting, see pages 14–15.

The following statement and questions are similar to those you considered earlier in "A Moment of Reflection." This time, you may want to write along with your group.

Think of a time when you were treated unfairly by someone who had power over you, such as a parent, teacher, supervisor, or boss. What happened? How did you handle the situation? Did you get angry, or were you able to control your temper? If the situation happened again, would you change anything about your behavior? What would you change?

After the freewriting, invite volunteers to share what they wrote. Allow time for brief discussion.

NOTE: Avoiding Roadblocks

Teens in your group may react strongly to the unfair way Christopher was treated by Robert. They could go off on tangents about similar confrontations in their own lives and lose sight of the larger themes of the story. The tangents can be instructive if you use them to show the importance of using insight to handle anger in a mature way. Ask the group:

What similarities or differences do you see between your experiences and Christopher's? Are you happy with the way you handled your situation? What have you learned from the way Christopher handled his?

2. Discussion: Understanding Events

To be sure group members have understood the story, ask questions such as:

- **What does Christopher want to do with the money he feels he's earned?**

- **Why doesn't Robert give Christopher the correct amount of money? Why doesn't Robert want to give Christopher his savings bond?**

- **What does Robert do when Christopher reaches into the filing cabinet to take his savings bond?**

- **How does Christopher show his *disrespect* for Robert? How does Robert show his disrespect for Christopher?**

- **Why is Christopher nervous when his cousin Eric goes into Robert's office?**

- **How does Eric handle the situation with Robert? Why does this surprise and impress Christopher?**

- **What does Christopher do now to control his temper?**

3. Discussion: Understanding Issues

Christopher's Insight

Review with the group what insight is, why it's sometimes hard to come by, and how it can be helpful. Then, referring as necessary to "How Insight Works in the Story" (page 32), ask questions such as:

- Why do you think Christopher gets so angry when Robert doesn't pay him the right amount and refuses to give him his savings bond?

- Despite his anger at Robert, why does Christopher say, "I should have handled myself better"? What does he *acknowledge* about his own behavior?

- Does Christopher take full responsibility for what happened between him and Robert? Explain.

- What does Christopher say he learned from the way his cousin Eric handled the situation with Robert? Why do you think Eric's behavior had such a big impact on him?

- What do you think of Christopher's advice to his readers?

Connecting with the Issues

Suggest that group members silently review what they wrote during freewriting. Then ask questions such as:

- How do you think Christopher might have handled the disagreement with Robert? What would you have done?

- Why do you think it's especially hard to ask yourself tough questions and give honest answers when you've been treated unfairly?

- Christopher feels that Robert treated him unfairly and handled the situation badly himself, as an adult. Still, Christopher is able to admit he has a temper problem and take steps to change his behavior. What does this tell you about him? Do you think you'd have the courage and honesty—the insight—to look at yourself as he did? Why or why not?

- Can you *reflect* back on a time when your temper got you into trouble? How would you handle the situation differently now?

- Have you ever been able to *anticipate*—see ahead—that you were going to lose your temper, before you actually lost it? What did you do to control yourself? What was the result?

- Do you have someone to look up to and learn from, as Christopher had Eric? How important is a role model like Eric? Explain.

4. Role Plays

For guidelines on role playing, see pages 15–16.

Objective: Group members will practice ways of using insight to avoid conflict.

Scenario A

Characters: Christopher, Robert

Procedure
Ask for volunteers to enact this scene:

Christopher and Robert are disagreeing about the payment for chores. Both want to make their views known, but without losing their tempers. Robert wants Christopher to respect his authority. Christopher wants Robert to pay him what he's owed.

Allow five to ten minutes for the role play. Afterward, discuss questions such as:

- What did you see happening in this scene?

- If you were Robert, how would you feel about the way Christopher spoke to you? If you were Christopher, how would you feel about the way Robert spoke to you?

- How did this role play affect or change your understanding of Christopher's story?

Scenario B

Characters: Christopher, another teenage resident of the group home, a staff member

Procedure

Ask for volunteers to enact this scene:

The staff member and the teen are arguing over payment for chores. Christopher wants to step in, speak to both, and help end the argument.

Allow five to ten minutes for the role play. Afterward, discuss questions such as:

- **What did you see happening in this scene?**

- **If you were Christopher, how would you feel about using your new skills to help someone else? If you were the people arguing, would Christopher have convinced you to end your dispute?**

- **How did this role play affect or change your understanding of Christopher's story?**

5. Writing Activities: Taking It Further

Ask students to complete one or more of the following activities individually, in small groups, or at home. Modify the activities as needed to suit the writing ability of group members. When activities are completed, invite volunteers to read their work to the group. Discuss how teens felt about the purpose and value of the writing.

Activity A

Objective: Group members will explain Christopher's insight in their own words.

Pretend you're Christopher. Write a letter to your cousin Eric. Explain how you were inspired to work at controlling your temper by the way he handled the situation with Robert.

Activity B

Objective: Group members will consider the role models in their own lives.

Eric becomes a positive role model for Christopher. Write about two role models in your life: one whose influence is negative, and one whose influence is positive. These people could be parents, friends, teachers, relatives, celebrities, and so forth. Write one paragraph about the influence of each.

Activity C

Objective: Group members will practice seeing both sides of a conflict.

Draw a line down the middle of your paper. On one side, write about Robert's view of the conflict with Christopher. On the other side, write about Christopher's view of the conflict. Try to see the situation through each person's eyes.

6. In Your Journal: Making It Personal

Encourage group members to reflect on the following topic in their journals:

As Christopher recognizes, his temper causes him to react without thinking. As he gains insight, he learns that staying calm and talking about what's bothering him are better ways to handle anger. How do you behave when you get angry? Do you lash out at people, withdraw, sulk, get sarcastic? If so, what's the usual result? Is there a more effective way you might handle anger? How could you develop this new way of reacting?

THE ANSWER WAS ME
by Eliott Castro

Pages 25–27 in *The Struggle to Be Strong*

PREPARING TO LEAD THE ACTIVITIES

Story Summary

Eliott's girlfriend breaks up with him because he has a drinking problem and abuses her verbally. He's very hurt, both by losing her and by his mother's abuse. Trying to handle his loss, he drinks more and gets caught in a vicious cycle—drinking, becoming violent and self-destructive, and then drinking more to hide his embarrassment. The turning point for Eliott comes when he admits he has a problem and looks at the roots of his pain. He accepts responsibility for his behavior but also forgives himself for the pain he's caused himself and others. The story ends with Eliott's advice to readers about the importance of facing problems rather than avoiding them.

A Moment of Reflection

To connect with the story's themes, consider from your own perspective the questions group members will address during freewriting: Think of a time when you had a problem in your life that was hard for you to face. What got in the way of facing the problem or taking action? Did you eventually take any steps to solve your problem? What happened? How did you feel about the situation?

How Insight Works in the Story

Seeing Eliott's Insight

Eliott's insight emerges out of his pain over losing his girlfriend. He realizes she broke up with him because of his drinking and verbal abuse—and that he drank to escape his mother's abuse. Knowing he has "to start somewhere," he moves out of his mother's house. Then he asks himself some difficult questions and answers honestly: "I realized that I had to make changes in my attitude and behavior. There was no one else to blame." Eliott won't hide from his problems anymore. At the same time, he comes to the crucial understanding that he needs to have compassion for himself. Eliott also discovers the power of introspection: ". . . sitting down and focusing my mind on solving my problems and not avoiding them." At the end of the story, Eliott is no longer self-destructive. He's a clear-thinking young man with some hard-won insights about himself.

Why Insight Is a Struggle for Eliott

After Eliott's girlfriend breaks up with him and his drinking problem worsens, he goes to a quiet park and asks himself some tough questions: "Why was everything around me falling apart? What made me lose everything? Who was causing all this to happen?" Though answering honestly is hard, Eliott musters the courage to face himself, admitting, "I was going through so much pain and hurt that hiding from my problems in alcohol only made them worse." Once Eliott achieves this insight, his next struggle is to temper his probing self-examination with compassion for himself: "The next step was hard. I realized that until I forgave myself, my problems wouldn't go away." Eliott shows tremendous willpower and persistence. Balancing insight with self-forgiveness, he changes his life for the better.

Useful Concept Words

To assist teens in understanding and discussing this story, you may want to introduce some or all of the following concept words by making them part of discussions and activities. Write them on the board in advance and plan to explain each word when it appears in a suggested discussion question or activity (where the words are shown in italics). Here are the concept words, with definitions and sentences relating them to the story.

commitment: *a pledge to do something*

*Eliott makes a **commitment** to face his problems, rather than avoid them.*

diversion: *something that distracts you or shifts your attention*

*Eliott realizes that he drank partly as a **diversion** from the pain of living with his mother and losing his girlfriend.*

introspective: *looking inside yourself*

*Sitting quietly in the park, Eliott becomes **introspective** about his alcohol problem.*

self-pity: *feeling sorry for yourself*

*Eliott realizes that he drank partly out of **self-pity** over losing his girlfriend.*

self-respect: *feeling good about your own character and actions*

*Eliott gains **self-respect** after he both accepts responsibility and forgives himself.*

ACTIVITIES

1. Freewriting: Finding Yourself in the Story

After group members have finished reading the story, ask them to take out writing materials. If you'll be writing also, have handy your own journal and tell students you'll be participating. For a description of freewriting, see pages 14–15.

The following statement and questions are similar to those you considered earlier in "A Moment of Reflection." This time, you may want to write along with your group.

Think of a time when you had a problem in your life that was hard for you to face. What got in the way of facing the problem or taking action? Did you ever take any steps to solve your problem? If so, what happened? If not, what happened? How did you feel about the situation?

After the freewriting, invite volunteers to share what they wrote. Allow time for brief discussion.

NOTE: Avoiding Roadblocks

If teens in your group bring up their own struggles with alcohol or other substances, gently steer the discussion back to the story. (If appropriate, suggest that an individual see you privately. Also see, "Handling Sensitive Issues," pages 7–8.) Highlight Eliott's strength and insight in facing his drinking problem. Discourage judgmental comments about alcohol abuse, which can distract teens from Eliott's courage in asking himself tough questions and making a commitment to change. Stay focused on the way Eliott handled his situation. Ask the group:

What similarities and differences do you see between Eliott's experience and your own? What is the most important lesson Eliott learned? How does it apply to your own life?

If students wonder how Eliott used his insight to stop drinking, you might point out that most people with a substance abuse problem also need professional help to overcome it. Insight, however, can be an important first step. Ask the group:

What qualities besides insight do you think are needed by most people fighting an addiction to alcohol or drugs?

2. Discussion: Understanding Events

To be sure group members have understood the story, ask questions such as:

- **Why does Eliott's girlfriend break up with him?**

- **What is Eliott's home life like?**

- **What does Eliott say would happen to him when he drank? What would happen when he sobered up?**

- Once Eliott admits he has a drinking problem, what's the first thing he does to change his life? Why does he take that first step?

- Where does Eliott go to think quietly about what to do? Why is it a good place?

- Who does Eliott decide is responsible for his problems? Why does he decide that he must forgive himself?

- What does Eliott do now when he has a problem? What's his advice to his readers?

3. Discussion: Understanding Issues

Eliott's Insight

Review with the group what insight is, why it's sometimes hard to come by, and how it can be helpful. Then, referring as necessary to "How Insight Works in the Story" (page 36), ask questions such as:

- Why do you think it's so hard for Eliott to face the reasons for his drinking?

- Do you think there's a connection between the way Eliott's mother treats him and the way Eliott treats his girlfriend? Explain.

- Eliott decides that the first step in solving his problems is to leave his mother. Do you think that was the right thing for him to do? Explain.

- What does Eliott realize about his life and behavior as he sits quietly in the park? What *commitment*—promise—does he make to himself about how he'll handle his problems?

- How does Eliott move from *self-pity* to *self-respect*?

Connecting with the Issues

Suggest that group members silently review what they wrote during freewriting. Then ask questions such as:

- Why does Eliott say that dealing with problems by lifting weights or watching TV can be as bad as drinking? Do you agree? Why or why not?

- Eliott forgives himself "for the physical and mental damage" his drinking has caused him and others. Why do you think he doesn't say that he forgives his mother? Do you think he'll eventually be able to forgive her? Explain your answer.

- Why do you think it's especially hard for someone to ask tough questions and give honest answers when the person has a drinking problem? What qualities besides insight would you say are needed by most people fighting an addiction like alcoholism?

- What's the difference between activities that help you to be *introspective*—to look inside yourself— and activities that are a *diversion*, distracting you from your problems? Is there an activity you do that helps you face your problems, rather than avoid them? If so, what is it? How does it help?

- Think of a problem you're going through. What's helped you face it? If you haven't been able to face it, what could be standing in the way?

4. Role Play

For guidelines on role playing, see pages 15–16.

Objective: Group members will practice communicating how important it is to face problems in order to change self-destructive behavior.

Characters: Eliott, his friend

Procedure
Ask for volunteers to enact this scene:

Eliott's friend drinks a lot but wants to convince Eliott that he or she doesn't have a problem with alcohol. Eliott wants to convince his friend that the drinking is out of control and that the friend should give it up.

Allow five to ten minutes for the role play. Afterward, discuss questions such as:

- What did you see happening in this scene?

- If you were Eliott's friend, would Eliott have persuaded you to stop drinking?

- How did this role play affect or change your understanding of Eliott's story?

5. Writing Activities: Taking It Further

Ask students to complete one or more of the following activities individually, in small groups, or at home. Modify the activities as needed to suit the writing ability of group members. When activities are completed, invite volunteers to read their work to the group. Discuss how teens felt about the purpose and value of the writing.

Activity A

Objective: Group members will explain Eliott's insight in their own words.

Pretend you're Eliott. Write a letter to a friend explaining why you've stopped drinking and what you do now when you have problems.

Activity B

Objective: Group members will reflect on the importance of self-forgiveness.

Why does Eliott feel it was as important for him to forgive himself as it was to take responsibility for his troubles? Write about whether you agree or disagree with him. Then write about which is harder for you: forgiving others or forgiving yourself.

Activity C

Objective: Group members will describe a favorite place for quiet thought.

Do you have a quiet place where you can go to think? If so, describe it. How important do you think it is to have such a place?

6. In Your Journal: Making It Personal

Encourage group members to reflect on the following topic in their journals:

Part of Eliott's insight is to realize that he has been using drinking to hide from his problems. Most of us, at one time or another, have used some activity as an escape. For example, maybe you've gone out with friends instead of working on a difficult school assignment. Write about an activity you've used to keep from facing a problem. What problem were you avoiding? What steps could you have taken to face the problem? How might facing a problem instead of avoiding it be helpful to you?

PREPARING TO LEAD THE ACTIVITIES

Story Summary

Jamal, an African-American teen, feels like an outcast because he doesn't conform to common stereotypes of blacks and isn't fully accepted by whites. Jamal doesn't use slang, listen to rap or reggae, play basketball well, or dance with a lot of hip movement. Although he seems similar to "a stereotypical white kid from the suburbs," he doesn't feel completely at home with white people, either. As he says, white people see him "not as 'that nice kid who is friends with my son or daughter' but rather as 'that nice *black* kid who is friends with my son or daughter.'" Feeling there's no place where he really belongs, Jamal reflects on the meaning and importance of race. He decides it's both wrong and unfair for anyone to expect him to act a certain way just because he's black.

A Moment of Reflection

To connect with the story's themes, consider from your own perspective the questions group members will address during freewriting: Think of a time when someone assumed something about you because of your race, religion, gender, age, appearance, accent, or any other reason. How was the stereotype different from the real you? How did it feel to be stereotyped? How did you respond?

How Insight Works in the Story

Seeing Jamal's Insight

We see Jamal's insight as his story opens: "I am black," he says, but "I'm not all that different from a stereotypical white kid from the suburbs." To answer his difficult questions—Where do I belong? Am I defined by the color of my skin or by the person I am?—he carefully examines the ways he's treated in various situations by family and friends. He looks beneath the surface for logical flaws in the ways people apply stereotypes. For example: "If we really believe everyone should be treated equally, then my Jewish friends should be expected to know just as much about black history as I do." Jamal also looks for role models and dictionary definitions supporting his view that race is determined by physical characteristics, not behavior. However, he understands that no matter what he's like, some people will always think of him in terms of his race. He knows he'll always be "something of an outcast."

Why Insight Is a Struggle for Jamal

Like all teens, Jamal wants to belong. Trying to understand why he doesn't quite belong requires ingenuity and probing self-analysis. Though he seems more comfortable with himself because of his efforts to figure out who he is, Jamal comes to the painful realization that he's not likely to be fully accepted by many black or white people.

Useful Concept Words

To assist group members in understanding and discussing this story, you may want to introduce some or all of the following concept words by making them part of discussions and exercises. Write them on the board in advance and plan to explain each word when it appears in a suggested discussion question or exercise (where the words are shown in italics). Here are the concept words, with definitions and sentences relating them to the story.

ambiguous: *unclear; uncertain; having more than one interpretation*

*In a society where many hold stereotypes about black people, Jamal's identity is **ambiguous** both to himself and to others.*

associate: to connect; to join together
*Jamal realizes that some people **associate** certain kinds of behavior with black people.*

stereotype: an oversimplified opinion or belief
*Some of Jamal's friends hold the **stereotype** that all black people dance well.*

tolerance: respect for the opinions and behavior of others
*Jamal wants people to have **tolerance** for him as a person.*

ACTIVITIES

1. Freewriting: Finding Yourself in the Story

After group members have finished reading the story, ask them to take out writing materials. If you'll be writing also, have handy your own journal and tell students you'll be participating. For a description of freewriting, see pages 14–15.

The following statement and questions are similar to those you considered earlier in "A Moment of Reflection." This time, you may want to write along with your group.

Think of a time when someone thought they knew what you were like because of your race, religion, gender, age, appearance, accent, or any other reason. How did you feel about that? How was the *stereotype*—what the person assumed about you— different from the real you? Did you say or do anything to show the person who you really were? If so, what happened? If not, what could you have said or done?

After the freewriting, invite volunteers to share what they wrote. Allow time for brief discussion.

2. Discussion: Understanding Events

To be sure group members have understood the story, ask questions such as:

- **What are some reasons Jamal feels "a certain distance" between himself and other black people?**

- **Why does the girl from his journalism workshop think he's "not a genuine black person"? How does Jamal feel about this?**

- **What is Jamal's explanation for why he prefers Mickey Mantle's baseball card to Jackie Robinson's? Why does this annoy his cousins?**

- **Why does Jamal mention Paul Olden, Lennox Lewis, and Clarence Thomas? What's his point?**

- **What are the two definitions of race that Jamal finds in the dictionary? Which one does he like better? Why?**

NOTE: Avoiding Roadblocks

Discussing core identity issues—racial or otherwise—isn't easy. Try to move beyond a debate over whether Jamal is "really black" or trying to "act white." Focus the discussion on how Jamal deals with his predicament. Within the group, there are bound to be students who have felt confined by stereotypes based on gender, ethnicity, race, religion, socioeconomic status, age, accent, and so on. By getting them to talk about Jamal's experiences, you'll help them understand and handle their own. Ask the group:

Why is it painful for Jamal to feel like an outcast from both black people and white people? How would you feel in his place?

3. Discussion: Understanding Issues

Jamal's Insight

Review with the group what insight is, why it's sometimes hard to come by, and how it can be helpful. Then, referring as necessary to "How Insight Works in the Story" (page 40), ask questions such as:

- **Why does Jamal feel out of place with both black and white people? Why is his identity *ambiguous*—unclear or confusing to him?**

- **Jamal found two definitions of race in the dictionary. Which definition do you think is more accurate? Why?**

- **Do you think Jamal will ever feel completely comfortable with who he is? Why or why not?**

Connecting with the Issues

Suggest that group members silently review what they wrote during freewriting. Then ask questions such as:

- **Jamal thinks it's unfair to *associate* black people with a certain kind of speech and music, and with skills in dancing and basketball. Do you agree? Why or why not?**

- **Jamal believes he shouldn't be expected to know more about black history and culture than white people do. Do you agree? Why or why not?**

- **How do you feel about the way Jamal handles his situation? How would you have handled it?**

- **Why do you think it's hard for people to have *tolerance*—acceptance—of behavior different from theirs?**

- **Have you ever had the experience of people thinking you're not a "real" black person—or white person or Hispanic person or Asian person or male person or female person—if you don't behave a certain way? Explain.**

4. Role Play

For guidelines on role playing, see pages 15–16.

Objective: Group members will identify with Jamal's frustration at not being considered a "real" black person.

Characters: Jamal, the girl from his journalism class

Procedure
Ask for volunteers to enact this scene:

The girl from Jamal's journalism class wants Jamal to know why she thinks he's not a "real" black person. Jamal wants her to know that he's as much a "real" black person as she is.

Allow five to ten minutes for the role play. Afterward, discuss questions such as:

- **What did you see happening in this scene?**

- **Which argument did you think was stronger, Jamal's or the girl's? Why?**

- **How did this role play affect or change your understanding of Jamal's story?**

5. Group Activity

Objective: Teens will discover the importance of getting to know people, rather than making assumptions about them.

Procedure
Tell the group that the object of this activity is to show that we don't really know people as well as we think we do. Ask them to write three things about themselves, two true and one untrue. The true items should be things they think most people in the group won't know (for example, "I sing in the church choir," "I play drums," "I like to write," "My favorite color is blue," "I have five brothers"). The untrue item should not be completely unbelievable or stand out too much from the true ones. Each person reads his or her list aloud. The others vote on which item is untrue; then the person indicates whether they've guessed right or wrong. Keep a tally on the board of right and wrong guesses. Afterward, discuss what surprised the group and what they learned from this activity. Ask:

- **What's the value of getting to know a person, rather than assuming you know what the person's like?**

- **How did this activity affect or change your understanding of Jamal's story?**

6. Writing Activities: Taking It Further

Ask students to complete one or more of the following activities individually, in small groups, or at home. Modify the activities as needed to suit the writing ability of group members. When activities are completed, invite volunteers to read their work to the group. Discuss how teens felt about the purpose and value of the writing.

Activity A

Objective: Group members will explain Jamal's insight in their own words.

Pretend you're Jamal. Write a letter to a friend explaining how you've learned to define for yourself who you are and where you belong, rather than accept what others think about you.

Activity B

Objective: Group members will reflect on their own views about race.

Jamal finds that race can be defined two ways: by shared interests and behavior, or by physical characteristics. Write about the definition you like better, explaining why it makes more sense to you.

Activity C

Objective: Group members will reflect on their own tendency to stereotype others.

Do you ever think you know people just because of the particular group they belong to? Write honestly about the assumptions you sometimes make about others based on their race, religion, gender, neighborhood, athletic skills, taste in music, style of dress, attitude toward school, and so on. What problems can be caused by assuming you know someone, rather than really getting to know the person?

7. In Your Journal: Making It Personal

Encourage group members to reflect on the following topic in their journals:

Jamal, who is stereotyped because he's black, learns that insight can mean asking yourself: "How should I react when people make assumptions about me?" Think of a time when someone stereotyped you because of your age, gender, racial or ethnic group, living situation, neighborhood, appearance, religion, choice of music or clothes, or for any other reason. Why do you think this person made assumptions about you? What's the best way to react when people judge you or stereotype you? Underneath your differences, what did you have in common with the person who stereotyped you? What steps could people take to see their similarities, instead of their differences?

FIVE TEENS: THE IMPORTANCE OF INSIGHT

As necessary, refer to pages 10 and 11 in the anthology to review with your group what insight is and why it's a resilience. Then invite group members to compare how insight works in the lives of the five teen writers in this section. (To help students recall each writer, you might list their first names on the board.) Ask questions such as:

- Which writer do you think has to ask the toughest questions about her or his life or situation? Why do you think so?

- Which writer do you think shows the most courage in facing the truth and taking personal responsibility? Why do you think so?

- Which writer do you think changes the most because of his or her insight? Why do you think so?

- Which story in this section do you like best? Which teen writer do you admire most? Explain your choices.

Many of the teen writers in this book demonstrate more than one resilience. If your group has read other stories, you might ask members to discuss how writers in other sections also demonstrate insight.

INDEPENDENCE
BEING YOUR OWN PERSON

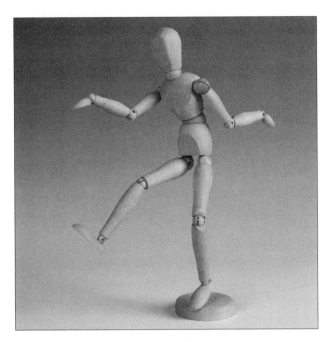

Before discussing the stories in this section, ask the group to read the introductory material about independence in their anthology, pages 34 and 35. Allow time for questions and brief discussion. Be sure teens understand the following:

- **Independence** is being your own person and keeping an emotional distance between you and the pressures of family, friends, and circumstances.

- The opposite of **independence** is doing things only to get the approval of others or to avoid feeling alone or rejected.

- **Independence** is hard because it sometimes means breaking or limiting connections with people who are important to you.

- **Independence** helps you feel safe and know you can rely on yourself.

As teens read each story, encourage them to look for ways the writer demonstrates independence. Also suggest that they reflect on—and possibly jot down ideas about—the questions that follow each story ("Think About It"). Refer them to the introductory section "'Think About It'—and Maybe Write About It," pages 7–8 in the anthology.

I WAS A BEAUTY SCHOOL SUCKER
by Tonya Leslie

Pages 36–39 in *The Struggle to Be Strong*

PREPARING TO LEAD THE ACTIVITIES

Story Summary

Tonya is taken in by an ad for a modeling school that appeals to her vanity. For a high fee that her parents pay, she and her sister sign up for a one-year course. The classes are boring and standardized, offering the same makeup and hair advice to everyone, regardless of skin color, facial features, or hair type. They're pressured to pay added costs for professional grooming, pictures, and so on. When Tonya receives her graduation pictures, which look ridiculous and cost an extra three hundred dollars, she knows she's been duped. At the end of the story she's approached with another modeling school offer, but this time she rejects it out of hand.

A Moment of Reflection

To connect with the story's themes, consider from your own perspective the questions group members will address during freewriting: Think of a time when you bought something because a promise or advertisement appealed to your vanity, your self-image, your desire for wealth, or something else. Why did you let yourself be deceived? What happened? Do you think you could be taken in again?

How Independence Works in the Story

Seeing Tonya's Independence

When the story opens, Tonya is not her own person. She wants to conform to the image of a fashion model: "How often had I dreamed of having my face on a magazine cover, of being sought after by the press and loved by the public." When she sees an ad in a magazine for Barbara's Beauty School, her vanity overpowers her good judgment, and she is lured into enrolling. Gradually, she realizes she's being exploited. At the end of her story, when a salesman for Barbara's Beauty School tells Tonya she looks "like a model," she rips up his business card. She's learned from experience the cost of trying to be someone else. We feel certain she's gained enough independence to avoid being taken in again.

Why Independence Is a Struggle for Tonya

It's hard to resist media promises that play to one's desire for beauty, success, riches, or whatever. Though Tonya has a hunch she's being exploited, she wants to be a famous model so badly that she fools herself into believing Barbara's Beauty School can make her into one: "I'd never seen runway shows like that, but I figured the teachers at Barbara's knew the deal better than I did. That was my first and constant mistake." Caught between a willing self-deception and knowing better, Tonya doesn't speak up. It's not until her parents have thrown away lots of money that she sees how her vanity undermined her independence.

Useful Concept Words

To assist the group in understanding and discussing this story, you may want to introduce some or all of the following concept words by making them part of discussions and activities. Write them on the board in advance and plan to explain each word when it appears in a suggested discussion question or activity (where the words are shown in italics). Here are the concept words, with definitions and sentences relating them to the story.

cloud: *to hide; to conceal*

*Tonya's sense of judgment is **clouded** by what the school tells her.*

defer: *to submit to the wishes or opinions of someone else*

*Against her better judgment, Tonya **defers** to her teachers, figuring they know best.*

exploit: *to selfishly make use of someone or something*

*Tonya is **exploited** by the beauty school.*

self-assured: *confident about oneself*

*By the end of the story, Tonya is a more **self-assured** person.*

vanity: *excessive pride in one's appearance or accomplishments*

*The beauty school appeals to Tonya's **vanity**.*

ACTIVITIES

1. Freewriting: Finding Yourself in the Story

After group members have finished reading the story, ask them to take out writing materials. If you'll be writing also, have handy your own journal and tell students you'll be participating. For a description of freewriting, see pages 14–15.

The following statement and question are similar to those you considered earlier in "A Moment of Reflection." This time, you may want to write along with your group.

Think of a time when you bought something because you thought it would make you popular, happy, good-looking, successful, or rich—for example, the latest sneakers, a haircut, a lottery ticket. Did it work? Why or why not? Looking back, how do you feel about the situation? Would you buy the same thing again? Explain.

After the freewriting, invite volunteers to share what they wrote. Allow time for brief discussion.

NOTE: Avoiding Roadblocks

Some group members may not be able to see themselves in Tonya. They might say, "I'd never be taken in like that. I'd never shell out that kind of money." Some boys might say, "Only a girl would fall for this." Keep the focus on why Tonya is taken in by the modeling ad and on the courage it takes for her to admit her mistakes. Ask the group:

How do you make decisions about spending money? What pressures do you feel to wear certain kinds of clothes or to project a certain image? How hard is it to be independent of these pressures?

2. Discussion: Understanding Events

To be sure group members have understood the story, ask questions such as:

- **When Tonya first enrolls in the beauty school, why don't her parents complain about "the $1,000-plus they kicked out"?**

- **What is Tonya's "first and constant mistake"?**

- **Why are the makeup classes "more like makeup disaster classes"?**

- **How do Tonya's parents react to the girls' graduation pictures?**

- **When Tonya is approached on the train by a salesman for Barbara's Beauty School, what does she do? Why does she do it?**

3. Discussion: Understanding Issues

Tonya's Independence

Review with the group what independence is, why it's sometimes hard to come by, and how it can be helpful. Then, referring as necessary to "How Independence Works in the Story" (page 46), ask questions such as:

- **Why do you think Tonya tells herself that the teachers at Barbara's Beauty School know what they're talking about? What prevents her from trusting her own instincts?**

- **The teacher tells Tonya that her hair and makeup "hardly looked professional" and that she needs experts to prepare her for photography. Why do you think Tonya lets this comment *cloud* her judgment? Why does she *defer* to her teacher's viewpoint?**

- **What do you think might have happened if Tonya hadn't gradually become *self-assured* and independent about how she wants to look?**

- **What lessons do you think Tonya learned from being *exploited* by the beauty school?**

Connecting with the Issues

Suggest that group members silently review what they wrote during freewriting. Then ask questions such as:

- **Before her beauty school experience, what kinds of messages about beauty do you think Tonya got from the media, her family, and her friends? What kinds of messages have you gotten about your looks? What impact do those messages have on you?**

- **Why is it so difficult for people to stay independent of the appeals of advertisers who promise beauty, success, riches, or other desirable things? Why do you think an appeal to people's *vanity* is so effective?**

- **Have you ever bought something that you thought would change you or your image? What happened? Do you think you could be persuaded to buy something similar again? Why or why not?**

- **Have you ever followed a dream that seemed realistic at the time, but didn't turn out as you'd hoped? How do you feel about that dream now?**

4. Role Plays

For guidelines on role playing, see pages 15–16.

Objective: Group members will practice staying independent when they're tempted by attractive promises and offers.

Scenario A

Characters: Tonya, her friend

Procedure
Ask for volunteers to enact this scene:

Tonya's friend wants to sign up for Barbara's Beauty School. Tonya wants to convince her she's making a mistake.

Allow five to ten minutes for the role play. Afterward, discuss questions such as:

- **What did you see happening in this scene?**

- **If you were Tonya's friend, would Tonya have persuaded you not to sign up for the beauty school?**

- **How did this role play affect or change your understanding of Tonya's story?**

Scenario B

Characters: Door-to-door salesperson, teen

Procedure
Before asking for volunteers, describe the scenario and ask the group to brainstorm a phony product for the door-to-door salesperson to sell. Suggest that teens think about products that people have actually tried to get them to buy. Here's the scene:

A door-to-door salesperson tries to sell a teen some product that the salesperson insists will change the teen's life in some way. The teen tries hard to resist the sales pitch.

Once the group has settled on a product, ask for volunteers. Allow five to ten minutes for the role play. Afterward, discuss questions such as:

- **What did you see happening in this scene?**

- **If you were the teen, would you have been persuaded to buy the product?**

- **How did this role play affect or change your understanding of Tonya's story?**

5. Group Activity

Objective: Teens will explore how advertisements appeal to our dreams and desires.

Materials: Paper, pencils, drawing/painting supplies, audiovisual supplies

Procedure

Tell the group that the object of this exercise is to show that most people are capable of being deceived by an attractive sales pitch. Have teens help you generate a list of desires most people have; for example, to get rich, to be loved, to have a good job, to have friends, and so on. Write all ideas on the board. Then ask each teen to choose one desire from the list that he or she personally wants very much. Ask each group member to create an advertisement for a product that would appeal to someone who wanted this particular thing. (They might also work with partners or in small groups.) The advertisement might be done as a poster, collage, song, jingle, rap, recording, video, and so on. Encourage everyone to be as wild, creative, funny, or inspiring as it takes to create an ad that would manipulate someone into spending money. When they've finished, ask everyone to present and describe their ads. Briefly discuss each one. Conclude by encouraging discussion about how teens might stay independent of the claims of advertisers, regardless of how much they want something. Ask:

- How can you be your own person and stay independent of advertisers' sales pitches?

- How did this activity affect or change your understanding of Tonya's story?

6. Writing Activities: Taking It Further

Ask students to complete one or more of the following activities individually, in small groups, or at home. Modify the activities as needed to suit the writing ability of group members. When activities are completed, invite volunteers to read their work to the group. Discuss how teens felt about the purpose and value of the writing.

Activity A

Objective: Group members will describe Tonya's independence in their own words as they try to persuade a friend not to sign up for Barbara's Beauty School.

Pretend you're Tonya. Write a letter to a friend who's just about to sign up for Barbara's Beauty School and wants your opinion. Describe how you were treated and how your bad experience at Barbara's made you more independent and *self-assured*, less likely to fall for a sales pitch again. Try to persuade your friend not to sign up.

Activity B

Objective: Group members will describe Tonya's independence in their own words as they write a letter of complaint to Barbara's Beauty School.

Pretend you're Tonya. Write a letter to the president of Barbara's Beauty School. Show your newly found independence by explaining why you feel you were treated poorly, why you stopped going to the school, and how you intend to respond to sales pitches in the future.

7. In Your Journal: Making It Personal

Encourage group members to reflect on the following topic in their journals:

Tonya let the people at the beauty school convince her that they knew better than she did. From the experience, she learned the value of independence: stepping back and asking yourself what you really want. Write about a time when you mistakenly trusted someone's advice and *deferred* to the person's judgment because you thought she or he knew more than you. Ask yourself: Why did I believe the person knew more than I did? What *clouded* my judgment? How long did it take me to discover my mistake? In the future, how do I decide whether to trust someone's advice or follow what I think is best for me?

MY WEIGHT IS NO BURDEN
by Charlene Johnson

Pages 40–43 in *The Struggle to Be Strong*

PREPARING TO LEAD THE ACTIVITIES

Story Summary

When Charlene starts junior high, she becomes obsessed with her weight and wants to be as thin as the fashion models she sees in magazines. Between purposely throwing up after meals and eating child-size portions, she manages to lose twenty pounds rather quickly. But she regains the weight and becomes deeply depressed, thinking she's fat and ugly. She writes a suicide note and gives it to her sister, who accuses Charlene of writing it for attention. The next day, Charlene hides some pills under her pillow and writes good-bye letters, which she again gives to her sister. This time the sister alerts their foster mother, who intervenes before Charlene can harm herself. She urges Charlene to see a therapist. Therapy helps Charlene worry less about her weight. Though she's still concerned, she realizes "there's more to life than being slim like a model in a magazine."

A Moment of Reflection

To connect with the story's themes, consider from your own perspective the questions group members will address during freewriting: Think of a time when you felt dissatisfied or self-conscious about your appearance. What brought on those feelings? How did you deal with them? Were you able to cast them off? Are you still bothered by your body image or appearance? If so, what could you do to feel good about yourself?

How Independence Works in the Story

Seeing Charlene's Independence

Charlene shows her growing independence as she shifts from measuring herself by a standard of appearance set by others to measuring herself by her own standards. We see the first signs of this shift in her realization that her weight obsession has gotten out of control: "I realized I was getting worse. I knew I needed some kind of help." Her suicide note and good-bye letters are attempts to get help. Finally, with her foster mother's support, Charlene begins therapy. She benefits greatly from the therapist's advice: "She said I was an intelligent, caring, and beautiful young adult, and that I should not let my weight be my burden." Using these words as her touchstone, Charlene brings her behavior under control by accepting and sticking to a diet plan that the therapist offers. She achieves an independent perspective on her appearance and tells her readers, "Young women should not make body image their first priority."

Why Independence Is a Struggle for Charlene

Charlene's experience is an example of the enormous social pressures young women face to be thin. She feels that pressure so strongly that she purposely throws up after meals and denies herself food to the point of getting sick. She's depressed, cries a lot, and can't sleep. She even contemplates killing herself. Charlene has a difficult struggle rejecting society's image of beauty and accepting herself as she is. Yet she persists until she wins the independence that allows her to put her physical appearance in perspective: "I realize I have a life to live, not just a body to get thin. I'm smart. I know that with my good brain I can be anything I want to be." By story's end, however, Charlene is not totally immune to the pressure to be thin. She lets us know she will continue to struggle: "I still worry about my weight a lot. . . . But now I don't take it to the extreme of thinking about suicide."

Useful Concept Words

To assist teens in understanding and discussing this story, you may want to introduce some or all of the following concept words by making them part of discussions and activities. Write them on the board in advance and plan to explain each word when it appears in a suggested discussion question or activity (where the words are shown in italics). Here are the concept words, with definitions and sentences relating them to the story.

balance: *stability; harmony; steadiness*
*Charlene eventually finds a **balance** between the media ideal of beauty and what's comfortable for her.*

burden: *something difficult to bear physically or emotionally*
*Charlene's weight becomes an emotional **burden** for her.*

conform: *to change or adjust behavior or opinions to fit society's standards*
*Charlene tries to **conform** to the media's emphasis on being thin.*

perspective: *a clear view of the true importance of things*
*Charlene gains **perspective** on her weight.*

self-acceptance: *comfort or ease with who one is*
*Charlene achieves greater **self-acceptance** as she becomes less obsessed with her weight.*

ACTIVITIES

1. Freewriting: Finding Yourself in the Story

After group members have finished reading the story, ask them to take out writing materials. If you'll be writing also, have handy your own journal and tell students you'll be participating. For a description of freewriting, see pages 14–15.

The following statement and questions are similar to those you considered earlier in "A Moment of Reflection." This time, you may want to write along with your group.

Think of a time when you felt unhappy or self-conscious about the way you look. What brought on those feelings? How did you deal with them? Were you able to get rid of them and feel good about yourself? Are you still unhappy with the way you look? If so, what could you do to feel good about yourself?

After the freewriting, invite volunteers to share what they wrote. Allow time for brief discussion.

NOTE: Avoiding Roadblocks

This story raises several serious issues that may come up during discussion: eating disorders, depression, suicidal thoughts or threats. Refer as necessary to "Handling Sensitive Issues," pages 7–8. Know when to make a referral to a program or professional outside the classroom if a teen in your group discloses that she or he is struggling with one of these issues. You might also simply encourage group members to seek professional help if they are personally concerned about these issues, and to seek help for anyone they know who seems at risk. Encourage individuals to see you privately for referral possibilities, and have resources available.

Another roadblock is that some teens may dismiss Charlene's obsession with her weight as "a girl's issue." Remind group members that eating disorders affect boys as well as girls, and that all teens face pressures about their appearance. Ask the group:

What pressures do you face about how you should look, dress, wear your hair, or whatever? How have you handled them?

2. Discussion: Understanding Events

To be sure group members have understood the story, ask questions such as:

- When does Charlene start feeling self-conscious about her weight?

- How does she try to lose weight? How does she feel after she gains all the weight back?

- How does Charlene's sister react to her suicide note?

- What happens after Charlene gives her sister her good-bye letters?

- What does the therapist tell Charlene? What's the effect of the therapy session on Charlene?

- What is Charlene's advice to young women "who think that being thin is all you need to get somewhere"?

3. Discussion: Understanding Issues

Charlene's Independence

Review with the group what independence is, why it's sometimes hard to come by, and how it can be helpful. Then, referring as necessary to "How Independence Works in the Story" (pages 50–51), ask questions such as:

- Why does Charlene start feeling self-conscious about her appearance? Why does her weight become a *burden* to her?

- What image is Charlene trying to *conform* to? Is it realistic or unrealistic? Why?

- Charlene writes a suicide note and good-bye letters but makes sure her sister sees them. Why do you think she does this?

- How does therapy help Charlene become more independent in her thinking and behavior? How does she learn *self-acceptance*?

- What helps Charlene put her feelings about her weight into *perspective?* How does she find a *balance* between media pressure to be thin and her own sense of independence?

Connecting with the Issues

Suggest that group members silently review what they wrote during freewriting. Then ask questions such as:

- Do you agree that society places too much importance on physical appearance? Explain. Why do you think it's so hard for people—teens especially—to break free from this pressure and be happy with themselves?

- Who do you think feels greater pressure to look a certain way: boys or girls? Explain your answer.

- Have you ever felt uncomfortable about your appearance? If so, what did you do to feel less uncomfortable?

- When have you *conformed* to how people think you should look? When have you gone against the crowd?

4. Role Play

For guidelines on role playing, see pages 15–16.

Objective: Group members will identify with Charlene's struggle to be independent of society's pressure to look a certain ideal way.

Characters: Charlene, her foster mother

Procedure
Ask for volunteers to enact this scene:

Charlene's foster mother has read Charlene's good-bye letters. Charlene is depressed and feeling hopeless about her weight. Her foster mother wants to convince her that she's okay as she is, but that she may need help from a therapist to accept herself.

Allow five to ten minutes for the role play. Afterward, discuss questions such as:

- What did you see happening in this scene?

- If you were Charlene, how would you feel about what your foster mother said?

- How did this role play affect or change your understanding of Charlene's story?

5. Writing Activities: Taking It Further

Ask students to complete one or more of the following activities individually, in small groups, or at home. Modify the activities as needed to suit the writing ability of group members. When activities are completed, invite volunteers to read their work to the group. Discuss how teens felt about the purpose and value of the writing.

Activity A

Objective: Group members will explain Charlene's independence in their own words.

Pretend you're Charlene. Write a letter to your therapist explaining how what she told you started you on the road to independence and a healthy *self-acceptance*.

Activity B

Objective: Group members will reflect on their own struggle with media pressures about appearance.

Charlene eventually found a *balance* between how the media said she should look and what was comfortable and possible for her. Have you learned to resist media pressure to *conform* to a particular look? If so, how? If not, would you like to? Why or why not?

Activity C

Objective: Group members will consider what self-acceptance means in their own lives.

How important is it to accept yourself as you are? If you accept yourself, does that mean you'll never change? Write about what you've learned to accept about yourself and your life. Then write about what you haven't learned—or don't want to learn—to accept.

6. In Your Journal: Making It Personal

Encourage group members to reflect on the following topic in their journals:

Charlene thought she needed to be as thin as the fashion models she saw in magazines. Think of a time you tried to look like or act like someone you weren't. Why did you do this? Are you still trying to do it? Do you like your image, or do you wish you could change it? What steps have you taken—or could you take—to be your own person, not the person others want you to be?

LOSING MY FRIENDS TO WEED
by Jamel A. Salter

Pages 44–47 in *The Struggle to Be Strong*

PREPARING TO LEAD THE ACTIVITIES

Story Summary

At fourteen, Jamel is still close to his childhood friends: he regularly plays basketball with them and enjoys their company. When they begin smoking marijuana, however, he's faced with a choice: smoke with them or lose their friendship. Jamel feels torn. He wants to keep his friends' approval, but he doesn't want to smoke. Though he's tempted to go along, he decides not to. As a result, they tease and ostracize him. As he continues to stand firm and refuse to smoke, they break off the friendship completely.

A Moment of Reflection

To connect with the story's themes, consider from your own perspective the questions group members will address during freewriting: Think about a time when you were pressured to go along with the negative behavior of others. Maybe your peers used drugs or alcohol, or engaged in other behavior you considered inappropriate. Or maybe you didn't want to go along with colleagues, a boss, or family members. Did you stand your ground? If so, how were you treated? If not, how did you feel about going against your principles?

How Independence Works in the Story

Seeing Jamel's Independence

When Jamel's friends decide to buy marijuana, Jamel doesn't put any money in, thinking his friends won't let him smoke and that he'll "pretend to be disappointed." However, his friends expect him to smoke anyway. He takes the blunt in his hand but then passes it on. Although it's painful when his friends tease him, he doesn't cave in to the pressure. When he's completely rejected by the group, even excluded from basketball games, he wonders if he should smoke "just one time" but he doesn't give in. The struggle to be his own person tests Jamel to the limit. At the end of the story, Jamel still feels hurt about losing his friends, but through his independence he's also learned something about friendship. He sees that the people he thought were his friends weren't true friends: "I know it was just a game." Jamel sees that a true friend would allow him to be independent *and* to feel he belongs. Neither should come at the expense of the other.

Why Independence Is a Struggle for Jamel

It's very hard to stand firm and not go along with the crowd. Although Jamel knows he made the right decision not to smoke, the consequences are hard for him to accept. In fact, he keeps trying to mend the rift with his friends, wondering whether he should relent and smoke in order to win them back. He knows that if they were true friends, they wouldn't have shut him out as they did. The struggle to be his own person tests Jamel's independence to the limit. As he says, "You might be wondering why I don't stop trying to stay close to them, why I don't make new friends. But it isn't so easy to lose friends you've grown up with." No sentence in this section better captures the pain that independence sometimes brings.

Useful Concept Words

To assist teens in understanding and discussing this story, you may want to introduce some or all of the following concept words by making them part of discussions and activities. Write them on the board in advance and plan to explain each word when it appears in a suggested discussion question or activity (where the words are shown in italics). Here are the concept words, with definitions and sentences relating them to the story.

compensate: *to make up for something*
To become truly independent, Jamel needs to **compensate** *for the loss of his friends.*

conform: *to change or adjust behavior or opinions to fit society's standards*
Jamel refuses to **conform** *to his friends' pressure to smoke marijuana.*

integrity: *quality of staying true to what you consider important*
Jamel shows he has **integrity** *when he doesn't give in to peer pressure.*

ostracize: *to banish, exclude, or keep out of a group*
Jamel's friends **ostracize** *him when he won't smoke marijuana.*

principles: *values; what you believe is right*
Jamel sticks to his **principles** *by not smoking marijuana.*

sacrifice: *to give up something*
Jamel **sacrifices** *his friends when he decides not to smoke marijuana.*

ACTIVITIES

1. Freewriting: Finding Yourself in the Story

After group members have finished reading the story, ask them to take out writing materials. If you'll be writing also, have handy your own journal and tell students you'll be participating. For a description of freewriting, see pages 14–15.

The following statement and questions are similar to those you considered earlier in "A Moment of Reflection." This time, you may want to write along with your group.

Think of a time when you were pressured to go along with something you didn't want to do. Maybe your friends wanted you to use drugs or alcohol, or take part in some other activity you didn't approve of. Maybe you didn't want to go along with people

you work with, a boss, or family members. Did you resist the pressure to go along? If so, how were you treated? How did you feel? If you decided to go along, how did you feel about doing something you didn't think was right?

After the freewriting, invite volunteers to share what they wrote. Allow time for brief discussion.

NOTE: Avoiding Roadblocks

Being judgmental about marijuana could sidetrack discussion of this story. Try to keep the focus on Jamel's independence, not on pot smoking. Let your group know you're interested in Jamel's courage and willpower in doing what he thinks is best for him. Point out the obstacle in his way—the pain of losing childhood friends—and the enormous effort it takes to get past it. If teens argue that they like marijuana or that Jamel should have smoked, stay close to the story. Try to build empathy for Jamel's struggle to be independent. You might also rely on the differing opinions within your group to carry the discussion. Encourage a variety of viewpoints so teens can see a range of options and consequences. Ask the group:

Do you think Jamel made the right decision for himself? If he'd decided to smoke marijuana, how do you think he'd have felt about himself? Do you know people who've been in a situation similar to Jamel's?

2. Discussion: Understanding Events

To be sure group members have understood the story, ask questions such as:

- **What does Jamel hope will happen when he doesn't put money in to buy marijuana? What does happen?**

- **Why does Jamel sit at the end of the line as the blunt is being passed? What does he do when the blunt is passed to him? How do his friends treat him?**

- What effect does smoking marijuana have on Jamel's friends?

- What happens when Jamel tries to steal the basketball from Dave during a game?

- How does Jamel feel when he finds out that his friends are playing basketball without him?

- Was there a time when you "went along with the crowd," even though you didn't want to? How do you feel about the incident now?

- Was there a time when you stayed independent and didn't "go along with the crowd"? How do you feel about the incident now?

3. Discussion: Understanding Issues

Jamel's Independence

Review with the group what independence is, why it's sometimes hard to come by, and how it can be helpful. Then, referring as necessary to "How Independence Works in the Story" (page 54), ask questions such as:

- What do you think of Jamel's decision not to smoke marijuana, even though his friends are all doing it? Should he have gone along with them for the sake of friendship? Explain your answer.

- What did Jamel gain from his decision not to smoke? What did he *sacrifice,* or lose?

- Why was Jamel's decision so hard to make?

- How would Jamel be a different person today if he'd gone along with his friends?

Connecting with the Issues

Suggest that group members silently review what they wrote during freewriting. Then ask questions such as:

- What would you have done if you were Jamel? Explain your reasoning.

- Do you think other people can make you do something you really don't want to do? Why or why not?

- Do you think it's difficult to stay independent of peer pressure? Is it hard to keep your *integrity*— to stay true to your *principles* of right and wrong? Why or why not?

- How much do you pay attention to the views of your friends in deciding what you want to do? Explain your answer.

4. Role Plays

For guidelines on role playing, see pages 15–16.

Objective: Group members will identify with Jamel's struggle to stand firm against his friends' pressure to smoke.

Scenario A

Characters: Jamel, his friend

Procedure
Ask for volunteers to enact this scene:

Jamel's friend wants Jamel to smoke marijuana. Jamel doesn't want to smoke.

Allow five to ten minutes for the role play. Afterward, discuss questions such as:

- What did you see happening in this scene?

- If you were Jamel, would your friend have convinced you to smoke? If you were Jamel's friend, how would you feel about Jamel's reasons for not smoking?

- How did this role play affect or change your understanding of Jamel's story?

Scenario B

Characters: Jamel, his old friend Dave

Procedure
Ask for volunteers to enact this scene:

Jamel wants Dave to know he's not been a true friend ever since he pressured Jamel to smoke marijuana. Dave wants Jamel to know he's not been a true friend since he refused to smoke.

Allow five to ten minutes for the role play. Afterward, discuss questions such as:

- What did you see happening in this scene?

- Who was more convincing: Jamel or Dave?

- How did this role play affect or change your understanding of Jamel's story?

5. Writing Activities: Taking It Further

Ask students to complete one or more of the following activities individually, in small groups, or at home. Modify the activities as needed to suit the writing ability of group members. When activities are completed, invite volunteers to read their work to the group. Discuss how teens felt about the purpose and value of the writing.

Activity A

Objective: Group members will describe Jamel's independence in their own words.

Pretend you're Jamel. Write a letter to Dave explaining that, although you're sorry to have lost him as a friend, you want him to understand why you've refused to smoke marijuana.

Activity B

Objective: Group members will speculate on what Jamel should do now.

What do you think Jamel should do now? Should he try harder to make new friends? Should he keep some contact with his old friends? How should he *compensate* for losing them? Write your opinion and explain your reasoning.

Activity C

Objective: Group members will consider their own definitions of independence.

To Jamel, independence means not doing something you think is wrong or harmful, even if your friends want you to—and even if your friends *ostracize* you for not *conforming.* Write about a time when you found it hard to be independent. What was hard about it? What did you do? What does independence mean to you?

6. In Your Journal: Making It Personal

Encourage group members to reflect on the following topic in their journals:

Although Jamel has been rejected by his friends, he still tries to keep in contact with them. Think about a time you were rejected by a group or couldn't become part of a group you wanted to belong to. Why do you think you were rejected or not allowed to join? What was the conflict between you and the group? Did you keep trying to be accepted? If so, what eventually happened? If not, did you find another group? If so, what made it different from the first one? What's the hardest thing about being your own person when you're part of a group? How do you find a balance in your life between being independent of others and still having friends?

OUT, WITHOUT A DOUBT
by Craig J. Jaffe

Pages 48–54 in *The Struggle to Be Strong*

PREPARING TO LEAD THE ACTIVITIES

Story Summary

As a young boy, Craig holds traditional stereotypes of manliness and is prejudiced against gay people. At thirteen and fourteen, he is terrified to find himself attracted to men. When he turns fifteen, he moves into a group home and is placed with a gay roommate, Mike. Craig tries to hold on to his negative stereotypes of gays, but he is also envious of Mike, who is out of the closet, doesn't fit the stereotypes, and is proud of who he is. Finally, Craig works up the courage to admit to Mike that he's gay. He experiences a tremendous sense of relief. One by one, he tells other people who are important to him. Most are supportive, but one close friend rejects him, using the same stereotypes Craig used to hold. Forced to compare himself to those stereotypes, Craig decides to be himself. He hesitates, however, to come out to his mother, with whom he's always had a bad relationship. When he finally tells her, she at first rejects him completely, but then comes around to grudging acceptance. At the end of the story, Craig is "out, without a doubt."

A Moment of Reflection

To connect with the story's themes, consider from your own perspective the questions group members will address during freewriting: Think of a time when you kept something important about yourself secret. It might have been something in your past, a relationship you didn't choose to reveal, a political opinion, a religious belief, or something else. How did it feel to keep a secret from those around you? Did you wish you could tell? Did you eventually decide to reveal the secret? If so, how did people react and how did you feel? If not, how did you feel about holding back?

How Independence Works in the Story

Seeing Craig's Independence

Craig takes the first step toward accepting himself and being his own person when he gets to know and admire Mike, his gay roommate. Discovering that Mike doesn't fit homophobic stereotypes and that he and Mike share many interests, Craig begins to feel more comfortable with his sexuality. Taking a second step toward independence, he sheds his own stereotypes and fears about gay people. When he musters the courage to tell Mike he's gay, he feels greatly relieved, "like I could even breathe a little bit easier now that I'd gotten this off my chest." Though "a straight female friend" doesn't believe he's gay because he doesn't fit the stereotypes, Craig becomes more and more determined to be himself, "regardless of what anybody said." The final test of Craig's independence comes when he decides to reveal his homosexuality to his homophobic mother. Though she rejects him at first, she gradually comes to accept him. By the end of the story, Craig's independence is solid. He rejects his mother's advice to hide his true identity, stands up to her criticism, vows never to hide behind a false front again, and feels proud of himself.

Why Independence Is a Struggle for Craig

Becoming comfortable with their sexuality is part of most teens' struggle toward independence. Since many people continue to hold negative, stereotyped views of homosexuality and gay people, it requires an especially difficult struggle for Craig to be his own person. He himself has believed negative stereotypes of gays for as long as he can remember: "I was going against everything I thought I believed in." Furthermore, coming from a painful family history, he now risks further disapproval and rejection from his mother. However, he stands to gain the freedom that comes from self-acceptance. Though his story ends on a note of success, we know his struggle isn't over. Craig will probably continue to encounter hurtful prejudice against gays that will test his capacity to be independent.

Useful Concept Words

To assist teens in understanding and discussing this story, you may want to introduce some or all of the following concept words by making them part of discussions and activities. Write them on the board in advance and plan to explain each word when it appears in a suggested discussion question or activity (where the words are shown in italics). Here are the concept words, with definitions and sentences relating them to the story.

conceal: *to hide or keep secret*
Craig **conceals** the fact that he's gay.

homophobic: *afraid of gay people or of homosexuality itself*
Craig's mother is **homophobic.**

liberate: *to set free*
Craig feels **liberated** when he accepts who he is.

reveal: *to make known*
Craig first **reveals** he's gay to his roommate, Mike.

ACTIVITIES

1. Freewriting: Finding Yourself in the Story

After group members have finished reading the story, ask them to take out writing materials. If you'll be writing also, have handy your own journal and tell students you'll be participating. For a description of freewriting, see pages 14–15.

The following statement and questions are similar to those you considered earlier in "A Moment of Reflection." This time, you may want to write along with your group.

Think of a time when you kept something important about yourself secret. It might have been something in your past, a family situation, a relationship you didn't want anyone to know about, a religious or political belief, or something else. How did it feel to keep a secret from those around you? Did you wish

you could tell someone? Did you eventually decide to reveal the secret? If so, how did people react and how did you feel? If not, how did you feel about holding back?

After the freewriting, invite volunteers to share what they wrote. Allow time for brief discussion.

NOTE: Avoiding Roadblocks

Many people have strong feelings about gay people and homosexuality. It's important to provide a safe atmosphere for gay kids, for kids who have gay family members or friends, and for everyone who believes people should be accepted for who they are. While some students may be uneasy about discussing the topic, or even homophobic, others will be supportive of Craig. You're the best judge of whether your group members have sufficient trust in and respect for each other to discuss this story appropriately. If you feel they're ready, expect and encourage a wide range of opinions, but don't allow inappropriate humor, name-calling, or stereotyping about gays, just as you wouldn't allow them about any other group. (As necessary, remind students of the guidelines for group discussion that you've established.) Instead of dwelling on Craig's homosexuality, try to keep the discussion focused on how he managed to reveal a secret that was at the heart of his identity. Help teens see Craig's difficulties in the broad context of the struggle to be independent. Ask the group:

What made Craig's struggle to be independent so difficult? How is he a different person at the end of the story?

2. Discussion: Understanding Events

To be sure group members have understood the story, ask questions such as:

- **As a young boy, how did Craig feel about gay people? When he was thirteen and fourteen, how did his feelings change?**

- How does Mike change Craig's view of gay people?

- How does Craig feel after he tells Mike he's gay?

- How does Craig's "straight female friend" react when he tells her he's gay?

- Why is Craig slow to tell his mother he's gay? What kind of relationship have they had? When he finally tells his mother, what's her reaction? How's their relationship now?

- Why does Craig now enjoy telling people he's gay?

3. Discussion: Understanding Issues

Craig's Independence

Review with the group what independence is, why it's sometimes hard to come by, and how it can be helpful. Then, referring as necessary to "How Independence Works in the Story" (pages 58–59), ask questions such as:

- What does Craig admire most about Mike? Why do you think Mike is the first person Craig tells about his homosexuality?

- Why do you think Craig comes out as a gay person gradually, in stages? Why doesn't he "tell the whole world"?

- Why is Craig so relieved to tell everyone— including his mother—that he's gay? In what ways does he feel *liberated,* or set free?

- How difficult do you think Craig's struggle for independence is? Why do you think so?

- What does Craig risk when he decides to *reveal* his sexuality? What's at stake for him?

Connecting with the Issues

Suggest that group members silently review what they wrote during freewriting. Then ask questions such as:

- Craig says that before he came out as a gay person, "I was sacrificing being happy for my reputation." What does he mean? Have you ever

felt that way about something you hadn't told anyone?

- Have you ever secretly admired someone else's confidence or independence, as Craig admired Mike's? How do you think that person got to be that way? What impact did that person have on you?

- Do you see any similarities between Craig's experiences and your own struggle to be independent? If so, what are they?

4. Role Plays

For guidelines about role playing, see pages 15–16.

Objective: Group members will identify with Craig's struggle to become independent.

Scenario A

Characters: Craig, Mike

Procedure
Ask for volunteers to enact this scene:

Craig wants to back down about telling his mother he's gay and continue to *conceal* his identity from her. Mike wants to convince Craig to tell her.

Allow five to ten minutes for the role play. Afterward, discuss questions such as:

- What did you see happening in this scene?

- If you were Craig, would Mike have convinced you to tell your mother?

- How did this role play affect or change your understanding of Craig's story?

Scenario B

Characters: Craig, his "straight female friend"

Procedure
Ask for volunteers to enact this scene:

Craig tells his friend that he's gay. She wants to convince him that he can't be gay because he doesn't "act feminine." Craig wants to explain that not all gay men behave or look the same way.

Allow five to ten minutes for the role play. Afterward, discuss questions such as:

- **What did you see happening in this scene?**

- **If you were Craig's friend, would Craig have convinced you to change your views about gay men?**

- **How did this role play affect or change your understanding of Craig's story?**

5. Group Activity

Objective: Teens will empathize with peers who are burdened by secrets.

Procedure
Tell the group that the object of this activity is to show how difficult it is to share important secrets about ourselves. First, have them brainstorm a list of secrets that teens typically keep, such as failing in school, losing an important relationship, abusing alcohol or drugs, being in foster care, having no mother or father at home, not having much money, being fired from a job, and so on. Next, ask everyone to choose one secret either from the list or from their own lives (they can choose how personal they want to get) and write it on a piece of paper. Then ask them to write one reason why someone would want to keep that secret, and one reason why someone might want to reveal it.

Now ask them to imagine that a friend of theirs has just revealed to them the secret they've written about. Each teen, knowing how hard it was for the friend to reveal the secret, is to write one or two paragraphs saying how she or he would respond to this friend.

When everyone's done, encourage volunteers to read aloud what they've written. Conclude by discussing what group members felt they learned from this activity. Ask:

- **Why is it useful to practice what you might say to a friend who *revealed* a personal secret to you?**

- **How did this activity affect or change your understanding of Craig's story?**

6. Writing Activities: Taking It Further

Ask students to complete one or more of the following activities individually, in small groups, or at home. Modify the activities as needed to suit the writing ability of group members. When activities are completed, invite volunteers to read their work to the group. Discuss how teens felt about the purpose and value of the writing.

Activity A

Objective: Group members will describe Craig's independence in their own words.

Pretend you're Craig. Write a letter to Mike explaining how knowing him helped you accept yourself and learn to be your own person.

Activity B

Objective: Group members will reflect on someone in their own lives who has helped them become independent.

Mike helps Craig to feel comfortable with who he is and to stop feeling *homophobic*. Write about someone in your life who has helped you become comfortable with yourself. You might write a short letter to that person.

Activity C

Objective: Group members will describe a secret they once kept, but have now revealed.

Write a paragraph titled, "Something I Once Kept Secret." In the first sentence, tell about the thing you once *concealed*. Then describe why you kept the secret, why you *revealed* it, how people responded, and what the differences were for you after you revealed it. How do you feel now about having revealed that secret?

7. In Your Journal: Making It Personal

Encourage group members to reflect on the following topic in their journals:

Craig is gay, yet he held prejudiced beliefs about gay people. He realized that until he freed himself from these prejudices, he couldn't fully accept himself. Think of a prejudice you hold (or others hold) about a group you belong to or are identified with. The group could be based on your gender, age, weight, religion, sexual preference, interests, dress, taste in music, circle of friends, or something else. (For example, if you're an athlete, people might think you don't do well in school. You might even believe that about yourself.) Ask yourself: What is the prejudiced belief you have (or other people have) about this group? Where do you think the belief comes from? (Your family? Friends? The media?) How has this belief affected your view of yourself? Do you think you can fully accept yourself while having this belief or knowing others believe it? What could you do to change the way you or other people feel about the group you belong to?

I'M BLACK, HE'S PUERTO RICAN . . . SO WHAT?
by Artiqua S. Steed

Pages 55–59 in *The Struggle to Be Strong*

PREPARING TO LEAD THE ACTIVITIES

Story Summary

Artiqua gets to know Johnny and soon begins dating him. Since she's African-American and he's Puerto Rican, she's surprised at how the relationship progresses. She's always been "very into black pride," believing black women should only date black men. Meeting Johnny, however, has changed her attitudes. Now she feels "that if a black woman dates a man of another race, it doesn't mean she's given up on black men." However, Artiqua is pressured to break off the relationship by family and friends, who feel she is betraying her people. She's also confused by her own stereotypes of Puerto Ricans, which she eventually drops: "I've learned they're not true. It hurts me when people dis Puerto Ricans because they're talking about my boyfriend." Despite the pressures, Artiqua continues seeing Johnny. Gradually, the negative comments seem less important. She realizes that being loyal to her African-American heritage does not require her to reject people of other races. "If you ask me, being of different races hasn't made our lives together more difficult, but more interesting."

A Moment of Reflection

To connect with the story's themes, consider from your own perspective the questions group members will address during freewriting: Think of a time when people close to you disapproved of your friendship or relationship with someone you cared for (or think about a friend who had this experience). Why did they disapprove? How did it feel to be friends with or date someone your family or friends didn't like (or, what was the experience like for your friend)? What happened? Did you (or your friend) eventually break off with this person? If so, was the breakup because of your (or your friend's) family or friends' disapproval, or for some other reason? How did you (or your friend) feel about what happened?

How Independence Works in the Story

Seeing Artiqua's Independence

We first see Artiqua's independence when she pursues her friendship with Johnny despite being laughed at by her sister and her friend, and despite her own negative feelings about interracial dating. She is open-minded enough to realize that she likes Johnny and is "excited to learn more about him. . . . to see the world from his perspective." Although Artiqua moderates her stand against interracial relationships as her feelings for Johnny grow, members of her family and some of her friends don't. As the disapproval mounts, Artiqua continues to stand firm. She learns to get past her own stereotypes about Puerto Ricans and the pressures of family and friends. She also makes a conscious decision not to conform to the bigoted attitudes of "outsiders," even though the choice causes her some pain. She evaluates the flaws in other people's opinions, and she forms her own opinions in contrast to theirs. Faced with a conflict between the group's view and her own principles, she thinks for herself: "Now when I hear racial slurs against Puerto Ricans, I'm offended by them. I've learned they're not true." She cherishes her relationship with Johnny and is happy, proud, and confident that she is being her own person.

Why Independence Is a Struggle for Artiqua

From the moment Artiqua finds herself attracted to a man who isn't black, she experiences the scorn and disapproval of some family members and friends. She also must battle her own prejudices against Puerto Ricans. Going against what one's group believes and changing one's own beliefs are difficult matters for anyone, particularly for a young person. It would have been easier for Artiqua to break off the relationship to please her relatives and friends. Instead, she reexamines her own views, decides what she thinks, and then sticks to her beliefs even when others disapprove. Still, "the hard part is dealing with other people's attitudes."

Useful Concept Words

To assist teens in understanding and discussing this story, you may want to introduce some or all of the following concept words by making them part of discussions and activities. Write them on the board in advance and plan to explain each word when it appears in a suggested discussion question or activity (where the words are shown in italics). Here are the concept words, with definitions and sentences relating them to the story.

distance: *to disconnect from; to withdraw*
*By being her own person, Artiqua **distances** herself from her family's views on relationships.*

evaluate: *to judge or determine the worth or value of something*
*Artiqua **evaluates** her family's arguments and her own feelings and does what's right for her.*

loyalty: *staying true to a person, group, or idea*
*Despite the disapproval of family and friends, Artiqua maintains her **loyalty** to Johnny and her feelings for him.*

prejudice: *a negative opinion of a person or group which is not based on fact*
*At first, like some of her family and friends, Artiqua is **prejudiced** toward Puerto Ricans.*

steadfast: *faithful; sticking to a position, even when one is being pressured*
*Artiqua is **steadfast** in rejecting pressure not to date a Puerto Rican boy.*

ACTIVITIES

1. Freewriting: Finding Yourself in the Story

After group members have finished reading the story, ask them to take out writing materials. If you'll be writing also, have handy your own journal and tell students you'll be participating. For a description of freewriting, see pages 14–15.

The following statement and questions are similar to those you considered earlier in "A Moment of Reflection." This time, you may want to write along with your group.

Think of a time when people close to you disapproved of your friendship or relationship with someone you cared for (or think about a friend who had this experience). Why did they disapprove? How did it feel to be friends with or date someone your family or friends didn't like (or, what was the experience like for your friend)? What happened? Did you (or your friend) eventually break off with this person? If so, was the breakup because of your (or your friend's) family or friends' disapproval, or for some other reason? How did you (or your friend) feel about what happened?

After the freewriting, invite volunteers to share what they wrote. Allow time for brief discussion.

2. Discussion: Understanding Events

To be sure group members have understood the story, ask questions such as:

- **How does Artiqua meet Johnny?**

- **Why does she say that dating Johnny caught her by surprise?**

- **How do Artiqua's brother, her sister, and some of her friends react to her relationship with Johnny?**

- **What was Artiqua's attitude toward Puerto Ricans before she met Johnny? What's her attitude now?**

- How do Johnny's family and friends react to his relationship with Artiqua?

- What sometimes happens when "outsiders" see Artiqua and Johnny together?

NOTE: Avoiding Roadblocks

Interracial dating is a controversial topic, and your group may have strong feelings about it—for and against. Your challenge will be to allow teens to express their feelings on the topic and then to link their comments to the story's underlying theme of independence. Focus discussion on the independence theme: what Artiqua did in the story, how she made her decision, the consequences of her decision. Help group members relate to her struggle for independence by asking open-ended questions that go beyond interracial dating and racial identity. For example, ask them:

Would it be easy or difficult for you to continue in a relationship your family or friends disapproved of? Why do you think so?

---

3. Discussion: Understanding Issues

Artiqua's Independence

Review with the group what independence is, why it's sometimes hard to come by, and how it can be helpful. Then, referring as necessary to "How Independence Works in the Story" (pages 63–64), ask questions such as:

- What does Artiqua mean when she says, "I have to admit that the fact that Johnny isn't black is one of the reasons I started liking him so much"?

- How did meeting Johnny change Artiqua's attitude about "black pride"? How did knowing him change her opinions about Puerto Ricans?

- How does Artiqua show her independence when her friends, family, or other people "dis Puerto Ricans"?

- Why do you think Artiqua's family and friends disapprove of her relationship with Johnny? How does Artiqua *evaluate* and then *distance* herself from their views?

Connecting with the Issues

Suggest that group members silently review what they wrote during freewriting. Then ask questions such as:

- How do you feel about the way Artiqua handled the situation? Do you think she made the right choice by continuing to date Johnny? Why or why not? What would you have done?

- When Artiqua started dating Johnny, some of the people close to her felt she was going against "black pride." Have you ever been accused of doing something that went against your racial, ethnic, or social group? Explain.

- Have you ever dated someone or had a friend from a different ethnic or racial background than yours? What was the reaction of your friends and family? What did you learn from the experience?

- How do you feel about interracial dating? Do you think you could be as independent and *steadfast* as Artiqua is, especially if your family and friends made disrespectful remarks about the person you were dating?

---

4. Role Play

For guidelines on role playing, see pages 15–16.

Objective: Group members will identify with Artiqua's struggle to stay independent in the face of pressure to conform.

Characters: Artiqua, her friend

Procedure
Ask for volunteers to enact this scene:

Artiqua is talking with her friend about her relationship with Johnny. Her friend wants her to break off the relationship. Artiqua wants to continue seeing Johnny.

Allow five to ten minutes for the role play. Afterward, discuss questions such as:

- **What did you see happening in this scene?**

- **If you were Artiqua, would your friend have convinced you to break off the relationship?**

- **How did this role play affect or change your understanding of Artiqua's story?**

5. Writing Activities: Taking It Further

Ask students to complete one or more of the following activities individually, in small groups, or at home. Modify the activities as needed to suit the writing ability of group members. When activities are completed, invite volunteers to read their work to the group. Discuss how teens felt about the purpose and value of the writing.

Activity A

Objective: Group members will describe Artiqua's independence in their own words.

Pretend you're Artiqua. Write a letter to Johnny, explaining the pressures you're feeling from friends and family, and how and why you're resisting them.

Activity B

Objective: Group members will reflect on a common expression about love.

What does the expression "love is blind" mean to you? Do you agree with it? Why or why not? How does the expression apply to Artiqua's story? How does it apply to your life?

6. In Your Journal: Making It Personal

Encourage group members to reflect on the following topic in their journals.

Dating Johnny causes Artiqua to change strong beliefs she had about race, relationships, *loyalty*, and *prejudice*. Think of a person or situation that caused you to change a strong belief. Describe the belief you had and how you developed it. What caused you to change your belief? Did the experience lead you to question other beliefs? Explain.

FIVE TEENS: THE IMPORTANCE OF INDEPENDENCE

As necessary, refer to pages 34 and 35 in the anthology to review with your group what independence is and why it's a resilience. Then invite group members to compare how independence works in the lives of the five teen writers in this section. (To help students recall each writer, you might list their first names on the board.) Ask questions such as:

- **Which writer do you think has the toughest time stepping back from outside pressures and being his or her own person? Why do you think so?**

- **Which writer do you think shows the most courage in standing apart from the group and staying true to personal values? Why do you think so?**

- **Which writer do you think changes the most because of her or his independence? Why do you think so?**

- **Which story in this section do you like best? Which teen writer do you admire most? Explain your choices.**

Many of the teen writers in this book demonstrate more than one resilience. If your group has read other stories, you might ask members to discuss how writers in other sections also demonstrate independence.

RELATIONSHIPS
CONNECTING WITH PEOPLE WHO MATTER

Before discussing the stories in this section, ask the group to read the introductory material about relationships in their anthology, pages 60 and 61. Allow time for questions and brief discussion. Be sure teens understand the following:

- **Relationships** are connections with other people based on sharing, mutual respect, and openness.

- The opposite of building **relationships** is cutting yourself off from others, protecting yourself by hiding behind a false front, or valuing other people only for what they can do for you.

- **Relationships** are hard because you must *give* of yourself as well as *take*. **Relationships** require you to take risks and trust others.

- **Relationships** give you understanding, friendship, and sometimes even love.

As teens read each story, encourage them to look for ways the writer builds relationships. Also suggest that they reflect on—and possibly jot down ideas about—the questions that follow each story ("Think About It"). Refer them to the introductory section "'Think About It'—and Maybe Write About It," pages 7–8 in the anthology.

ALL TALK AND NO ACTION
by Elizabeth Thompson

Pages 62–65 in *The Struggle to Be Strong*

PREPARING TO LEAD THE ACTIVITIES

Story Summary

Out of the blue, Elizabeth receives a phone call from a boy she's never met. Soon she and the boy she calls Stormie are talking on the phone regularly and become close friends. Their conversations range from silly to serious, and they help each other solve problems—particularly, problems connected with understanding the opposite sex. Elizabeth can talk to Stormie much more freely than she can to her boyfriend. At one point, she and Stormie make plans to meet, but somehow they miss each other at the meeting place. The story ends with Elizabeth's reflection on how her telephone relationship with Stormie allows her to achieve a greater level of intimacy than if she had actually met him: "Boys are hard to have friendships with in person."

A Moment of Reflection

To connect with the story's themes, consider from your own perspective the questions group members will address during freewriting: Think about the possibility of developing a close friendship with someone you've never met in person—only over the phone, through letters or email, or in an Internet chat room. How might such a relationship be different from a face-to-face friendship? What qualities would you like such a friend to have? What kinds of things might you talk about? Do you think you'd eventually like to meet the person? Why or why not?

How Relationships Work in the Story

Seeing Elizabeth's Relationships

Through Elizabeth's comparisons of her friendships with Stormie and her boyfriend, we see her view of what she wants in a relationship. Since she avoids meeting Stormie face to face—and perhaps being attracted to him—Elizabeth can freely talk with him, as she feels she never could if they met. Stormie gives her insights into the male mind. On the phone with him, Elizabeth listens and is heard. She trusts and is trusted. She likes her boyfriend too, but for different reasons. Though he hides his emotions and doesn't know how to cope with hers, they have fun together. As she says, "My boyfriend and Stormie make me see that there's no boy in this world who has every detail I want." It seems no accident that when she and Stormie do try to meet, the plan fails: "Actually, I'm kind of beating around the bush when it comes to meeting Stormie, because I'm afraid it might change our relationship." At the end of the story, Elizabeth seems comfortable being emotionally close to a boy she's never met and proud of her unconventional relationship.

Why Relationships Are a Struggle for Elizabeth

Most teens struggle with how to form real, lasting relationships with members of the opposite sex. Neither Elizabeth's relationship with Stormie nor her relationship with her boyfriend is complete. Each boy supplies what the other can't or won't. Stormie is a comforting voice, but he's physically unavailable. Her boyfriend, on the other hand, is unavailable emotionally. He's not good at making conversation or coping with feelings. Elizabeth's challenge is to find the emotional fulfillment she gets from the friendship with Stormie with a person she can meet face-to-face.

Useful Concept Words

To assist teens in understanding and discussing this story, you may want to introduce some or all of the following concept words by making them part of discussions and activities. Write them on the board in advance and plan to explain each word when it appears in a suggested discussion question or activity (where the words are shown in italics). Here are the concept words, with definitions and sentences relating them to the story.

anonymous: *unknown*
Stormie is Elizabeth's **anonymous** *friend.*

divided: *pulled by conflicting interests*
Elizabeth feels **divided** *in both her relationships.*

intimate: *very close; very familiar*
Although they don't meet, Stormie and Elizabeth have an emotionally **intimate** *relationship.*

mutual: *shared; in common*
Stormie and Elizabeth have many **mutual** *interests and concerns.*

platonic: *close without being sexual*
Stormie and Elizabeth have a **platonic** *relationship.*

ACTIVITIES

1. Freewriting: Finding Yourself in the Story

After group members have finished reading the story, ask them to take out writing materials. If you'll be writing also, have handy your own journal and tell students you'll be participating. For a description of freewriting, see pages 14–15.

The following statement and questions are similar to those you considered earlier in "A Moment of Reflection." This time, you may want to write along with your group.

Think about the possibility of developing a close friendship with someone you've never met in person—only over the phone, through letters or email, or in an Internet chat room. How do you think a relationship like that would be different from a face-to-face friendship? What qualities would you like such a friend to have? What kinds of things might you talk about? Do you think you'd eventually like to meet the person? Why or why not?

After the freewriting, invite volunteers to share what they wrote. Allow time for brief discussion.

2. Discussion: Understanding Events

To be sure group members have understood the story, ask questions such as:

- How does Elizabeth's relationship with Stormie begin?

- What kinds of things do Elizabeth and Stormie talk about?

- What does Elizabeth like about having Stormie for a friend?

- How is Stormie different from Elizabeth's boyfriend? What does she like about each?

- What happens when Elizabeth and Stormie make plans to meet?

3. Discussion: Understanding Issues

Elizabeth's Relationships

Review with the group what relationships are, why they're sometimes hard to come by, and how they can be helpful. Then, referring as necessary to "How Relationships Work in the Story" (pages 68–69), ask questions such as:

- What do each of Elizabeth's relationships—with Stormie and with her boyfriend—offer her that the other doesn't? Why do you think she feels so *divided* between them? Which relationship do you think is more important to her? Why do you think so?

- Why do you think Elizabeth and Stormie arranged to meet "at the train station at 3:30" but never did meet? What do you think happened?

- If you were Stormie or Elizabeth, would you want to meet your *anonymous* "phone friend"? Why or why not?

Connecting with the Issues

Suggest that group members silently review what they wrote during freewriting. Then ask questions such as:

- Elizabeth says, "Boys are hard to have friendships with in person." What does she mean by that? Do you agree that it's difficult to have friendships or *platonic* relationships—as opposed to romantic or dating relationships—with people of the opposite sex? Why or why not?

- Is there a Stormie in your life, an *intimate* friend you've never met or only see once in a while? If so, what makes this person a good friend?

- Have you ever had a close friendship—but not a romantic relationship—with someone of the opposite sex? If so, how did you feel about it? If not, would you like to? Why or why not?

- What do you look for in friendships? Is it important for friends to have *mutual* interests? Why or why not? What makes you a good friend? What's hard about keeping friends?

4. Role Plays

For guidelines on role playing, see pages 15–16.

Objective: Group members will practice discussing what qualities make for real, lasting relationships.

Scenario A

Characters: Elizabeth, her boyfriend

Procedure
Ask for volunteers to enact this scene:

Elizabeth's boyfriend has found out about her relationship with Stormie. Elizabeth wants to explain what Stormie offers that he doesn't. The boyfriend wants to convince Elizabeth that their relationship is better than the one she has with Stormie.

Allow five to ten minutes for the role play. Afterward, discuss questions such as:

- What did you see happening in this scene?

- If you were Elizabeth's boyfriend, would Elizabeth have convinced you that she needs both you and Stormie as friends?

- How did this role play affect or change your understanding of Elizabeth's story?

Scenario B

Characters: Stormie, a male friend

Procedure
Ask for volunteers to enact this scene:

Stormie tells his friend about his phone relationship with Elizabeth. The friend is doubtful that any guy could have that kind of relationship with a girl. Stormie defends and explains his relationship with Elizabeth.

Allow five to ten minutes for the role play. Afterward, discuss questions such as:

- What did you see happening in this scene?

- If you were the friend, would Stormie have convinced you that it's possible to have a close relationship with a girl you've never met?

- How did this role play affect or change your understanding of Elizabeth's story?

5. Writing Activities: Taking It Further

Ask students to complete one or more of the following activities individually, in small groups, or at home. Modify the activities as needed to suit the writing ability of group members. When activities are completed, invite volunteers to read their work to the group. Discuss how teens felt about the purpose and value of the writing.

Activity A

Objective: Group members will describe Elizabeth's view of relationships in their own words.

Pretend you're Elizabeth. Write a letter to your boyfriend explaining why you value both the relationship with him and the relationship with Stormie.

Activity B

Objective: Group members will consider the story from Stormie's point of view.

Pretend you're Stormie. Write a letter to a male friend, explaining your relationship with Elizabeth.

Activity C

Objective: Group members will reflect on what they want from relationships.

What do you think is more important in a relationship: being able to talk to someone about your personal life, as Elizabeth and Stormie do, or having fun, as Elizabeth and her boyfriend do? Explain why.

6. In Your Journal: Making It Personal

Encourage group members to reflect on the following topic in their journals:

Elizabeth and her good friend Stormie have an unusual relationship. Think about an important friendship of your own. Why are you and this person such good friends? How do you keep the relationship strong and lasting? What's hard about keeping the relationship strong over time? What do you think makes you a good friend? What makes this person a good friend?

SHE'S MY SISTER (NOT FOSTER)
by Tamara Ballard

Pages 66–69 in *The Struggle to Be Strong*

PREPARING TO LEAD THE ACTIVITIES

Story Summary

When Tamara moves to a new foster home, she has to share a room with Cheryl, an older girl who has a job. Unused to roommates, Tamara finds Cheryl bossy. She responds "with a real snotty attitude," and the girls argue a lot. Gradually, however, things change. The two begin talking, and Tamara finds that they like many of the same things. She stops viewing Cheryl as an intruder in her space, recognizes her good qualities, and begins to see her as a role model and potential friend. Most of all, Tamara comes to understand that she and Cheryl have something powerful in common: they're both foster children. As she puts it, "I began to see that we were sailing along in the same boat, only she was more equipped than I was and I needed her." They begin confiding in one another and feeling like sisters. Tamara's change in attitude leads to a respectful, caring relationship with Cheryl.

A Moment of Reflection

To connect with the story's themes, consider from your own perspective the questions group members will address during freewriting: Think of a time when you started out disliking someone who later became a good friend. Why didn't you like the person at first? What happened to change your feelings? Did one of you change your behavior toward the other? Did you both change? How hard was it to begin to see the person as a friend?

How Relationships Work in the Story

Seeing Tamara's Relationships

Having longed for a sister, Tamara builds this kind of connection with Cheryl step by step. First she decides to put aside her initial dislike and talk to Cheryl: "Despite what went down, she was my roommate, and I realized that if I put down my guard, we might actually have a friendship." Tamara then starts to see their similarities instead of their differences. Most of all, she realizes that the experience of foster care is an important bond between them. As Tamara's connection to Cheryl grows, she notices positive qualities she hadn't seen before. She begins to appreciate that Cheryl is "very smart and has her life in perspective." Cheryl responds to Tamara's new attitude and opens up. Their conversations become more intimate. As a result of her efforts at friendship, Tamara begins to have the sense of security and connection she has longed for in a relationship. She learns that behind negative first impressions lie possibilities for satisfying relationships.

Why Relationships Are a Struggle for Tamara

As a foster child who has lived in various homes, Tamara is slow to form relationships. She wants a sister and envies Cheryl for the respect she's shown by their foster mother's biological kids: "They didn't have that respect for me." Tamara is also used to having her own bedroom, as in her previous foster home. Against this background, it's hard for Tamara to recognize Cheryl's potential as a friend. It's also not easy for her to see beyond Cheryl's bossy behavior and to stop being angry long enough to recognize what she and Cheryl have in common. But by opening up to Cheryl and looking at her from a new perspective, Tamara changes a casual, sometimes hostile relationship into a friendship that's close to a family tie.

Useful Concept Words

To assist teens in understanding and discussing this story, you may want to introduce some or all of the following concept words by making them part of discussions and activities. Write them on the board in advance and plan to explain each word when it appears in a suggested discussion question or activity (where the words are shown in italics). Here are the concept words, with definitions and sentences relating them to the story.

assume: *to accept something as truth without proof*
Tamara at first assumes that she and Cheryl won't ever get along.

impression: *a feeling about something or someone*
Tamara's first impression is that Cheryl is too bossy.

invade: *to intrude; to encroach on*
Tamara feels that Cheryl invades her space when they first share a room.

label: *a term or name used to identify someone*
For Tamara, "foster sister" isn't an accurate label for her relationship with Cheryl.

provocative: *causing anger or resentment*
Tamara feels that Cheryl's behavior is provocative.

ACTIVITIES

1. Freewriting: Finding Yourself in the Story

After group members have finished reading the story, ask them to take out writing materials. If you'll be writing also, have handy your own journal and tell students you'll be participating. For a description of freewriting, see pages 14–15.

The following statement and questions are similar to those you considered earlier in "A Moment of Reflection." This time, you may want to write along with your group.

Think of a time when you started out disliking someone who later became a good friend. Why didn't you like the person at first? What happened to change your feelings? Did one of you change your behavior toward the other? Did you both change? How hard was it to begin to see the person as a friend?

After the freewriting, invite volunteers to share what they wrote. Allow time for brief discussion.

2. Discussion: Understanding Events

To be sure group members have understood the story, ask questions such as:

- Why does Cheryl become Tamara's roommate?

- At first, what's the only thing Tamara envies Cheryl for?

- Why do Tamara and Cheryl argue so much?

- What's the most important thing Tamara discovers she has in common with Cheryl?

- Why does Tamara decide that Cheryl is "a good influence" on her?

- What has Cheryl taught Tamara about what lies behind the *labels* "foster" and "roommate"?

3. Discussion: Understanding Issues

Tamara's Relationships

Review with the group what relationships are, why they're sometimes hard to come by, and how they can be helpful. Then, referring as necessary to "How Relationships Work in the Story" (pages 72–73), ask questions such as:

- How does Tamara's relationship with Cheryl develop? How does Cheryl change from someone who *invades* Tamara's space and behaves *provocatively* to "a sister and a friend"?

- Tamara says that she and Cheryl "were sailing along in the same boat, only she was more equipped than I was and I needed her." What does she mean?

- What do you think of Tamara's view of what a "sisterly" relationship involves? If you have a friend or sibling you feel particularly close to, how is your relationship like Tamara and Cheryl's? How is it different?

- Do you think Tamara's relationship with Cheryl will last? Why or why not?

Connecting with the Issues

Suggest that group members silently review what they wrote during freewriting. Then ask questions such as:

- Tamara finds a "sister" in Cheryl. Do you feel "like family" with someone who's not a member of your family? If so, what qualities does this person have?

- If you were Tamara, would you have tried to overcome your differences with Cheryl? If so, how would you have gone about it? If not, why not?

- How do you become a good friend with someone? What would you say is most important? Why do you think so?

4. Role Play

For guidelines on role playing, see pages 15–16.

Objective: Group members will practice talking about getting beyond first impressions to form real, lasting relationships.

Characters: Tamara, a new girl in the foster home

Procedure
Ask for volunteers to enact this scene:

A new girl in Tamara's foster home doesn't like her roommate and *assumes* they'll never be friends. Tamara wants her to move beyond her assumptions and first *impressions,* and to try being a friend.

Allow five to ten minutes for the role play. Afterward, discuss questions such as:

- What did you see happening in this scene?

- If you were the new girl, would Tamara have convinced you to try and make friends with your roommate?

- How did this role play affect or change your understanding of Tamara's story?

5. Writing Activities: Taking It Further

Ask students to complete one or more of the following activities individually, in small groups, or at home. Modify the activities as needed to suit the writing ability of group members. When activities are completed, invite volunteers to read their work to the group. Discuss how teens felt about the purpose and value of the writing.

Activity A

Objective: Group members will describe Tamara's relationship with Cheryl in their own words.

Pretend you're Tamara. You've gone away to college. Write a letter to Cheryl, explaining how important her friendship has been in your life.

Activity B

Objective: Group members will consider the effects of labeling people.

Tamara learns to get behind the *labels* "foster" and "roommate" to find "an actual person." Have you (or has someone you know) ever been labeled? Did the label get in the way of making friends? If so, how? If not, how did you get beyond the label?

6. In Your Journal: Making It Personal

Encourage group members to reflect on the following topic in their journals:

Tamara at first had a difficult relationship with Cheryl, but eventually Cheryl became a close friend, almost like the sister Tamara always longed for. Think about the friendships you have. How are they different from your relationships with family members? In what ways are your ties with your friends closer than your ties with family? What do your friends offer you that your family can't? What does your family offer that your friends can't?

BONDING THROUGH COOKING
by Aurora Breville

Pages 70–76 in *The Struggle to Be Strong*

PREPARING TO LEAD THE ACTIVITIES

Story Summary

When Aurora enters a foster home at thirteen, she doesn't know how to cook. She's dismayed to find that she's expected to learn. Deciding to be honest with the other girls in the house, Aurora admits she's never cooked. They teach her, and in the process Aurora forms friendships with girls her own age for the first time in her life.

A Moment of Reflection

To connect with the story's themes, consider from your own perspective the questions group members will address during freewriting: Think of a time when you made a friend through an activity you both liked. How did your friendship develop? How did the activity help you develop the friendship? Do you think you would have become friends with this person if you hadn't gotten to know them through the activity?

How Relationships Work in the Story

Seeing Aurora's Relationships

In thirteen years of living with her parents, Aurora was never encouraged to bond with girls her own age. In her foster home she learns to do that in the process of learning to cook. The bonding starts when, instead of trying to hide her ignorance, Aurora admits to needing help from her housemates and accepts their terms: she's the learner and they're the teachers. She asks questions; they have the answers. They tease her; she takes what they dish out. Despite the teasing, Aurora recognizes the girls' good intentions, and she perseveres.

As a result, she makes friends. She learns how to cook, and she grows emotionally: "Whenever I'm cooking, I feel like I'm working on something that will help to make a bigger and better me."

Why Relationships Are a Struggle for Aurora

It's not easy for Aurora to form relationships with girls her age for the first time. She's not sure she wants them to see her vulnerability. She's embarrassed, afraid that everyone will talk behind her back, and tempted to lie about not knowing how to cook. Driven by hunger, when she does ask for help, she must battle her resentment: "'Fine!' I snapped. 'Then show me how to cook the stupid thing, doggonit!'" Nevertheless, Aurora works hard both at learning how to cook and at making friends. In the process, she moves from helpless dependency to a more mature relationship with others. At the end of the story she reflects proudly on the change: "I felt a little more like an adult because I didn't have to depend on anyone. . . . And making friends has become second nature to me because, just like cooking, it's no longer a crazy idea."

Useful Concept Words

To assist teens in understanding and discussing this story, you may want to introduce some or all of the following concept words by making them part of discussions and activities. Write them on the board in advance and plan to explain each word when it appears in a suggested discussion question or activity (where the words are shown in italics). Here are the concept words, with definitions and sentences relating them to the story.

bond: *to form a close relationship*

*By learning how to cook, Aurora **bonds** with the other girls in her foster home.*

dependent: needing support or aid

At first, Aurora is **dependent** on others because she can't cook for herself.

novice: someone who is new to an experience

As a **novice** cook, Aurora needs the other girls to teach her.

self-sufficient: capable of providing for oneself

Aurora becomes **self-sufficient** by learning how to cook.

vulnerable: easily hurt; sensitive; open to criticism or attack

When Aurora realizes she has to learn to cook, she feels **vulnerable** to teasing from her housemates.

ACTIVITIES

1. Freewriting: Finding Yourself in the Story

After group members have finished reading the story, ask them to take out writing materials. If you'll be writing also, have handy your own journal and tell students you'll be participating. For a description of freewriting, see pages 14–15.

The following statement and questions are similar to those you considered earlier in "A Moment of Reflection." This time, you may want to write along with your group.

Think of a time when you made a friend through an activity you both liked. How did your friendship develop? How did the activity help you develop the friendship? Do you think you would have become friends with this person if you hadn't gotten to know them through the activity? Why or why not?

After the freewriting, invite volunteers to share what they wrote. Allow time for brief discussion.

2. Discussion: Understanding Events

To be sure group members have understood the story, ask questions such as:

- When Aurora asks her foster mother to cook for her, what response does she get?

- What cooking chore does Aurora swear she will never do in her life? Why does she change her mind?

- How does Aurora feel about herself once she learns to cook?

- As she learns to cook, what does Aurora do that her parents "had never encouraged"?

3. Discussion: Understanding Issues

Aurora's Relationships

Review with the group what relationships are, why they're sometimes hard to come by, and how they can be helpful. Then, referring as necessary to "How Relationships Work in the Story" (page 75), ask questions such as:

- Aurora says her cooking lessons "weren't all bad." What does she mean? What, besides cooking, does she learn during the lessons?

- How does Aurora change in the process of learning to cook?

- Why do you think Aurora's parents never encouraged her to make friends with girls her own age?

- What do you think was hardest for Aurora about her cooking experience?

- If Aurora's foster mother had cooked for her, how do you think Aurora would have gotten along with the other girls in the house?

- How does learning to cook help Aurora make friends? What else does cooking do for her?

Connecting with the Issues

Suggest that group members silently review what they wrote during freewriting. Then ask questions such as:

- Aurora says, "Whenever I'm cooking, I feel like I'm working on something that will help to make a bigger and better me." What does she mean? Is there an activity that makes you feel this way? Explain your answer.

- Have you ever been in a situation like Aurora's, where you were a *novice*—a beginner—at some skill that everyone else had? What happened?

- How hard is it for you to admit you don't know something or you need help? Do you like or dislike being *dependent* on someone else for help? Explain your answer.

- Have you ever made a friend through an activity you both liked? Do you think you would have become friends with this person if you hadn't gotten to know them through the activity? Why or why not?

- What activities have helped you *bond* with people your age?

4. Role Play

For guidelines on role playing, see pages 15–16.

Objective: Group members will identify with the importance of forming relationships based on equality and self-sufficiency.

Characters: Aurora, a new girl in the foster home

Procedure
Ask for volunteers to enact this scene:

A new girl in Aurora's foster home doesn't know how to cook and expects others to cook for her. Aurora wants the girl to understand why she should learn to cook.

Allow five to ten minutes for the role play. Afterward, discuss questions such as:

- What did you see happening in this scene?

- If you were the new girl, would Aurora have convinced you to learn to cook?

- How did this role play affect or change your understanding of Aurora's story?

5. Group Activity

Objective: Group members will experience teaching and learning a skill.

Procedure
Tell the group that the object of this exercise is to experience how it feels to teach a skill and to learn a skill. First, brainstorm a list of skills or activities that individuals in the group are good at; for example, a current dance step or move, an athletic skill, an artistic technique, a cooking technique, an academic skill. (You may want to include a few of your own skills.) Next, ask everyone to write down two skills or activities from the list: one they can't do or aren't good at, and one they think they could teach someone else. Pair teachers with learners and allow five to ten minutes for lessons. (For skills that would require materials or equipment, ask students to pantomime the process.) Then reverse roles and again form pairs: teachers become learners and learners become teachers. Allow another five to ten minutes for lessons. Afterward, discuss how it felt to teach a skill and to learn one. Ask the group:

- How did you feel about your teacher? How did you feel about your student?

- How did this activity affect or change your understanding of Aurora's story?

6. Writing Activities: Taking It Further

Ask students to complete one or more of the following activities individually, in small groups, or at home. Modify the activities as needed to suit the writing ability of group members. When activities are completed, invite volunteers to read their work to the group. Discuss how teens felt about the purpose and value of the writing.

Activity A

Objective: Group members will describe Aurora's view of relationships in their own words.

Pretend you're Aurora. Write a letter to your social worker describing how learning to cook helped you make friends.

Activity B

Objective: Group members will reflect on why doing activities together can help people form relationships.

Write about how participating in an activity with other people (for example, group lessons, sports, school clubs, study groups) can sometimes lead to friendships. If you have found this true in your own life, describe what happened.

Activity C

Objective: Group members will reflect on their ability to admit they don't know something.

Aurora had to admit to the other girls that she couldn't cook. How hard is it for you to admit that you don't know something or aren't *self-sufficient*? If you find it hard, has this gotten in the way of relationships you'd have liked to develop? If you don't find it hard, have you made friends by asking others for help? Write about it.

7. In Your Journal: Making It Personal

Encourage group members to reflect on the following topic in their journals:

Diane and the other girls go out of their way to help Aurora learn her way around the kitchen and become *self-sufficient*. Think of a time someone your age helped you learn something new. How did you feel as the learner? *Vulnerable? Dependent? Independent?* Frustrated? Embarrassed? Happy? How did you feel about your teacher? Did working with this person help you know him or her better? Did it lead to a friendship? Why or why not?

A LOVE TOO STRONG
by Tamecka Crawford

Pages 77–80 in *The Struggle to Be Strong*

PREPARING TO LEAD THE ACTIVITIES

Story Summary

At sixteen, Tamecka enters a group home where, for the first time, she is given attention, love, and care. At first, unaccustomed to positive interactions with people, she retreats to her room. Gradually, however, she begins to respond to the staff's concern. Tamecka grows especially close to one staff member, Ms. Thomas, who she feels has taken a special interest in her. When Ms. Thomas is transferred, Tamecka is devastated and retreats again to her room. Ms. Thomas, she feels, is "the only person who could ever take away my feelings of being unloved." Ms. Smith, the director of social work, tries to explain to Tamecka that her strong attachment to Ms. Thomas is unrealistic and inappropriate, that no staff member can ever provide the intimate relationship Tamecka craves. Tamecka resists hearing this and goes through "an emotional hell." By the end of the story, however, Tamecka realizes that her expectations of Ms. Thomas "were unrealistic and sometimes unfair." She also feels that her attachment to Ms. Thomas was "just another bond that had been broken by the foster care system." She becomes willing to open herself up to people again, but realizes she can't expect anyone to provide the parental love she never received.

A Moment of Reflection

To connect with the story's themes, consider from your own perspective the questions group members will address during freewriting: Think of a time when, as a teenager, you developed a strong attachment to a teacher, coach, neighbor, or other adult figure. Why do you think you felt so close to this person? Were your expectations for the relationship realistic or unrealistic? How did this person

treat you? How did the relationship turn out? How do you feel about the experience now?

How Relationships Work in the Story

Seeing Tamecka's Relationships

The love and attention Tamecka receives from adults in her group home encourage her to connect to others. She begins to feel especially close to one staff member, Ms. Thomas: she "really touched my heart." When Ms. Thomas cries at a group meeting, Tamecka shares her pain. For Tamecka, so used to retreating from emotional situations, experiencing empathy is a big step forward in her ability to form relationships. However, because she's unable to maintain any emotional distance from Ms. Thomas, when the woman is transferred Tamecka feels abandoned. She slips back into isolation and goes through "an emotional hell." Yet she rallies. Despite her pain, Tamecka is finally able to accept Ms. Smith's advice: "I realize that Ms. Smith was partly right, that my expectations were unrealistic and sometimes unfair." By the end of the story, Tamecka has learned that relationships can give her some of the support and affection she craves, but can never completely heal her childhood wounds. That recognition is painful for her, but it's also a healthy lesson.

Why Relationships Are a Struggle for Tamecka

Because of her family's lack of love, Tamecka closes off from people to protect herself from being hurt. When she permits herself to feel close to Ms. Thomas and then feels abandoned, as she was in the past, Tamecka suffers a devastating sense of loss. Having learned the comfort of being connected, she's torn between her attachment to Ms. Thomas and her growing understanding that her expectations are unrealistic. Through great effort, Tamecka reconciles her need for closeness with the reality of what she can expect from relationships. Given her vulnerability, it's remarkable that she achieves this balanced understanding.

Useful Concept Words

To assist teens in understanding and discussing this story, you may want to introduce some or all of the following concept words by making them part of discussions and activities. Write them on the board in advance and plan to explain each word when it appears in a suggested discussion question or activity (where the words are shown in italics). Here are the concept words, with definitions and sentences relating them to the story.

devastated: *very hurt; overwhelmed by something*
*Tamecka is **devastated** when Ms. Thomas leaves the group home.*

idealize: *to think of something or someone as perfect*
*Tamecka **idealizes** Ms. Thomas as the "perfect mother figure."*

isolated: *alone; apart; away from others*
*The care and concern of the group home staff made it hard for Tamecka to stay **isolated.***

needy: *lacking something one strongly desires*
*Tamecka feels **needy** for affection from adults.*

substitute: *a replacement for something else*
*Tamecka wants Ms. Thomas to be a **substitute** parent.*

ACTIVITIES

1. Freewriting: Finding Yourself in the Story

After group members have finished reading the story, ask them to take out writing materials. If you'll be writing also, have handy your own journal and tell students you'll be participating. For a description of freewriting, see pages 14–15.

The following statement and questions are similar to those you considered earlier in "A Moment of Reflection." This time, you may want to write along with your group.

Think of a time when you developed a strong attachment to a teacher, coach, neighbor, or other adult figure. Why do you think you felt so close to this person? What did you expect from your relationship with him or her? How did the relationship actually turn out? How do you feel about the experience now?

After the freewriting, invite volunteers to share what they wrote. Allow time for brief discussion.

NOTE: Avoiding Roadblocks

Some teens may have trouble understanding the depth of Tamecka's attachment to Ms. Thomas. You might review with them what foster care is (see page 6 in the anthology), asking them to consider how being in foster care may have contributed to Tamecka's great need for a parent figure. Also remind students of Tamecka's painful family history. Other teens may feel Ms. Thomas didn't respond in the right way to Tamecka and should have been a close friend to her. Discuss the qualities of healthy relationships: balance, willingness to risk rejection, realistic expectations. Ask teens to consider what makes a relationship between a teen and an adult healthy and appropriate. Point out that Ms. Thomas was willing to support Tamecka, but couldn't be her parent or make up for the past. Ask the group:

- **Do you think it was realistic for Tamecka to think Ms. Thomas could be her close friend? Or was she expecting too much? Explain your answer.**

- **What do you expect from teachers, social workers, or other adult figures in your life?**

---

2. Discussion: Understanding Events

To be sure group members have understood the story, ask questions such as:

- **What does Tamecka find in the group home that she's never found before?**

- Why does Tamecka stay in her room during the first few months at the group home?

- Tamecka describes an incident in which she sees Ms. Thomas cry. What effect does the incident have on Tamecka?

- What does Tamecka do when Ms. Thomas is transferred to another home?

- What does Ms. Smith tell Tamecka about her attachment to Ms. Thomas? At first, how does Tamecka feel about what Ms. Smith says?

- How does Tamecka feel now about what Ms. Smith told her?

- What does Tamecka say she has learned from the experience with Ms. Thomas?

3. Discussion: Understanding Issues

Tamecka's Relationships

Review with the group what relationships are, why they're sometimes hard to come by, and how they can be helpful. Then, referring as necessary to "How Relationships Work in the Story" (pages 79–80), ask questions such as:

- Why do you think seeing Ms. Thomas cry has such a big impact on Tamecka?

- Why do you think Tamecka forms such a strong attachment to Ms. Thomas? Why does she feel so *devastated* by the loss of Ms. Thomas?

- Ms. Smith warns Tamecka that her feelings toward Ms. Thomas are "unrealistic" and "inappropriate." Do you agree with Ms. Smith? Why or why not?

- Do you think Ms. Thomas was right in her attitude toward Tamecka? Should she have offered more support? Why or why not?

- How well do you think Tamecka will be able to form relationships in the future? What do you think she's learned from her experience with Ms. Thomas?

Connecting with the Issues

Suggest that group members silently review what they wrote during freewriting. Then ask questions such as:

- Why do you think teens sometimes form strong attachments to adults who aren't family members? What do you think of relationships like these? Explain.

- What do you think the relationship should be between a teen and an adult such as a teacher, coach, member of the clergy, and so forth? Explain.

- What does it mean to *idealize* someone? In what ways did Tamecka idealize Ms. Thomas? How did idealizing Ms. Thomas lead to Tamecka's feeling *isolated* and *needy* once again?

- Have you ever *idealized* someone? Did the person live up to your expectations? Explain.

4. Role Plays

For guidelines on role playing, see pages 15–16.

Objective: Group members will see the difficulty of having unrealistic expectations for relationships and will practice expressing what's needed for healthy relationships.

Scenario A

Characters: Tamecka, Ms. Thomas

Procedure
Ask for volunteers to enact this scene:

Tamecka tells Ms. Thomas that she wants them to be close friends. Ms. Thomas wants to explain to Tamecka that she's happy to support and encourage her, but that she can't really be her close friend.

Allow five to ten minutes for the role play. Afterward, discuss questions such as:

- What did you see happening in this scene?

- If you were Tamecka, would Ms. Thomas have convinced you that she can't really be your close friend? If you were Ms. Thomas, would Tamecka have convinced you to be her close friend?

- How did this role play affect or change your understanding of Tamecka's story?

Scenario B

Characters: Tamecka, her friend

Procedure
Ask for volunteers to enact this scene:

Tamecka expects Ms. Thomas to be like a parent to her and wants her friend to give Ms. Thomas that message. Her friend has been through a similar experience and wants Tamecka to understand why she won't deliver such a message.

Allow five to ten minutes for the role play. Afterward, discuss questions such as:

- What did you see happening in this scene?

- If you were Tamecka, would your friend have convinced you that what you expected from Ms. Thomas was unrealistic?

- How did this role play affect or change your understanding of Tamecka's story?

5. Writing Activities: Taking It Further

Ask students to complete one or more of the following activities individually, in small groups, or at home. Modify the activities as needed to suit the writing ability of group members. When activities are completed, invite volunteers to read their work to the group. Discuss how teens felt about the purpose and value of the writing.

Activity A

Objective: Group members will describe Tamecka's maturing view of relationships in their own words.

Pretend you're Tamecka. Write a letter to Ms. Smith explaining how you now understand the value of her advice about your feelings toward Ms. Thomas.

Activity B

Objective: Group members will reflect on Tamecka's future relationships.

Write about what you think will be the main challenges facing Tamecka in her future relationships. What do you think she's learned? What do you think may still be a problem for her?

Activity C

Objective: Group members will reflect on their own experience with unrealistic expectations.

Have you ever known someone who expected more from you than you could give? How did you feel about this person's expectations? Write about the experience.

6. In Your Journal: Making It Personal

Encourage group members to reflect on the following topic in their journals:

Tamecka realizes that she's been unrealistic in expecting Ms. Thomas to be a *substitute* parent. Think about a person you felt close to who didn't return your strong feelings. How would you describe the person and the situation? Why do you think the relationship didn't work? How did this experience change your thinking about relationships? Were you able to find what you were looking for from someone else? If so, describe.

LEARNING TO FORGIVE
by Christopher A. Bogle

Pages 81–85 in *The Struggle to Be Strong*

PREPARING TO LEAD THE ACTIVITIES

Story Summary

Christopher's relationship with his mother has been troubled for a long time. While he's living in a group home, his social worker urges him to see a therapist. Reluctantly, Christopher agrees. The therapist gradually wins Christopher's trust, but he still won't speak to his mother. He feels she verbally abuses him just as his father had verbally abused her. One day Christopher confides to his therapist how he wound up in a detention center. He'd returned home very late one night and been disrespectful to his mother. When she became violent, Christopher's sister's boyfriend got between mother and son and was wounded. In court, Christopher's mother accused him of injuring the boyfriend and her. He was sent to a detention center and then to a juvenile prison for a year and a half. Christopher's therapist urges him to forgive his mother, for both their sakes. Gradually, Christopher sees that "everybody makes mistakes and deserves a second chance." He goes to visit his mother, realizing that he's been at fault for some of their problems. They apologize to one another. By the end of the story, Christopher and his mother are in regular contact and have begun joint therapy. He acknowledges his love for her but knows they still have work to do before they can live together again.

A Moment of Reflection

To connect with the story's themes, consider from your own perspective the questions group members will address during freewriting: Think of a person, perhaps a family member, with whom you have a difficult relationship. Why do you think the relationship is difficult? In what ways is it difficult? What would it take to repair it? Have you tried? Has the other person tried? What happened?

How Relationships Work in the Story

Seeing Christopher's Relationships

Although Christopher doesn't want "to go to any 'stupid' therapy," he uses the opportunity to learn how to repair his broken relationship with his mother. He decides to trust his therapist, confide in her, and begin to let go of his anger. When his therapist tells him that the first step in forgiving someone "is to really mean it from the heart," Christopher opens himself to the idea. He realizes his mother's weaknesses and mistakes, and at the same time admits his own. "I left therapy that day feeling like a better person. . . . I knew everybody makes mistakes and deserves a second chance." He also accepts responsibility for his part in their problems. Christopher decides to visit his mother for the first time in two years. When she tells him how sorry she is for the behavior that landed him in a detention center, Christopher forgives her and tells her he wants "to start a new relationship with her and just move on." Afterward, he takes steps to protect his new relationship with his mother. He guards against expecting too much by keeping their past difficulties in mind. He doesn't return home to live with her, preferring not to rush things. He allows his mother to join him in therapy, a step that comes with a cost: "When I was in therapy alone it was easier to express myself and the room was less tense, but eventually I got used to being in therapy with her." By the end of the story, Christopher is happy about his improved relationship with his mother. He's also realistic about the limits of the relationship and their shared responsibility for maintaining it.

Why Relationships Are a Struggle for Christopher

Christopher is understandably reluctant to forgive his mother for the behavior that cost him a year and a half in juvenile detention. He has convinced himself that he doesn't need her: "... I didn't want to have anything to do with her. I had been making it without her, so why did I need her now?" He has bitter memories, and he and his mother fight whenever they're together: "She'd bring up things that happened in the past and throw them in my face." He's concluded that his relationship with her isn't going to improve. Reconnecting with her involves a considerable struggle, yet, on the advice of his therapist, Christopher tries. He and his mother forgive each other, but he knows his struggle isn't over. "I feel our relationship is better, but I wouldn't want to destroy it by rushing home before I'm ready. I want to take it slow."

Useful Concept Words

To assist teens in understanding and discussing this story, you may want to introduce some or all of the following concept words by making them part of discussions and activities. Write them on the board in advance and plan to explain each word when it appears in a suggested discussion question or activity (where the words are shown in italics). Here are the concept words, with definitions and sentences relating them to the story.

affirm: to state something firmly and positively
At the end of the story, Christopher affirms his love for his mother.

forgive: to stop feeling angry or resentful toward someone
Christopher forgives his mother for their past troubles.

hostile: unfriendly; antagonistic
At the beginning of the story, Christopher and his mother have a hostile relationship.

risk: the chance of suffering harm or loss
Christopher takes a risk by allowing his mother to be part of his therapy.

sustain: to keep something going; to maintain something
Christopher knows it will take work to sustain his new relationship with his mother.

ACTIVITIES

1. Freewriting: Finding Yourself in the Story

After group members have finished reading the story, ask them to take out writing materials. If you'll be writing also, have handy your own journal and tell students you'll be participating. For a description of freewriting, see pages 14–15.

The following statement and questions are similar to those you considered earlier in "A Moment of Reflection." This time, you may want to write along with your group.

Think of a person, maybe a family member, you have a difficult relationship with. Why do you think the relationship is difficult? In what ways is it difficult? What would it take to make the relationship better? Have you tried? Has the family member tried? Why or why not? What do you think will happen between you in the future?

After the freewriting, invite volunteers to share what they wrote. Allow time for brief discussion.

NOTE: Avoiding Roadblocks

Group members may think Christopher should not have forgiven his mother. They may voice their own anger about what she did. Help them see that although Christopher's anger and feelings of betrayal are great, he *wants* to forgive his mother. He believes his therapist when she says that forgiving his mother will "release the pain" inside him. Focus on why Christopher wanted to do what he did, what he gained as a result, and why learning to forgive is a valuable lesson. Ask the group:

What does Christopher say about the value of *forgiving* his mother? How do you think he'd feel if he hadn't forgiven her?

2. Discussion: Understanding Events

To be sure group members have understood the story, ask questions such as:

- At the beginning of the story, how does Christopher feel about his mother? What does he do when she calls or when he sees her on the streets?

- How does Christopher's mother treat him differently than she treats his sisters? Why does he think she does this?

- What was his mother's role in the events that sent Christopher to a detention center?

- Why does Christopher's therapist say he has to learn to *forgive* his mother? What does she say is the first step?

- What happens when Christopher goes to see his mother for the first time in two years?

- At the end of the story, what does Christopher *affirm* about his feelings for his mother?

3. Discussion: Understanding Issues

Christopher's Relationships

Review with the group what relationships are, why they're sometimes hard to come by, and how they can be helpful. Then, referring as necessary to "How Relationships Work in the Story" (pages 83–84), ask questions such as:

- Why does Christopher feel so *hostile* toward his mother? Why is it so difficult for him to *forgive* her? How does he feel after he does?

- How does Christopher's mother treat him differently from the way she treats his sisters?

- Who do you think is more responsible for their painful relationship: Christopher or his mother? Or are they equally responsible? Explain your answer.

- Why is it a *risk* for Christopher to include his mother in his therapy sessions?

- Do you think Christopher is realistic about what he can and can't expect from his mother in the future? What do you think will happen between them? How can they *sustain* their improved relationship?

Connecting with the Issues

Suggest that group members silently review what they wrote during freewriting. Then ask questions such as:

- If you were in Christopher's shoes, how would you have handled the situation with your mother?

- What does it mean to *forgive* someone? Do you think being able to forgive someone who's hurt you is important in forming healthy relationships? Explain your answer.

4. Role Plays

For guidelines on role playing, see pages 15–16.

Objective: Group members will identify with the steps Christopher went through to rebuild his relationship with his mother.

Scenario A

Characters: Christopher, his mother, their therapist

Procedure
Ask for volunteers to enact this scene (you may want to play the therapist yourself):

Christopher and his mother are in a therapy session together. Both want to express how much they care for each other. But first, Christopher wants his mother to know how hurt he was by her past behavior. His mother wants him to know how she's been hurt by his behavior. The therapist wants both of them to open up about their feelings for each other.

Allow five to ten minutes for the role play. Afterward, discuss questions such as:

- What did you see happening in this scene?

- If you were Christopher's mother, how would you feel about what Christopher told you? If you were Christopher, how would you feel about what your mother told you?

- How did this role play affect or change your understanding of Christopher's story?

Scenario B

Characters: Christopher, his friend

Procedure
Ask for volunteers to enact this scene:

Christopher's friend is angry with his own mother and wants Christopher to know he can never *forgive* her. Christopher has learned to forgive his mother and wants his friend to understand what he's gained from forgiving her.

Allow five to ten minutes for the role play. Afterward, discuss questions such as:

- What did you see happening in this scene?

- If you were Christopher's friend, would Christopher have convinced you to *forgive* your mother?

- How did this role play affect or change your understanding of Christopher's story?

5. Writing Activities: Taking It Further

Ask students to complete one or more of the following activities individually, in small groups, or at home. Modify the activities as needed to suit the writing ability of group members. When activities are completed, invite volunteers to read their work to the group. Discuss how teens felt about the purpose and value of the writing.

Activity A

Objective: Group members will describe Christopher's improved relationship with his mother in their own words.

Pretend you're Christopher. Write a letter to your therapist explaining how her advice about *forgiving* your mother and rebuilding your relationship with her has changed your life for the better.

Activity B

Objective: Group members will reflect on their own experience of forgiving someone.

Write about someone you've *forgiven* for hurting you. Why did you decide to forgive this person? How difficult was it to forgive him or her? How do you feel about having forgiven the person? Are you glad you did? Why or why not?

Activity C

Objective: Group members will reflect on their own experience of being forgiven.

Write about someone who's *forgiven* you. How do you feel about being forgiven by this person? What difference has it made in your life? How would you describe your relationship with the person now?

6. In Your Journal: Making It Personal

Encourage group members to reflect on the following topic in their journals:

Although Christopher had broken his ties with his mother, he worked very hard to build and *sustain* a new relationship with her. Think of someone with whom you have a close but difficult relationship. What makes the relationship difficult? What steps are you willing to take to improve it? What steps would you like to see the other person take?

FIVE TEENS: THE IMPORTANCE OF RELATIONSHIPS

As necessary, refer to pages 60 and 61 in the anthology to review with your group what relationships are and why they're a resilience. Then invite group members to compare how relationships work in the lives of the five teen writers in this section. (To help students recall each writer, you might list their first names on the board.) Ask questions such as:

- Which writer do you think has the toughest time building relationships based on sharing, mutual respect, and openness? Which writer do you think has the easiest time doing this? Why do you think so?

- Which writer do you think takes the greatest risks in order to build healthy relationships? Why do you think so?

- Which writer do you think changes the most because of his or her relationships? Why do you think so?

- Which story in this section do you like best? Which teen writer do you admire most? Explain your choices.

Many of the teen writers in this book demonstrate more than one resilience. If your group has read other stories, you might ask members to discuss how writers in other sections also build and maintain relationships.

INITIATIVE
TAKING CHARGE

Before discussing the stories in this section, ask the group to read the introductory material about initiative in their anthology, pages 86 and 87. Allow time for questions and brief discussion. Be sure teens understand the following:

- **Initiative** is taking action, meeting challenges, solving problems.

- The opposite of taking **initiative** is giving up or feeling helpless.

- Taking **initiative** is hard because some problems seem too overwhelming to solve.

- **Initiative** helps you see that you can make a difference in your own life.

As teens read each story, encourage them to look for ways the writer demonstrates initiative. Also suggest that they reflect on—and possibly jot down ideas about—the questions that follow each story ("Think About It"). Refer them to the introductory section "'Think About It'—and Maybe Write About It," pages 7–8 in the anthology.

IT TAKES WORK TO FLIRT
by Danny Gong

Pages 88–92 in *The Struggle to Be Strong*

PREPARING TO LEAD THE ACTIVITIES

Story Summary

Quiet, shy Danny wants to meet more girls and find "that special someone." He's tired of his friends' flirting techniques: "I wanted to open myself up to a larger world." First he changes his hairstyle and wardrobe; then he tries to improve his flirting. He doesn't have much success, but he perseveres, convinced that practice and patience will do the trick. One day, rather impulsively, he takes the initiative and buys a book, *101 Ways to Flirt*. The tips he reads help him get over his anxiety. He recommends self-help books: "What's wrong with a little assistance?"

A Moment of Reflection

To connect with the story's themes, consider from your own perspective the questions group members will address during freewriting: Think of a time—perhaps during your teenage years—when you were attracted to someone but felt embarrassed about admitting it or talking to the person. What happened? Why do you think you felt embarrassed? Did you ever manage to talk to the person? If you did, how did it go? If you didn't, how do you feel about that now?

How Initiative Works in the Story

Seeing Danny's Initiative

We see Danny's initiative in the way he thinks about his problem with flirting: it's something he can fix by taking action. He doesn't defeat himself by deciding the problem is too big to solve. When Danny first decides he's not good at flirting, he tells himself that knowing how to flirt isn't an inborn quality. It's something you can become

better at through practice. He also regards failure as something he can learn from, rather than as evidence that he's deficient or hopeless. He's motivated to persist. He experiments with different styles of flirting, and when these fail he buys a self-help book. By the end of the story, Danny has come to the realization that the way we view problems affects the way we respond to them: "So if you buy a flirting book, don't think of it as, 'I'm desperate, I can't get a date.' Think of it as, 'Hey, I'm smart, gonna get me some more dates and meet new people.'"

Why Initiative Is a Struggle for Danny

Taking initiative is a struggle for Danny because he's afraid he'll make a fool of himself. ". . . I was shaking, biting my lips, scratching my head. . . . So my first attempt was pretty sad, but I had to start somewhere." He also feels clueless around girls: ". . . I had some mega-problems with flirting. I didn't know the first thing to do." Although practice and his self-help book have improved his technique, he knows he still has a way to go: "Flirting books are like the *Princeton Review* of dating. They don't guarantee a perfect 1600, but they can raise your score."

Useful Concept Words

To assist teens in understanding and discussing this story, you may want to introduce some or all of the following concept words by making them part of discussions and activities. Write them on the board in advance and plan to explain each word when it appears in a suggested discussion question or activity (where the words are shown in italics). Here are the concept words, with definitions and sentences relating them to the story.

awkward: *clumsy*
*Danny feels **awkward** around girls.*

charisma: personal charm or magnetism

Danny says books about flirting can help people who don't have **charisma.**

experiment: to try out different problem-solving approaches

Danny **experiments** *with different methods of flirting.*

vulnerable: open to injury or hurt

Danny feels **vulnerable** *when he tries to flirt.*

ACTIVITIES

1. Freewriting: Finding Yourself in the Story

After group members have finished reading the story, ask them to take out writing materials. If you'll be writing also, have handy your own journal and tell students you'll be participating. For a description of freewriting, see pages 14–15.

The following statement and questions are similar to those you considered earlier in "A Moment of Reflection." This time, you may want to write along with your group.

Think of a time when you were attracted to someone but felt embarrassed about admitting it or talking to the person. What happened? Why do you think you felt embarrassed? Did you ever manage to talk to the person? If you did, how did it go? If you didn't, how do you feel about that now?

After the freewriting, invite volunteers to share what they wrote. Allow time for brief discussion.

2. Discussion: Understanding Events

To be sure group members have understood the story, ask questions such as:

- Why does Danny decide to break away from his friends' style of approaching girls?

- What happens when Danny's inline skating in the park and tries to talk to a girl?

- What does Danny mean when he says flirting is "like fishing"? What does he mean when he says

books can help "people who aren't born with high **charisma**"?

- What's one effect on Danny of reading *101 Ways to Flirt*?

- Danny disagrees with one point in the book. What is it?

3. Discussion: Understanding Issues

Danny's Initiative

Review with the group what initiative is, why it's sometimes hard to come by, and how it can be helpful. Then, referring as necessary to "How Initiative Works in the Story" (page 90), ask questions such as:

- What do you think of Danny's buying a book to help him talk to girls more easily?

- What's your reaction to Danny's techniques?

- What advice would you give Danny about being more comfortable approaching girls?

- How hard do you think it was for Danny to break off from his group of friends and develop his own style? Would it be hard for you? Why or why not?

Connecting with the Issues

Suggest that group members silently review what they wrote during freewriting. Then ask questions such as:

- Why do you think it's so hard to risk feeling *awkward* or being embarrassed?

- Have you ever read a self-help book to teach yourself something or to improve yourself in some way? If so, what was the result of your *experimenting*? If not, can you see yourself ever doing what Danny did? Why or why not?

- Instead of feeling hopeless, Danny saw his difficulties meeting girls as a challenge to be met. Have you ever solved a problem that you at first thought was hopeless? What changed your view of the problem? How did shifting your view of the problem change the way you responded to it?

4. Role Play

For guidelines about role playing, see pages 15–16.

Objective: Group members will identify with Danny's ability to take initiative.

Characters: Danny, his friend Peter

Procedure
Ask for volunteers to enact this scene:

Danny and his friend Peter are in a store. Danny wants to learn how to approach girls more easily and tells Peter he's going to buy _101 Ways to Flirt._ Peter believes you either know how to talk to girls or you don't.

Allow five to ten minutes for the role play. Afterward, discuss questions such as:

- **What did you see happening in this scene?**

- **If you were Peter, would Danny have convinced you that a book can help?**

- **How did this role play affect or change your understanding of Danny's story?**

5. Group Activities

Activity A

Objective: Group members will discuss various sources of information for self-improvement.

Procedure
Have teens pair off and discuss things they've learned, tips they've found useful, or behaviors they've changed using self-help books, advice columns, magazines or newspapers, television or movies, the Internet, and so on. Allow about ten minutes. Afterward, ask volunteers to share some of their discussion with the group. Then discuss what teens learned from this activity. Ask:

- **What kinds of self-help sources did you learn about? What kinds of advice do they offer?**

- **How did this activity affect or change your understanding of Danny's story?**

Activity B

Objective: Group members will consider their own favorite ways of meeting people.

Procedure
Ask group members to write down their favorite ways to meet potential dating partners or make new friends. Do they use a "line" or a certain icebreaker? Tell them not to put their names on the papers. Collect the papers, screen them as necessary, and read a few aloud.

After each, ask the group to discuss whether they think the method or "line" would be effective. If so, why do they think so? If not, how would they go about improving it? Then discuss what they learned from this activity. Ask:

- **How do these ways of meeting people compare with Danny's?**

- **How did this activity affect or change your understanding of Danny's story?**

6. Writing Activities: Taking It Further

Ask students to complete one or more of the following activities individually, in small groups, or at home. Modify the activities as needed to suit the writing ability of group members. When activities are completed, invite volunteers to read their work to the group. Discuss how teens felt about the purpose and value of the writing.

Activity A

Objective: Group members will describe Danny's initiative in their own words.

Pretend you're Danny. Write a letter to an old friend explaining how and why you changed your approach to meeting girls.

Activity B

Objective: Group members will consider a time when they took initiative to solve a problem.

Write about a time when you admitted to yourself that you needed help with something and took action. How hard was it to admit that you were *vulnerable* and needed help? What action did you take? What happened?

Activity C

Objective: Group members will describe a time they overcame anxiety and took action.

Danny learned to control his anxiety when he approached girls. Write about a time you overcame anxiety to try something new or scary. What helped you deal with your worries and take action, rather than give up?

Encourage group members to reflect on the following topic in their journals:

Danny identified a personal problem and took steps to solve it. Think of something you want to be better at or that doesn't come easily for you. What is it you'd like to improve? What might be a self-help improvement plan for you? For example, could you read books, take courses, get help from friends, or do something else? What do you think would help you most to improve? What's one specific step you could take to put your plan into action?

PREPARING TO LEAD THE ACTIVITIES

Story Summary

At thirteen, Craig runs away from his abusive mother and lives on the streets. He starts smoking marijuana to get his mind off his troubles. It doesn't work. Instead, when Craig is high, he is flooded with bad memories and often becomes angry, paranoid, and even violent. Later, he feels depressed and guilty. Resolving to quit smoking, he suffers the pains of withdrawal for seven weeks. Finally, his craving disappears. Now, after two years of being off marijuana, he's confident that he's kicked the habit for good.

A Moment of Reflection

To connect with the story's themes, consider from your own perspective the questions group members will address during freewriting: Think of a time when you had a habit you wanted to break. How or why did the habit start? Why did you want to break it? What techniques did you try? Which worked, and which didn't? If you weren't able to break the habit, what do you think got in the way? If you did manage to break the habit, how did you feel about your efforts? How do you feel about the experience now?

How Initiative Works in the Story

Seeing Craig's Initiative

Craig begins to take charge of his problem with marijuana when he acknowledges that smoking doesn't block out his pain, but instead makes him feel worse. Once he decides to quit, he's resourceful and exercises great persistence and willpower. To control his craving, he sleeps, eats, or takes long walks. He stops associating with friends who smoke and spends time with a new girlfriend. When he's tempted to smoke, he strengthens his resolve by remembering the problems marijuana caused him: ". . . I knew I had to stop if I wanted the memories to stop." By the end of the story, we see Craig's pride in his accomplishments—conquering his addiction and talking about his problem with an honesty he sees as rare: "My story may seem odd, because not many people come forward and tell the real reasons why they quit. Well, I may start a trend!!"

Why Initiative Is a Struggle for Craig

Kicking his marijuana habit is a struggle for Craig because of his painful childhood and his hope of escaping that pain through drugs. Also, as he says, "The craving was unbearable. It was like finding a million dollars on the street and then having to give it back." An added difficulty is that his friends continue to offer him marijuana. He finds the strength he needs by remembering the bad feelings marijuana gave him.

Useful Concept Words

To assist teens in understanding and discussing this story, you may want to introduce some or all of the following concept words by making them part of discussions and activities. Write them on the board in advance and plan to explain each word when it appears in a suggested discussion question or activity (where the words are shown in italics). Here are the concept words, with definitions and sentences relating them to the story.

aggravate: *to make something worse*
Smoking marijuana **aggravates** *Craig's problems.*

craving: *an intense desire for something*
Craig has a **craving** *for marijuana until he finally kicks the habit.*

paranoid: *having unreasonable distrust and suspicion*
Smoking marijuana makes Craig **paranoid.**

willpower: *strength of mind*
Craig shows great **willpower** *in giving up marijuana smoking.*

ACTIVITIES

1. Freewriting: Finding Yourself in the Story

After group members have finished reading the story, ask them to take out writing materials. If you'll be writing also, have handy your own journal and tell students you'll be participating. For a description of freewriting, see pages 14–15.

The following statement and questions are similar to those you considered earlier in "A Moment of Reflection." This time, you may want to write along with your group:

Think of a time when you had a habit you wanted to break. How or why did the habit start? Why did you want to break it? What techniques did you try? Which worked, and which didn't? If you weren't able to break the habit, what do you think got in the way? If you did manage to break the habit, how did you feel about your efforts? How do you feel about the experience now?

After the freewriting, invite volunteers to share what they wrote. Allow time for brief discussion.

2. Discussion: Understanding Events

To be sure group members have understood the story, ask questions such as:

- **Why does Craig smoke marijuana?**

- **What memories come back when he smokes?**

- **What stages does Craig go through when he smokes? Why does he keep on smoking?**

- **How does Craig quit? What does he do to keep from thinking about his *craving* for marijuana?**

- **What's the "trend" Craig thinks he may start?**

NOTE: Avoiding Roadblocks

Potential roadblocks in this story are similar to those you may have found in "Losing My Friends to Weed," page 55. Specifically, judgmental comments about marijuana could sidetrack discussion. Try to keep the focus on Craig's initiative, not on pot smoking. Let your group know you're interested in Craig's courage and willpower as he fights his addiction. Point out the obstacles in his way—his abusive childhood, a life on the streets, friends who smoke, the pains of withdrawal—and the enormous effort it takes to get past these obstacles. If teens argue that they like marijuana and that Craig's problems with it are unusual, stay close to the story. Emphasize that Craig struggles to give up something that he feels is bad for him; he wants to stop. You might also rely on the differing opinions within your group to carry the discussion. Encourage a variety of viewpoints so teens can see a range of options and consequences. Encourage their empathy with Craig. Ask the group:

Why did Craig want to stop smoking? Why is he glad he did?

3. Discussion: Understanding Issues

Craig's Initiative

Review with the group what initiative is, why it's sometimes hard to come by, and how it can be helpful. Then, referring as necessary to "How Initiative Works in the Story" (page 94), ask questions such as:

- **What do you think is the hardest thing for Craig about giving up marijuana? What takes the most *willpower*?**

- **Do you think giving up marijuana was a good thing for Craig to do? Why or why not?**

- **Do you think Craig is likely to smoke marijuana again? Why or why not?**

Connecting with the Issues

Suggest that group members silently review what they wrote during freewriting. Then ask questions such as:

- **Craig says that most of his friends never talk about the bad effects of marijuana. Is there a topic your friends avoid? Why don't they talk honestly about this subject?**

- **Why do you think people form habits and keep them, even when they're harmful? What would you tell a friend who continued to do something that you could see was dangerous or self-destructive?**

4. Role Play

For guidelines on role playing, see pages 15–16.

Objective: Group members will identify with Craig's struggle to take the initiative and kick his marijuana habit.

Characters: Craig, his friend

Procedure
Ask for volunteers to enact this scene:

Craig and his friend are talking together. The last time Craig smoked marijuana, his memories were particularly painful. He wants to quit. His friend wants him to keep smoking.

Allow five to ten minutes for the role play. Afterward, discuss questions such as:

- **What did you see happening in this scene?**

- **If you were Craig, would your friend have convinced you to keep smoking? If you were Craig's friend, would Craig have convinced you he shouldn't smoke?**

- **How did this role play affect or change your understanding of Craig's story?**

5. Writing Activities: Taking It Further

Ask students to complete one or more of the following activities individually, in small groups, or at home. Modify the activities as needed to suit the writing ability of group members. When activities are completed, invite volunteers to read their work to the group. Discuss how teens felt about the purpose and value of the writing.

Activity A

Objective: Group members will describe Craig's initiative in their own words.

Pretend you're Craig. Write a letter to a friend describing why and how you stopped smoking marijuana.

Activity B

Objective: Group members will reflect on a problem they analyzed before solving.

Before he decides to give up smoking, Craig analyzes how marijuana affects him—how, for example, marijuana made him *paranoid* and only *aggravated* his problems. Write about a positive action you took after analyzing a problem you were having. What was the problem? How did you go about understanding it? What did you do to solve it?

Activity C

Objective: Group members will consider why people use drugs.

Why do you think people use drugs? Why are drugs so hard to give up? Why do some people find the initiative to quit while others don't? Write about this issue.

6. In Your Journal: Making It Personal

Encourage group members to reflect on the following topic in their journals:

Most of us have habits we'd like to break. Craig smoked marijuana to escape painful memories, although marijuana only made the memories worse. Think about a habit you have (or had in the past). What purpose does it serve? Does the habit help you or hurt you? Do you want to break it? If not, why not? If so, what steps will you have to take? Do you think you'll take them? Why or why not?

COLLEGE CAN BE HELL

by Tamecka Crawford

Pages 96–100 in *The Struggle to Be Strong*

PREPARING TO LEAD THE ACTIVITIES

Story Summary

When Tamecka gets to college, she's filled with doubts and insecurities. Soon, involved with a new boyfriend, she begins missing classes and failing exams. Her first response is to blame her failure on being a foster child without parental support. She feels jealous of other students whose lives seem easier than hers because they have families. But by the end of the first semester she's tired of making excuses, tired of failing. Tamecka faces and controls her jealousy. Realizing that time is passing her by, she improves her academic performance by attending classes regularly; getting tutoring, counseling, and a part-time job; and asking for help from her professors. Contemplating her success, Tamecka remarks, "I learned that in order for anything to change, I first must care about myself. Then I'm able to care about the situation and do what I need to do."

A Moment of Reflection

To connect with the story's themes, consider from your own perspective the questions group members will address during freewriting: Think of a time when feeling sorry for yourself kept you from doing what you needed to do. How did your hurt feelings affect you? Were you able to get past them? If so, what happened? If not, how could you keep from feeling sorry for yourself in the future?

How Initiative Works in the Story

Seeing Tamecka's Initiative

For Tamecka, the first and hardest step in taking initiative is becoming aware that she can take charge of her life: "I got tired of using the fact that I was in foster care as an excuse." As she sees, "It wasn't being from a group home holding me back—it was me holding myself back." Tamecka's awareness launches her into action. She attends classes regularly, works with tutors, seeks help from professors, gets counseling, and takes a part-time job. She also changes her attitude that seeking help is a sign of weakness or an invitation for others to judge her. When her professors give her the help she needs, without judging her adversely, Tamecka's initiative is reinforced and she's able to succeed. She even sees that in some ways, foster care has given her certain advantages in adjusting to college life. By the end of the story, she confidently looks forward to finishing the school year.

Why Initiative Is a Struggle for Tamecka

Tamecka is burdened by the pain of her past. She feels stigmatized: "I felt as if the words 'group home child' were hanging over my head." Her self-pity and her jealousy of classmates with loving families undermine her self-esteem and ability to take charge of her life. Gradually, however, Tamecka takes initiative to succeed in school. The key is changing her attitude toward her hurtful past. She stops viewing her childhood solely as an obstacle or as her downfall. Instead, she realizes it also has benefits. Most important, says Tamecka, "I learned that in order for anything to change, I first must care about myself."

Useful Concept Words

To assist teens in understanding and discussing this story, you may want to introduce some or all of the following concept words by making them part of discussions and activities. Write them on the board in advance and plan to explain each word when it appears in a suggested discussion question or activity (where the words are shown

in italics). Here are the concept words, with definitions and sentences relating them to the story.

competent: *well-qualified, capable*
After she seeks help and begins doing better in school, Tamecka feels more **competent.**

self-doubt: *doubt about one's own competence or worth*
When she doesn't do well in her classes, Tamecka feels **self-doubt.**

self-pity: *excessive concern with one's misfortunes*
Tamecka feels **self-pity** *because she's in foster care and doesn't have family support.*

stigma: *a mark of shame or disgrace*
Tamecka feels a sense of **stigma** *as a foster child.*

ACTIVITIES

1. Freewriting: Finding Yourself in the Story

After group members have finished reading the story, ask them to take out writing materials. If you'll be writing also, have handy your own journal and tell students you'll be participating. For a description of freewriting, see pages 14–15.

The following statement and questions are similar to those you considered earlier in "A Moment of Reflection." This time, you may want to write along with your group:

Think of a time when feeling sorry for yourself kept you from doing what you needed to do. How did your hurt feelings affect you? Were you able to get past them? If so, what happened? If not, how could you keep from feeling sorry for yourself in the future?

After the freewriting, invite volunteers to share what they wrote. Allow time for brief discussion.

2. Discussion: Understanding Events

To be sure group members have understood the story, ask questions such as:

- Why does Tamecka say that going off to college is especially scary for a foster child?

- When Tamecka misses a class or fails an exam, what excuse does she use?

- How does Tamecka feel when other students get calls or care packages from home?

- After Tamecka decides to take charge of her life, what are three things she does to improve her school performance? How does each make her feel more *competent* as a student?

- What happens when Tamecka lets her professors know she's having problems?

3. Discussion: Understanding Issues

Tamecka's Initiative

Review with the group what initiative is, why it's sometimes hard to come by, and how it can be helpful. Then, referring as necessary to "How Initiative Works in the Story" (page 97), ask questions such as:

- What are the steps Tamecka takes to do better in college? Why are they hard?

- Tamecka says, "I finally realized it wasn't because I was in foster care that I was failing my classes." Why was she failing?

- What effect does counseling have on Tamecka?

- In your opinion, what's the most important realization Tamecka has about herself?

Connecting with the Issues

Suggest that group members silently review what they wrote during freewriting. Then ask questions such as:

- Once Tamecka becomes determined to turn her life around, she takes a number of active steps: attending classes, getting tutoring and counseling, taking a part-time job. What qualities would you say she has that allow her to put such great effort into change?

- Have you ever felt jealous of people you thought had it easier than you did? If so, what steps did you take (or could you take) to stop comparing yourself negatively to others?

- How hard is it for you to seek help from others? Explain your answer.

4. Role Play

For guidelines on role playing, see pages 15–16.

Objective: Group members will identify with Tamecka's efforts to overcome self-doubt.

Characters: Tamecka, her roommate

Procedure
Ask for volunteers to enact this scene:

Tamecka's roommate was in foster care. She doubts she can succeed in college and is thinking of dropping out. Tamecka wants her to know that there are steps she can take to overcome her *self-doubt* and do well in college.

Allow five to ten minutes for the role play. Afterward, discuss questions such as:

- What did you see happening in this scene?

- If you were Tamecka's roommate, how would you feel about what Tamecka said?

- How did this role play affect or change your understanding of Tamecka's story?

5. Writing Activities: Taking It Further

Ask students to complete one or more of the following activities individually, in small groups, or at home. Modify the activities as needed to suit the writing ability of group members. When activities are completed, invite volunteers to read their work to the group. Discuss how teens felt about the purpose and value of the writing.

Activity A

Objective: Group members will describe Tamecka's initiative in their own words.

Pretend you're Tamecka. Write a letter to your friends in the group home explaining the steps you took to change your attitude about your past and improve your college performance. Describe what was hard, and why.

Activity B

Objective: Group members will reflect on ways that negative experiences can be seen as sources of strength.

Tamecka realized that being a foster child actually had some advantages in helping her adjust to college life. Write about a time when you realized that something negative in your past could actually be an advantage or source of strength for you in the present.

Activity C

Objective: Group members will reflect on their own experience with feeling stigmatized.

Tamecka feels a sense of *stigma* as a foster child—she feels she carries an invisible mark of shame that makes everyone think less of her. Write about a time you felt stigmatized about something (for instance, about your family background, your academic record, your interests or beliefs, or something else). How did feeling stigmatized affect you? Looking back, would you do anything differently to deal with the situation?

6. In Your Journal: Making It Personal

Encourage group members to reflect on the following topic in their journals:

Tamecka has a hard time overcoming *self-pity* and *self-doubt* about her painful childhood in foster homes. Are there painful experiences from your past that get in the way of your life today? Do you think it's possible to get over experiences like this and move on? Why or why not? What action could you take now to try and overcome the past?

PREPARING TO LEAD THE ACTIVITIES

Story Summary

Shaniqua starts writing poetry at age ten to express her feelings. She studies the work of famous poets and develops her own style. As she matures, she writes about all kinds of serious issues, from personal to universal, and becomes interested in reading her work in public. The thought of performing, however, scares her. When she notices a café that holds readings, she decides to override her fear of performing and sign up. When her name is called, she nervously steps up to the mike. She starts out clumsily but quickly wins the audience over and begins to enjoy herself. Shaniqua now reads her poetry in public regularly.

A Moment of Reflection

To connect with the story's themes, consider from your own perspective the questions group members will address during freewriting: Think of the first time you had to speak or perform in front of an audience. How did you feel about it, physically and emotionally? If you felt frightened or self-conscious, how did you try to control those feelings? How did your feelings affect your performance? How did you feel when your speech or performance was over? Was speaking or performing any easier the next time you did it?

How Initiative Works in the Story

Seeing Shaniqua's Initiative

Shaniqua shows initiative early, when she teaches herself to write poetry by studying the work of famous poets. As a teenager, eager to share her work but nervous about performing, she inquires about reading at a small, nearby café because, as she puts it, "what did I have to lose by asking?" Having come that far, Shaniqua regards her decision to read as a commitment; she even goes to the café alone. Although she's "feeling a little jittery," aware that she's the only black person in the room and that everyone's older than she, Shaniqua reminds herself what she's there for: "to enjoy myself, read my poetry, and have a good time." She focuses her attention outside herself, looking around the coffee shop and at the people there, enjoying the poetry she hears. When it's her turn, she covers her clumsiness with a joke and addresses the audience with friendly conversation: "Hi, my name's Shaniqua, and I'd like to read everyone a couple of poems. Is that cool with you?"

Why Initiative Is a Struggle for Shaniqua

As soon as Shaniqua begins to think of reading in public, anxiety sets in. "[N]othing scared me more than when I decided to read my poems out loud before an audience," she tells us. "Being the shy person I am, I couldn't believe I was doing this." Once she commits to the poetry reading, however, Shaniqua takes charge of the experience, does well, and enjoys herself. Through her initiative, she gains confidence and develops a solid vision of herself as a writer now and in the future: "Writing will always be my first love, and I will continue to write so I can get even better."

Useful Concept Words

To assist teens in understanding and discussing this story, you may want to introduce some or all of the following concept words by making them part of discussions and activities. Write them on the board in advance and plan to explain each word when it appears in a suggested discussion question or activity (where the words are shown

in italics). Here are the concept words, with definitions and sentences relating them to the story.

aspire: to seek to accomplish a particular goal
Shaniqua **aspires** *to be a prize-winning, best-selling author.*

overcome: to conquer
Shaniqua **overcomes** *her fears of reading in front of an audience.*

performance anxiety: fears about presenting or exhibiting oneself before an audience
Before she reads her poetry in public for the first time, Shaniqua feels **performance anxiety.**

ACTIVITIES

1. Freewriting: Finding Yourself in the Story

After group members have finished reading the story, ask them to take out writing materials. If you'll be writing also, have handy your own journal and tell students you'll be participating. For a description of freewriting, see pages 14–15.

The following statement and questions are similar to those you considered earlier in "A Moment of Reflection." This time, you may want to write along with your group:

Think of the first time you had to speak or perform in front of an audience. How did you feel about it, physically and mentally? Were you scared or self-conscious? If so, how did you try to control those feelings? How did your feelings affect your performance? How did you feel when your speech or performance was over? Was speaking or performing any easier the next time you did it? Why or why not?

After the freewriting, invite volunteers to share what they wrote. Allow time for brief discussion.

2. Discussion: Understanding Events

To be sure group members have understood the story, ask questions such as:

- **Why does Shaniqua begin writing?**

- **Where does she first read her poetry in public? Describe the place and audience.**

- **How does Shaniqua feel as she listens to other people's poetry and waits for her turn?**

- **What happens in the story from the time Shaniqua hears her name called until she finishes reading?**

- **What dreams does Shaniqua have for her future? What does she *aspire* to?**

3. Discussion: Understanding Issues

Shaniqua's Initiative

Review with the group what initiative is, why it's sometimes hard to come by, and how it can be helpful. Then, referring as necessary to "How Initiative Works in the Story" (page 100), ask questions such as:

- **As Shaniqua waits for her turn to read, what does she do to feel more relaxed and comfortable? How does she *overcome* her *performance anxiety*?**

- **Why does Shaniqua say, "Performing in front of an audience is as important to me as writing poetry"? What is the value, for her, of reading her work?**

- **Could you have done what Shaniqua did? Why or why not?**

Connecting with the Issues

Suggest that group members silently review what they wrote during freewriting. Then ask questions such as:

- **Do you have a talent or skill you'd like to share with others, but haven't yet? What has kept you from sharing it? What would help you share it?**

- **Have you ever shared a talent or skill, as Shaniqua did? If so, what was the experience like?**

- **Do you agree that talents should be shared? Why or why not?**

- Shaniqua was afraid at first to read her poetry in public, but eventually became skilled at it. What's something you're now good at (sports, writing, art, playing in a band, or something else) that you were at first afraid to try? How did you develop your skills? What steps did you take to *overcome* your fear of trying?

4. Role Play

For guidelines on role playing, see pages 15–16.

Objective: Group members will identify with Shaniqua's methods for overcoming performance anxiety.

Characters: Shaniqua, her friend

Procedure
Ask for volunteers to enact this scene:

Shaniqua's friend is afraid to read her poetry in public. Shaniqua wants to give her friend specific steps to take to *overcome* her fears.

Allow five to ten minutes for the role play. Afterward, discuss questions such as:

- What did you see happening in this scene?
- If you were Shaniqua's friend, would Shaniqua have convinced you to read your poetry in public?
- How did this role play affect or change your understanding of Shaniqua's story?

5. Group Activity

Objective: Teens will practice describing something in front of the group.

Procedure
Ask teens to think of something important to them that they'd be willing to describe for the group. For instance, they might talk about something they've written, a piece of artwork they made, a favorite possession, a favorite place, or something that's been in their family for a long time. They might also describe an important experience, a person who means a lot to them, or a funny incident. Before teens do their presentation, ask them to jot down what they're feeling. After the presentations, ask them to jot down how sharing felt. After everyone has presented, have them compare their "before" and "after" notes. Discuss any steps or strategies that could make public speaking easier in the future. Ask the group:

- What would help you feel more comfortable talking in front of a group?
- How did this activity affect or change your understanding of Shaniqua's story?

6. Writing Activities: Taking It Further

Ask students to complete one or more of the following activities individually, in small groups, or at home. Modify the activities as needed to suit the writing ability of group members. When activities are completed, invite volunteers to read their work to the group. Discuss how teens felt about the purpose and value of the writing.

Activity A

Objective: Group members will describe Shaniqua's initiative in their own words.

Pretend you're Shaniqua. Your friend has a good singing voice, but is afraid to perform in public. Write her a letter, telling her about your own experiences and encouraging her to perform.

Activity B

Objective: Group members will reflect on a time they overcame anxieties about doing something.

Write about a time when, like Shaniqua, you managed to *overcome* fears or anxieties and do something you wanted to do. How did it work out? How did you feel about your efforts?

Activity C

Objective: Group members will describe taking a risk that didn't work out well.

Shaniqua took a risk when she first read her poetry out loud. Describe a time you took a risk and things didn't work out well. How did you feel about it? Would you take the same risk again? If so, what would you do differently?

7. In Your Journal: Making It Personal

Encourage group members to reflect on the following topic in their journals:

Do you have a talent or skill that you haven't really worked on or developed? What do you think is holding you back from developing it? What steps could you take to get better? What would it be like for you to work on and develop this talent or skill to the fullest?

HOW I GRADUATED
by Angi Baptiste

Pages 106–109 in *The Struggle to Be Strong*

PREPARING TO LEAD THE ACTIVITIES

Story Summary

When Angi enters high school in ninth grade, she soon begins a pattern of sleeping in class and falling behind in schoolwork. Although her goal is to graduate, a negative inner voice holds her back from trying: "I used to put myself down all the time. I thought I was never gonna make it." When she recalls a remark once made to her, "Never say never, until you try," she decides to change. In tenth and eleventh grade, she works well at first but then slows down. Finally, in twelfth grade, Angi breaks the pattern and graduates.

A Moment of Reflection

To connect with the story's themes, consider from your own perspective the questions group members will address during freewriting: Think of a time when a poor self-image or negative "inner voice" threatened to hold you back from achieving something or moving forward in your life. What did that negative inner voice tell you about yourself? Where do you think those ideas came from? How did they affect your behavior? Have you been able to overcome your doubts about yourself? If so, how did you do it? If not, what do you think might help you?

How Initiative Works in the Story

Seeing Angi's Initiative

Inspired by the remark, "Never say never, until you try," Angi decides to buckle down in school so she can graduate. She acknowledges her challenges: to prevent her pain at being a foster child and her jealousy of other kids with supportive families

from getting in her way, and to quiet her own self-defeating inner voice. She begins by trying to work hard. She also focuses on a new goal—making her foster parents and herself proud: "I didn't want to disappoint my foster parents, because they believed I was gonna make it. That would have hurt me very much—to let them and everybody else down. Most of all, I wouldn't be proud of myself." When Angi finds she can't sustain her initiative despite her best efforts, she tries another approach: switching to night school. The switch helps her make headway with her academic difficulties and also has an unexpected benefit: gradually, she begins to see school as a refuge from the unhappiness she feels in her foster home. Her teachers help and care about her, and she learns something she can use the rest of her life: "Never think any less of yourself because you're in foster care. Never feel you're not gonna make it. . . . You have the power to make things happen for yourself."

Why Initiative Is a Struggle for Angi

Taking initiative is a struggle for Angi because she feels she can't succeed: "I couldn't stop worrying about what was going to happen to me, whether I'd be dead or alive by the age of twenty, whether I'd make it to see tomorrow." She is also frightened in a new school, finds classes hard, and can't concentrate. Most important, Angi struggles against the voice of her critical father that she hears over and over in her mind: ". . . I started to believe what my father used to say, that I would never graduate 'because you're nothing.'" Determined to prove him wrong, Angi switches to night school, gets tutoring with the help of her foster parents, and consistently works hard. Still, she continues to be tormented by jealousy of friends with supportive families, by unhappiness with her own living situation, and by negative thoughts. But her teachers help her, her foster parents support her struggle, and she graduates, proud of her newly gained sense that she has power over her life.

Useful Concept Words

To assist teens in understanding and discussing this story, you may want to introduce some or all of the following concept words by making them part of discussions and activities. Write them on the board in advance and plan to explain each word when it appears in a suggested discussion question or activity (where the words are shown in italics). Here are the concept words, with definitions and sentences relating them to the story.

focus: *to concentrate; to see clearly*
*Angi struggles to **focus** on her schoolwork, rather than on her unhappy home life.*

persevere: *to persist or keep trying in the face of obstacles or disappointment*
*Angi **perseveres** in her studies so she can graduate.*

refuge: *a place providing protection or shelter*
*School becomes a **refuge** for Angi.*

self-defeating: *serving to defeat or frustrate oneself*
*Angi's negative inner voice is **self-defeating.***

self-image: *one's view of oneself*
*Angi has a poor **self-image** because of her father's criticism and her unhappy home life.*

ACTIVITIES

1. Freewriting: Finding Yourself in the Story

After group members have finished reading the story, ask them to take out writing materials. If you'll be writing also, have handy your own journal and tell students you'll be participating. For a description of freewriting, see pages 14–15.

The following statement and questions are similar to those you considered earlier in "A Moment of Reflection." This time, you may want to write along with your group:

Think of a time when a poor *self-image* or negative "inner voice" was keeping you from achieving something or moving forward in your life. What did that negative inner voice tell you about yourself? Where do you think those ideas came from? How did they affect you? Have you been able to overcome your

doubts about yourself? If so, how did you do it? If not, what do you think might help you?

After the freewriting, invite volunteers to share what they wrote. Allow time for brief discussion.

2. Discussion: Understanding Events

To be sure group members have understood the story, ask questions such as:

- Why does Angi say she has trouble concentrating in school?

- What did Angi's father used to tell her?

- Why does Angi feel jealous of her friends?

- Why does school become "more like my real home" for Angi?

- How does Angi know that her social studies teacher cares a lot about her education?

- What happens when Angi calls her father to tell him she graduated?

- Why is she angry with her sister?

- What advice does Angi offer at the end of the story?

3. Discussion: Understanding Issues

Angi's Initiative

Review with the group what initiative is, why it's sometimes hard to come by, and how it can be helpful. Then, referring as necessary to "How Initiative Works in the Story" (page 104), ask questions such as:

- Angi says her main problem with school was laziness. Do you agree with her? Why or why not? What steps did she take to "stop being lazy"? Why was it hard to stop?

- Angi says she couldn't concentrate in school because she "couldn't stop worrying." What was she worried about? Do you worry about similar things? How can a person get over worries like these?

- Why do you think Angi calls her father to tell him she graduated? How do you think she felt about his reaction to her news? Explain your answer.

- Angi says, "You have the power to make things happen for yourself." Do you agree? Why or why not?

Connecting with the Issues

Suggest that group members silently review what they wrote during freewriting. Then ask questions such as:

- How can a negative *self-image*—feeling bad about yourself—make it hard to concentrate in school? What do you think a person could do about *self-defeating* thoughts like the ones Angi had? What helps you concentrate when you're feeling bad?

- Angi changes from seeing school as a burden to seeing it as a *refuge,* "more like my real home." Have you ever found a "second home" in an unexpected place or among people that you didn't feel comfortable with at first? Explain your answer.

- Think of a time you succeeded at something, despite negative thoughts or other problems. What helped you succeed?

4. Role Plays

For guidelines on role playing, see pages 15–16.

Objective: Group members will identify with Angi's struggle to overcome her poor self-image.

Scenario A

Characters: Angi, her friend

Procedure
Ask for volunteers to enact this scene:

Angi's friend is failing in school and feels she can't graduate. Angi wants to convince her that she can.

Allow five to ten minutes for the role play. Afterward, discuss questions such as:

- What did you see happening in this scene?

- If you were Angi's friend, would Angi have convinced you that you can graduate after all?

- How did this role play affect or change your understanding of Angi's story?

Scenario B

Characters: Angi, her negative inner voice

Procedure
Ask for volunteers to enact this scene:

Angi's inner voice tells her she can't succeed, that she's a loser just like her father told her. Angi wants to stand up to the voice by insisting on her positive qualities, strengths, and goals.

Allow five to ten minutes for the role play. Afterward, discuss questions such as:

- What did you see happening in this scene?

- If you were Angi, would you feel you'd defeated your negative inner voice?

- How did this role play affect or change your understanding of Angi's story?

5. Writing Activities: Taking It Further

Ask students to complete one or more of the following activities individually, in small groups, or at home. Modify the activities as needed to suit the writing ability of group members. When activities are completed, invite volunteers to read their work to the group. Discuss how teens felt about the purpose and value of the writing.

Activity A

Objective: Group members will describe Angi's initiative in their own words.

Pretend you're Angi. Write a letter to a friend, explaining why you couldn't concentrate in school and what steps you took to *focus* and to meet your goal of graduating.

Activity B

Objective: Group members will give advice on ways to sustain initiative.

Pretend you're a friend of Angi's. You know she's not doing well in school and is afraid she won't graduate. Write a letter to her, encouraging her to *persevere* in her efforts.

Activity C

Objective: Group members will consider ways to overcome a negative self-image.

What can people do to overcome a negative *self-image*? What actions can they take? Make a list of everything you can think of that a person could try. After you make your list, put a check next to the ones you've tried. Then write about the one that worked best for you.

6. In Your Journal: Making It Personal

Encourage group members to reflect on the following topic in their journals:

From time to time, all of us have negative inner voices, or inner "critics." Where do you think your negative inner voice comes from? What do you hear from your "inner critic"? List each criticism. Now answer each criticism from your inner voice with a positive response. For the next two days, try replacing your inner critic with these supportive voices. Then come back to your journal and write about what happened.

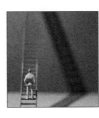

FIVE TEENS: THE IMPORTANCE OF INITIATIVE

As necessary, refer to pages 86 and 87 in the anthology to review with your group what initiative is and why it's a resilience. Then invite group members to compare how initiative works in the lives of the five teen writers in this section. (To help students recall each writer, you might list their first names on the board.) Ask questions such as:

- **Which writer do you think has the toughest time taking charge and meeting the challenges of his or her life? Why do you think so?**

- **Which writer do you think shows the most courage in overcoming fears and taking action? Why do you think so?**

- **Which writer do you think changes the most because of taking initiative? Why do you think so?**

- **Which story in this section do you like best? Which teen writer do you admire most? Explain your choices.**

Many of the teen writers in this book demonstrate more than one resilience. If your group has read other stories, you might ask members to discuss how writers in other sections also demonstrate initiative.

CREATIVITY
USING IMAGINATION

Before discussing the stories in this section, ask the group to read the introductory material about creativity in their anthology, pages 110 and 111. Allow time for questions and brief discussion. Be sure teens understand the following:

- **Creativity** is using your imagination to express yourself and to handle hurt feelings and difficult experiences.

- The opposite of **creativity** is keeping your feelings bottled up inside.

- **Creativity** is hard because hurt feelings and painful experiences can weigh you down, dull your mind, and block your imagination.

- **Creativity** helps you turn something that feels ugly and bad into something beautiful. **Creativity** helps you express your feelings in a positive, satisfying way.

As teens read each story, encourage them to look for ways the writer demonstrates creativity. Also suggest that they reflect on—and possibly jot down ideas about—the questions that follow each story ("Think About It"). Refer them to the introductory section "'Think About It'—and Maybe Write About It," pages 7–8 in the anthology.

HOW WRITING HELPS ME
by Terry-Ann Da Costa

Pages 112–114 in *The Struggle to Be Strong*

PREPARING TO LEAD THE ACTIVITIES

Story Summary

With the help and encouragement of her father, Terry-Ann starts writing when she's just four years old. At twelve, she leaves her father's home in Jamaica and comes to America to live with her mother. Though her mother makes fun of her writing, accuses her of copying others' work, and says she won't "be anything" when she grows up, Terry-Ann continues to write short stories and poems. At the end of the story, Terry-Ann expresses the hope that her writing will be published someday.

A Moment of Reflection

To connect with the story's themes, consider from your own perspective the questions group members will address during freewriting: Think of a time when you turned to a hobby or activity for comfort or to find strength. (For example, writing, praying, meditating, cooking, painting, reading, playing sports, and so on.) How did this activity help you? Why do you think it did? Do you still turn to this activity during difficult times? Why or why not?

How Creativity Works in the Story

Seeing Terry-Ann's Creativity

Terry-Ann relies on her creativity to deal with painful aspects of her life. She puts her hurt feelings, mainly over her mother's verbal abuse, into her poems, short stories, and diaries, thereby gaining control over her emotions. Putting her feelings into words also stops her from acting self-destructively: "I remember one day I was really depressed. I wrote about how I felt and what made me feel that way, and then I read over what I'd written. That helped me feel a lot better, because when I read it I couldn't believe I was capable of having those harmful, dangerous thoughts and feelings about myself." Writing reassures Terry-Ann about her ability to survive and gives her hope. She keeps writing despite criticism, believing that her work will someday change her mother's poor opinion of her. Terry-Ann also finds a sense of purpose in writing. When she shows a poem to a troubled cousin, the cousin feels better: "I know that if someone has a problem and they read my story or poem, it might make them feel a little (or even a lot) better about themselves."

Why Creativity Is a Struggle for Terry-Ann

Terry-Ann suffers considerable loss when she has to leave her loving father and live with a mother who ridicules what the girl cherishes most: her talent for writing. In part, Terry-Ann persists with her writing in the hope of proving her mother wrong. Her struggle is to keep believing in herself and to continue writing.

Useful Concept Words

To assist teens in understanding and discussing this story, you may want to introduce some or all of the following concept words by making them part of discussions and activities. Write them on the board in advance and plan to explain each word when it appears in a suggested discussion question or activity (where the words are shown in italics). Here are the concept words, with definitions and sentences relating them to the story.

despair: hopelessness; a sense of defeat

Terry-Ann's writing prevents her from slipping into **despair.**

endurance: the power to withstand hardship or stress

Terry-Ann has the **endurance** to continue writing despite the problems in her life.

hope: a wish for something with the expectation that it will happen

Terry-Ann's creativity enables her to have **hope.**

release: to set free

Terry-Ann **releases** her emotions through writing.

ACTIVITIES

1. Freewriting: Finding Yourself in the Story

After group members have finished reading the story, ask them to take out writing materials. If you'll be writing also, have handy your own journal and tell students you'll be participating. For a description of freewriting, see pages 14–15.

The following statement and questions are similar to those you considered earlier in "A Moment of Reflection." This time, you may want to write along with your group.

Think of a time when you felt unhappy and turned to a hobby or activity for comfort or to find strength. (For example, you may have turned to writing, praying, meditating, cooking, painting, reading, playing sports, and so on.) How did this activity help you? Why do you think it did? Do you still turn to this activity when you're going through difficult times? Why or why not?

After the freewriting, invite volunteers to share what they wrote. Allow time for brief discussion.

2. Discussion: Understanding Events

To be sure group members have understood the story, ask questions such as:

- **How did Terry-Ann's father encourage her to write when she was very young?**

- **What does her mother think about her writing? What does her mother say Terry-Ann will be when she grows up?**

- **When Terry-Ann feels unhappy or depressed, what's the effect of writing about her feelings and then reading what she's written?**

- **How does Terry-Ann help her cousin?**

- **What are the two reasons Terry-Ann wants to be a published writer someday?**

3. Discussion: Understanding Issues

Terry-Ann's Creativity

Review with the group what creativity is, why it's sometimes hard to come by, and how it can be helpful. Then, referring as necessary to "How Creativity Works in the Story" (page 110), ask questions such as:

- **Why do you think Terry-Ann's writing helps her deal with depression and unhappiness?**

- **Terry-Ann says that "writing is like both my friend and my family." What does she mean?**

- **If Terry-Ann's childhood had been happier, do you think she would still write? Why or why not?**

Connecting with the Issues

Suggest that group members silently review what they wrote during freewriting. Then ask questions such as:

- **Terry-Ann uses writing to *release* her strong feelings and as a way to strengthen herself and avoid *despair* in the face of her mother's put-downs. How have you used your own creativity (for instance, singing, playing an instrument, drawing, writing, cooking, sewing, meditating) to deal with painful feelings?**

- **Do you think creativity has to be shared with others in order for it to help you? Can it remain private and still help? Would you rather share your creativity or keep it to yourself? Why?**

4. Role Play

For guidelines on role playing, see pages 15–16.

Objective: Group members will identify with how creativity can help people deal with difficult emotions and situations.

Characters: Terry-Ann, her friend

Procedure
Ask for volunteers to enact this scene:

Terry-Ann's friend is unhappy. Terry-Ann wants her friend to try writing about these painful feelings. The friend thinks writing won't help at all.

Allow five to ten minutes for the role play. Afterward, discuss questions such as:

- **What did you see happening in this scene?**

- **If you were Terry-Ann's friend, would Terry-Ann have convinced you to try writing about your feelings?**

- **How did this role play affect or change your understanding of Terry-Ann's story?**

5. Group Activities

Activity A

Objective: Teens will practice using writing as a creative means of expressing feelings.

Procedure
Tell the group that the object of this activity is to practice using writing as a way to express feelings. Also tell them that they won't be asked to share what they write, unless they want to. Ask them to think about one of two things: either something in their lives that's making them unhappy, or something that's making them happy. Next, have them take about five minutes to write about the situation and to describe their feelings. Then ask them to write answers to these questions:

- **How was it to write about your feelings?**

- **Do you feel any different after getting your feelings down on paper? If so, how would you describe the difference? If not, do you think writing or some other form of self-expression could ever be helpful for you? Why or why not?**

Afterward, discuss what surprised the group and what they learned from this activity. Ask:

- **What's the value of writing about your feelings?**

- **How did this activity affect or change your understanding of Terry-Ann's story?**

Activity B

Objective: Teens will share examples of their own creativity.

Procedure
Ask group members to bring in something or prepare to explain something that demonstrates or exemplifies their creativity. For example, they might bring in writing, artwork, crafts, music, food they made, photographs they took, clothing or jewelry, a school project they're proud of, and so on. Ask everyone to talk about the experience of working creatively. For instance, does creativity help them solve problems or deal with strong feelings? What's hard about being creative? What do they enjoy most about it?

Afterward, summarize how creativity helps group members, and draw the connection between the activity and the story. Ask:

- **What are some of the ways people said creativity helps them?**

- **How did this activity affect or change your understanding of Terry-Ann's story?**

6. Writing Activities: Taking It Further

Ask students to complete one or more of the following activities individually, in small groups, or at home. Modify the activities as needed to suit the writing ability of group members. When activities are completed, invite volunteers to read their work to the group. Discuss how teens felt about the purpose and value of the writing.

Activity A

Objective: Group members will describe Terry-Ann's creativity in their own words.

Pretend you're Terry-Ann. Write a letter to your father explaining how your writing has given you *endurance* and *hope.*

Activity B

Objective: Group members will reflect on how creative expression can help people cope with unhappiness.

Write about how a favorite book, poem, song, painting, sculpture, movie, play, or some other creative work has helped you when you were going through hard times.

Activity C

Objective: Group members will consider the effects of writing about problems.

Do you think writing about a problem can sometimes make the problem worse? Why or why not? When does writing seem to help? When does it not seem to help?

7. In Your Journal: Making It Personal

Encourage group members to reflect on the following topic in their journals:

Terry-Ann uses her creative talent not only to keep herself from *despair,* but also to help her cousin. When did you use your creativity to help someone get through a painful or confusing situation? When did a friend use her or his creativity to help you get through a difficult situation?

PREPARING TO LEAD THE ACTIVITIES

Story Summary

As Cassandra's story opens, she's sitting on her bed with the TV on, fantasizing about singing with a fictional boyfriend in a fictional band. She's had an active fantasy life since the age of six, an "imaginary world" where "there are no blocks or barriers in the road." She assures us that she also works for her dreams in real life but considers it useful to picture her goals first in her imagination. Sometimes Cassandra's vivid imagination gets her so carried away that she's embarrassed "in the real world." Still, her imagination makes her happy.

A Moment of Reflection

To connect with the story's themes, consider from your own perspective the questions group members will address during freewriting: Think of a time when you used your imagination to deal with a situation that was boring, stressful, or painful. What made the situation difficult? How did you use your imagination to deal with it? Did using your imagination help make real life more bearable?

How Creativity Works in the Story

Seeing Cassandra's Creativity

When Cassandra and her father miss seeing Santa Claus in the mall, she comforts herself by imagining that Santa brings her "hundreds of presents." From that time on, she uses her imagination actively to find excitement, freedom, and a sense of confidence that reality sometimes denies. Her imagination also gets her through jobs she dislikes, relieves her bad moods, helps her solve problems, and shapes her dreams for the future. As she says, "It's good to imagine your goals so you have a picture of them and can believe in yourself. You can look ahead at your 'wished for' future. You can say, 'If I imagine it, then I can be it.'"

Why Creativity Is a Struggle for Cassandra

Cassandra worries that relying on her imagination too much might be unhealthy. "I get nervous because I live so much in my imagination, dreaming of things that can't be realities." Cassandra also worries about the way other people look at her when she's "caught imagining," and many times she feels let down when she returns to reality. In the end, Cassandra concludes that her creativity is her strength: "Imagination doesn't solve my problems, but it helps me find and follow the road to my goals."

Useful Concept Words

To assist teens in understanding and discussing this story, you may want to introduce some or all of the following concept words by making them part of discussions and activities. Write them on the board in advance and plan to explain each word when it appears in a suggested discussion question or activity (where the words are shown in italics). Here are the concept words, with definitions and sentences relating them to the story.

compensate: *to make up for something*
*Cassandra uses her imagination to **compensate** for disappointments in real life.*

consequences: *the effects or results of an action*
*Living in her imagination sometimes results in negative **consequences** for Cassandra.*

excessive: *beyond what is normal or reasonable*

*Cassandra worries that she spends an **excessive** amount of time fantasizing.*

fantasy: *a creation of the imagination*
*On the bus to Boston, Cassandra has a **fantasy** about being lost in a castle.*

reality: *that which is actual or true*
*In **reality,** people on the bus stare at Cassandra.*

ACTIVITIES

1. Freewriting: Finding Yourself in the Story

After group members have finished reading the story, ask them to take out writing materials. If you'll be writing also, have handy your own journal and tell students you'll be participating. For a description of freewriting, see pages 14–15.

The following statement and questions are similar to those you considered earlier in "A Moment of Reflection." This time, you may want to write along with your group.

Think of a time when you used your imagination to deal with a situation that was boring, stressful, or painful. What made the situation difficult? How did you use your imagination to deal with it? Did using your imagination help make real life more bearable? If so, how? If not, why not?

After the freewriting, invite volunteers to share what they wrote. Allow time for brief discussion.

2. Discussion: Understanding Events

To be sure group members have understood the story, ask questions such as:

- **How does Cassandra use her imagination to get over her disappointment at not seeing Santa Claus at the mall?**

- **How does she say imagination helps her in her "real life"?**

- **How do people usually react when they "catch" Cassandra daydreaming?**

- **What's her *fantasy* while on the bus to Boston?**

- **When Cassandra imagines her future, what does she see?**

- **What does she imagine when she's doing something she dislikes, such as washing dishes?**

3. Discussion: Understanding Issues

Cassandra's Creativity

Review with the group what creativity is, why it's sometimes hard to come by, and how it can be helpful. Then, referring as necessary to "How Creativity Works in the Story" (page 114), ask questions such as:

- **Cassandra says, "When I'm in my imaginary world, there are no barriers or blocks in the road." What do you think she means?**

- **What are Cassandra's two main concerns about living so much in her imagination? Do you think she's right to be concerned? Why or why not?**

- **Do you think Cassandra uses her imagination to face and deal with *reality,* or to escape from reality? Explain your answer.**

- **Cassandra says her imagination "has more good than bad effects" on her. Do you agree? Would you say her *fantasies* are healthy? Or would you say they're *excessive*—meaning unreasonable or even abnormal? Explain your answer.**

Connecting with the Issues

Suggest that group members silently review what they wrote during freewriting. Then ask questions such as:

- **To *compensate* for missing Santa at the mall, Cassandra imagines that he brings her "hundreds of presents." Have you ever used your imagination to help you compensate for disappointment? Is *fantasy* always a compensation for disappointment, depression, or boredom? Why or why not?**

- **If you were the man on the bus who was awakened by Cassandra laughing to herself, how would you have reacted?**

- **How do you use your imagination in your everyday life?**

4. Role Plays

For guidelines on role playing, see pages 15–16.

Objective: Group members will identify with the role of fantasy as a creative release.

Scenario A

Characters: Cassandra, the man on the bus

Procedure
Ask for volunteers to enact this scene:

Cassandra wants to convince the man sitting next to her on the bus (whom she's awakened with her laughter) that imagination is a great thing to have and use. The man thinks she's out of her mind.

Allow five to ten minutes for the role play. Afterward, discuss questions such as:

- **What did you see happening in this scene?**

- **If you were the man, would Cassandra have convinced you that imagination is valuable?**

- **How did this role play affect or change your understanding of Cassandra's story?**

Scenario B

Characters: Cassandra, friend 1, friend 2

Procedure
Ask for volunteers to enact this scene:

Cassandra and her two friends each like a different activity as a way to deal with stress. Friend 1 likes to watch TV. Friend 2 likes to hang out with friends. Cassandra likes to live for a while in her *fantasy* world. Each wants to convince the others that his or her activity is the best.

Allow five to ten minutes for the role play. Afterward, discuss questions such as:

- **What did you see happening in this scene?**

- **If you were friend 1 or friend 2, would Cassandra have convinced you that using imagination is the best way to deal with stress?**

- **How did this role play affect or change your understanding of Cassandra's story?**

5. Writing Activities: Taking It Further

Ask students to complete one or more of the following activities individually, in small groups, or at home. Modify the activities as needed to suit the writing ability of group members. When activities are completed, invite volunteers to read their work to the group. Discuss how teens felt about the purpose and value of the writing.

Activity A

Objective: Group members will describe Cassandra's imagination in their own words.

Pretend you're Cassandra. Write a letter to a friend explaining why your imagination makes you happy.

Activity B

Objective: Group members will reflect on the role of imagination in their own lives.

Cassandra says, "Imagination doesn't solve my problems, but it helps me find and follow the road to my goals." However, she admits, "I get nervous because I live so much in my imagination, dreaming of things that can't be realities." Which is true in your life? Does imagination help you reach your goals? Or do you think you spend too much time dreaming and avoiding situations you need to face? Can both of these *consequences* be true? Write about it.

6. In Your Journal: Making It Personal

Encourage group members to reflect on the following topic in their journals:

We all daydream, imagine, and have *fantasies.* Think of ways you use your imagination. What favorite fantasies do you have about your future, your family, or your friends? Do you daydream about the same things now as you did when you were younger? If not, how have your daydreams changed?

WALKING OUT THE ANGER

by Tamara Ballard

Pages 120–123 in *The Struggle to Be Strong*

PREPARING TO LEAD THE ACTIVITIES

Story Summary

Tamara has mood swings she can't control. When she's in a bad mood and doesn't want to be around people, she goes to the beach at Coney Island. There it's peaceful and she can be alone to think. When she can't get to the beach, Tamara takes long walks—very long walks, "from one part of the city to another." Walking helps her "burn off" her bad feelings. Tamara also writes poetry and stories and keeps a journal. She says that when she gets older she'd like to compile her various writings into an autobiography.

A Moment of Reflection

To connect with the story's themes, consider from your own perspective the questions group members will address during freewriting: Think of a time when you used an activity to help you deal with stress, anger, or tension. What did you do? Did you walk, run, hike, or play sports? Did you turn to a less physical activity like painting, writing, listening to music, or meditating? How did this activity help you?

Do you have a special place where you can go to think quietly? What is it like? How does it help you?

How Creativity Works in the Story

Seeing Tamara's Creativity

Tamara realizes that she must relieve stress in order "to stay centered." She approaches her bad moods creatively. By walking, she converts destructive anger into physical activity. In a key passage, she says, "Walking helps me burn off some of my negative emotions. It takes that adrenaline rush to hate and fight and does something good with it." Walking helps her leave her turmoil behind and think clearly. Tamara also writes to "release stress and anger." Through writing, she is transported from the pressures and intrusions of the real world into the privacy of her imagination: "I don't usually feel comfortable talking about my real feelings. . . . Writing is so easy for me because I can be as real as I want to be and not have to worry about being judged because of how I feel." While walking and writing help Tamara a lot, her favorite way to relieve stress is going to the beach early in the morning. There it's quiet, and she can think clearly.

Why Creativity Is a Struggle for Tamara

Tamara's bad moods are powerful and frequent. They make her feel helpless because she can't control them. Sometimes she doesn't want to get out of bed in the morning. Other times, she wants to snap at everybody. Her life is filled with noise, which is why she so loves the beach in the early morning: "At Coney Island there are no phones ringing, no teachers screaming, no kids crying." Her achievement—channeling her powerful moods into creative expression, both physical and artistic—takes hard work.

Useful Concept Words

To assist teens in understanding and discussing this story, you may want to introduce some or all of the following concept words by making them part of discussions and activities. Write them on the board in advance and plan to explain each word when it appears in a suggested discussion question or activity (where the words are shown in italics). Here are the concept words, with definitions and sentences relating them to the story.

authentic: real; genuine

In her writing, Tamara expresses her **authentic** emotions.

disguise: to conceal or hide something

Tamara feels she must **disguise** her true feelings when she's around people.

express: to communicate; to make known

Tamara **expresses** her feelings through walking and writing.

restore: to bring something back

The beach **restores** Tamara's sense of calm.

transform: to change the nature or condition of something

Walking and writing **transform** Tamara's bad feelings into purposeful activities.

ACTIVITIES

1. Freewriting: Finding Yourself in the Story

After group members have finished reading the story, ask them to take out writing materials. If you'll be writing also, have handy your own journal and tell students you'll be participating. For a description of freewriting, see pages 14–15.

The following statement and questions are similar to those you considered earlier in "A Moment of Reflection." This time, you may want to write along with your group.

Think of a time when you used an activity to help you deal with stress, anger, or tension. What did you do? Did you walk, run, work out, or play sports? Did you turn to a less physical activity like painting, writing, listening to music, or meditating? How did this activity help you? Do you have a special place where you can go to think quietly? What is it like? How does it help you sort out your feelings?

After the freewriting, invite volunteers to share what they wrote. Allow time for brief discussion.

2. Discussion: Understanding Events

To be sure group members have understood the story, ask questions such as:

- **How does Tamara describe her moods?**

- **Why does she avoid people when she's moody?**

- **Where is Tamara's "hideaway"? Why does she like being there?**

- **Why does Tamara take long walks?**

- **What's the third way she relieves stress and anger, besides walking and going to Coney Island?**

- **What does she plan to do someday with her writing?**

3. Discussion: Understanding Issues

Tamara's Creativity

Review with the group what creativity is, why it's sometimes hard to come by, and how it can be helpful. Then, referring as necessary to "How Creativity Works in the Story" (page 117), ask questions such as:

- **Why do you think it's easier for Tamara to write about her feelings than to talk about them?**

- **To relieve stress, *express* her emotions, and *restore* her sense of calm, Tamara visits the beach, takes long walks, and writes. What would you say these activities have in common? Why do you think they help Tamara?**

- **Based on her story, how would you describe Tamara's personality? What clues does she give about why she's so moody?**

Connecting with the Issues

Suggest that group members silently review what they wrote during freewriting. Then ask questions such as:

- **Tamara says her mood swings "are predictable, but not controllable." Do you feel that way about your moods? What would you say makes a mood controllable or uncontrollable?**

- **Tamara uses a physical activity (walking) and an imaginative activity (writing) to deal with stress. Which kind of activity works better for you when you're feeling stressed? Why?**

4. Role Play

For guidelines on role playing, see pages 15–16.

Objective: Group members will identify with positive ways to deal with angry feelings.

Characters: Tamara, her friend

Procedure
Ask for volunteers to enact this scene:

Tamara's friend feels angry a lot and doesn't know what to do about it. Tamara wants her friend to understand how both physical activity and creativity can help her manage and *transform* her feelings.

Allow five to ten minutes for the role play. Afterward, discuss questions such as:

- **What did you see happening in this scene?**

- **If you were Tamara's friend, how would you feel about what Tamara said?**

- **How did this role play affect or change your understanding of Tamara's story?**

5. Writing Activities: Taking It Further

Ask students to complete one or more of the following activities individually, in small groups, or at home. Modify the activities as needed to suit the writing ability of group members. When activities are completed, invite volunteers to read their work to the group. Discuss how teens felt about the purpose and value of the writing.

Activity A

Objective: Group members will describe Tamara's creativity in their own words.

Pretend you're Tamara. Write a letter to a friend who's going through a stressful situation. Describe how you use creativity to *transform* your moods and suggest ways your friend can use creativity in a similar way.

Activity B

Objective: Group members will reflect on ways they choose to reveal their true feelings.

Tamara says people know her true emotions only through her writing because she usually *disguises* her feelings. Write about ways you let people know your *authentic* emotions.

6. In Your Journal: Making It Personal

Encourage group members to reflect on the following topic in their journals:

Tamara says the best way to get to know her is to read her poetry, because she doesn't feel comfortable talking about her feelings. Write about a way you *express* your feelings besides talking about them (for example, dancing, singing, playing sports, walking, drawing, cooking or baking, playing a musical instrument, meditating, writing letters, writing stories or poetry, keeping a journal, and so forth). What do you like about expressing your feelings through this creative activity? Do you think expressing yourself through a creative outlet is sometimes easier than talking about your feelings? Why or why not?

THREE TEENS: THE IMPORTANCE OF CREATIVITY

As necessary, refer to pages 110 and 111 in the anthology to review with your group what creativity is and why it's a resilience. Then invite group members to compare how creativity works in the lives of the three teen writers in this section. (To help students recall each writer, you might list their first names on the board.) Ask questions such as:

- **Which writer do you think finds the most creative way to handle strong feelings and difficult experiences? Why do you think so?**

- **Which writer do you think finds the best balance between everyday life and the life of the imagination? Why do you think so?**

- **Which writer do you think is most likely to continue to be creative throughout her life? Why do you think so?**

- **Which story in this section do you like best? Which teen writer do you admire most? Explain your choices.**

Many of the teen writers in this book demonstrate more than one resilience. If your group has read other stories, you might ask members to discuss how writers in other sections also demonstrate creativity.

HUMOR
FINDING WHAT'S FUNNY

Before discussing the stories in this section, ask the group to read the introductory material about humor in their anthology, pages 124 and 125. Allow time for questions and brief discussion. Be sure teens understand the following:

- **Humor** is finding what's funny, even when you're sad or in pain.

- The opposite of **humor** is taking yourself and your situation too seriously.

- **Humor** is hard because pressures can blot out the lighter side of life.

- **Humor** helps you put pain in perspective. **Humor** helps you laugh and let others laugh with you.

As teens read each story, encourage them to look for ways the writer uses humor. Also suggest that they reflect on—and possibly jot down ideas about—the questions that follow each story ("Think About It"). Refer them to the introductory section "'Think About It'—and Maybe Write About It," pages 7–8 in the anthology.

MY HAIR IS BLUE—BUT I'M NOT A FREAK!
by Lenny Jones

Pages 126–129 in *The Struggle to Be Strong*

PREPARING TO LEAD THE ACTIVITIES

Story Summary

Lenny, now in high school, has always been teased about having a large head. Some kids call him "cartoon character names." When he's not allowed to wear a hat in school, he decides to try and stop the teasing by dyeing his hair "platinum white." A friend helps him with the process, but his hair comes out yellow, rather than white. At school he attracts a lot of attention and is still laughed at and called names, but he feels "much more comfortable" than before. He's able to make jokes and enjoy himself. Eventually, he dyes his hair "several different shades of blue" and plans to change it to "jet-black" soon. Then, says Lenny, "I'll leave it alone for a while."

A Moment of Reflection

To connect with the story's themes, consider from your own perspective the questions group members will address during freewriting: Think of a time when you felt self-conscious about your physical appearance—perhaps when you were a teen. How did you deal with your feelings? If you were teased, how did you react? Are you less self-conscious now? If so, why do you think you are? If not, how do you think you could learn to be?

How Humor Works in the Story

Seeing Lenny's Humor

After trying to hide his large head under a hat, Lenny attempts a new experiment to deal with being teased: he dyes his hair a ridiculous color. By doing so, he makes a display of his head rather than hiding it. As he says, "I hoped to distract people from making fun of my head and send all the attention to my hair." Lenny's dyed hair also makes a mockery of his classmates' emphasis on appearance and points out their hypocrisy. "When people said I wasn't keepin' it real, I asked them if they ever dyed their hair. They said yeah. Then they realized how stupid they sounded and just changed the subject." Humor allows Lenny to respond in a positive, healthy way to a painful situation. He's able to turn the tables on his teasing classmates and win a small triumph.

Why Humor Is a Struggle for Lenny

Lenny's classmates tease him mercilessly about something he can't control—the size of his head. First he tries to deal with his hurt feelings by ignoring them: "I try to flush these things out of my system, but they always come back." Frustrated and unhappy, he then decides to do something more dramatic and comes up with the idea of dyeing his hair. He expects the scheme to change his life: "I thought after I dyed my hair, people would stop making fun of me. . . ." However, he admits, "In some ways it worked, but it also backfired." His classmates still laugh at him, but it doesn't hurt as much. They aren't, at least, laughing at the size of his head anymore. Also, he says, "The comments didn't apply to me, so I just made jokes." By the end of the story, Lenny's more comfortable with himself. He's gained greater control of his hurt feelings and can deal better with the way his classmates treat him.

Useful Concept Words

To assist teens in understanding and discussing this story, you may want to introduce some or all of the following concept words by making them part of discussions and activities. Write them on the board in advance and plan to explain each word when it appears in a suggested discussion question or activity (where the words are shown in italics). Here are the concept words, with definitions and sentences relating them to the story.

backfire: *to produce an unexpected or undesired result*

Lenny feels his plan has **backfired** *because his classmates laugh at his dyed hair.*

freak: *someone considered unusual or abnormal*

Lenny doesn't like the fact that some kids treat him like a **freak.**

hypocrite: *someone who pretends to believe something*

Lenny thinks some people who criticize his hair are **hypocrites.**

ridicule: *to mock or make fun of someone*

For most of his life, Lenny has been **ridiculed** *for the size of his head.*

self-conscious: *uncomfortably conscious of oneself; ill at ease*

Lenny feels **self-conscious** *because of his large head.*

ACTIVITIES

1. Freewriting: Finding Yourself in the Story

After group members have finished reading the story, ask them to take out writing materials. If you'll be writing also, have handy your own journal and tell students you'll be participating. For a description of freewriting, see pages 14–15.

The following statement and questions are similar to those you considered earlier in "A Moment of Reflection." This time, you may want to write along with your group.

Think of a time when you felt *self-conscious* about the way you look. How did you deal with your feelings? If you were teased, how did you react? What happened? Are you less self-conscious now? If so, why do you think you are? If not, how do you think you could learn to be?

After the freewriting, invite volunteers to share what they wrote. Allow time for brief discussion.

2. Discussion: Understanding Events

To be sure group members have understood the story, ask questions such as:

- **What have Lenny's classmates always teased him about?**

- **What does Lenny try first to stop the teasing? Why doesn't it work?**

- **Why does Lenny decide to dye his hair? What effect does he think his dyed hair will have on the people who've been teasing him?**

- **When he evaluates the effects of his dyed hair, Lenny says, "In some ways it worked, but it also *backfired.*" What does he mean? How does it "work"? How does it "backfire"?**

- **What are some of the reactions Lenny gets to his dyed hair?**

3. Discussion: Understanding Issues

Lenny's Humor

Review with the group what humor is, why it's sometimes hard to come by, and how it can be helpful. Then, referring as necessary to "How Humor Works in the Story" (page 122), ask questions such as:

- **After dyeing his hair, Lenny is *ridiculed* for the color of his hair rather than the size of his head. He says the teasing after he dyes his hair doesn't hurt as much. Why do you think that's so?**

- **Why does Lenny think some of the people who criticize his hair are *hypocrites*?**

- **How else might Lenny have handled his situation? Which ways of handling it might have been worse than what he actually did? Which might have been better? Explain your answer.**

Connecting with the Issues

Suggest that group members silently review what they wrote during freewriting. Then ask questions such as:

- What should you do if you're teased? How should you react?

- Why do you think people tease others? Is it ever fun to be teased? Why or why not?

- Have you ever wanted to change your appearance? If so, why and in what way? If you did change the way you look, how did the change affect your life? How did it affect the way you felt about yourself?

- How can a sense of humor help when you're feeling *self-conscious*?

4. Role Play

For guidelines on role playing, see pages 15–16.

Objective: Group members will identify with using humor to deflect teasing.

Characters: Lenny, his friend

Procedure
Ask for volunteers to enact this scene:

Lenny's friend is very short. He's teased, feels like a *freak*, and hates to go to school. Lenny wants to convince his friend to make his life easier by using his sense of humor.

Allow five to ten minutes for the role play. Afterward, discuss questions such as:

- What did you see happening in this scene?

- If you were Lenny's friend, would Lenny have convinced you to help yourself by using your sense of humor?

- How did this role play affect or change your understanding of Lenny's story?

5. Writing Activities: Taking It Further

Ask students to complete one or more of the following activities individually, in small groups, or at home. Modify the activities as needed to suit the writing ability of group members. When activities are completed, invite volunteers to read their work to the group. Discuss how teens felt about the purpose and value of the writing.

Activity A

Objective: Group members will describe Lenny's humor in their own words.

Pretend you're Lenny. Write a letter to a friend who's being teased, explaining how you used your sense of humor when you were teased.

Activity B

Objective: Group members will consider how clothes and appearance can reflect one's sense of humor.

Lenny deals with teasing by letting his appearance reflect his sense of humor. Have your clothes, hairstyle, or general appearance ever reflected your sense of humor? If so, in what ways? If not, how would they change to show your sense of humor?

Activity C

Objective: Teens will reflect on what they consider funny.

What do you consider funny? Write about a favorite TV show, book, magazine, or movie that you think is funny. What do you like about the humor? How has the humor affected your view of the world?

6. In Your Journal: Making It Personal

Encourage group members to reflect on the following topic in their journals:

Lenny finds that his sense of humor helps him feel less *self-conscious* and isolated. Have you ever used your sense of humor as Lenny does—to deal with feelings of self-consciousness or with being teased? If so, how did your humor help? If you've found it hard to see the humor in painful situations, do you think you could learn to do that? Why or why not?

HOW TO SURVIVE SHOPPING WITH MOM
by Chris Kanarick

Pages 130–133 in *The Struggle to Be Strong*

PREPARING TO LEAD THE ACTIVITIES

Story Summary

Chris wants to go clothes shopping with his friends, but agrees to go with his mother instead because she's the one with the credit cards. As he humorously details, they can't agree on clothes to buy and she embarrasses him when he tries on jeans. Chris uses the experience to reassure others in the same situation who want to salvage their pride: "Just remember, you're not alone in this crazy, mixed-up world where mothers reign supreme. Someday, you'll be able to stand tall like me and say: 'Hi, my name is Chris, and I've gone shopping with my mother.'"

A Moment of Reflection

To connect with the story's themes, consider from your own perspective the questions group members will address during freewriting: Think of a time when you used your sense of humor to make the best of an unpleasant situation. What was the situation? How did you use humor to deal with it? Was it hard or easy to find humor in the situation? How did you see the situation differently as a result of using your sense of humor?

How Humor Works in the Story

Seeing Chris's Humor

We see Chris's humor as he tries to save himself from the embarrassment of clothes shopping with his mother. Although he goes along in body, his mind goes elsewhere—into the funny world of his own imagination. There he transforms his embarrassing experience by reversing his and his mother's roles. He's not the obedient child being dragged around. Rather, Chris's mother is like an out-of-control child crazed with shopping, while he's the patient parent who both endures his mom's strange behavior and tries various ploys to manage it. We also see Chris's humor in the way he writes about his experiences as a sort of advice column, giving tips to other kids in the same situation. For instance, "You put on a pair of jeans and they feel pretty comfortable. . . . So you go out to get Mom's opinion. 'How do they feel?' she asks. You tell her they feel fine. Next, she'll want you to walk around in them. . . . She'll ask you to squat. Then she'll start getting personal. 'How do they feel in the crotch?' 'Ma!' you exclaim. 'Not so loud!'" All of this has nothing to do with Chris, of course! He's just the expert, offering advice.

Why Humor Is a Struggle for Chris

Chris is embarrassed about shopping with his mother. He's also afraid his friends may be laughing at him. Having a sense of humor in a situation like this isn't easy. But instead of sulking or feeling sorry for himself, Chris gets himself through his shopping ordeal with wit and gentle satire: "Now, some of you may be laughing at me and saying, 'Oh, I don't know what you're talking about.' But there are others—you know who you are."

Useful Concept Words

To assist teens in understanding and discussing this story, you may want to introduce some or all of the following concept words by making them part of discussions and activities. Write them on the board in advance and plan to explain each word when it appears in a suggested discussion question or activity (where the words are shown in italics). Here are the concept words, with definitions and sentences relating them to the story.

comply: to obey; to go along

Chris feels he has no choice but to **comply** with his mother's wishes, since she has the credit cards.

dilemma: a situation without a satisfactory solution

Shopping with his mother is a **dilemma** for Chris.

exaggerate: to make greater than is actually the case; to overstate

Chris **exaggerates** to create humor, such as when he says that mothers "can smell a sale from a mile away."

impulse: a sudden urge

Chris has the **impulse** to say no when his mother says she wants to go shopping with him.

self-deprecating: making fun of oneself; putting oneself down

Chris uses **self-deprecating** humor when he writes about how his mother embarrasses him.

ACTIVITIES

1. Freewriting: Finding Yourself in the Story

After group members have finished reading the story, ask them to take out writing materials. If you'll be writing also, have handy your own journal and tell students you'll be participating. For a description of freewriting, see pages 14–15.

The following statement and questions are similar to those you considered earlier in "A Moment of Reflection." This time, you may want to write along with your group.

Think of a time when you used your sense of humor to make the best of an unpleasant situation. What was happening? How did you use humor to deal with it? Was it hard or easy to find humor in the situation? Why? How did you see the situation differently as a result of using your sense of humor?

After the freewriting, invite volunteers to share what they wrote. Allow time for brief discussion.

2. Discussion: Understanding Events

To be sure group members have understood the story, ask questions such as:

- What is Chris's first *impulse* when his mother proposes going shopping with him? Why does he feel he has to *comply* with her wishes?

- What does Chris's mother do when she "smell[s] a sale"?

- When they get to Macy's, which department does Chris's mother immediately head for? What happens when Chris tells her he belongs in the men's department, not the boys'?

- What happens when Chris tries on jeans?

3. Discussion: Understanding Issues

Chris's Humor

Review with the group what humor is, why it's sometimes hard to come by, and how it can be helpful. Then, referring as necessary to "How Humor Works in the Story" (page 125), ask questions such as:

- Why does Chris need to use his sense of humor to get through his shopping trip with his mother?

- How does he use humor "to survive shopping with Mom"?

- How would Chris's shopping trip with Mom have been different if he didn't have a sense of humor about it?

- What else might Chris have done to get through his shopping trip? What could he have done that might have had a negative effect?

Connecting with the Issues

Suggest that group members silently review what they wrote during freewriting. Then ask questions such as:

- If you were in Chris's situation, what would you have said to your mother during the shopping trip?

- Have you ever been in a *dilemma* similar to Chris's? How did you handle it?

- How does humor get you through embarrassing moments?

4. Role Plays

For guidelines on role playing, see pages 15–16.

Objective: Group members will practice using humor to deflect embarrassment.

Scenario A

Characters: Chris, his friend

Procedure
Ask for volunteers to enact this scene:

Chris's friend is about to go shopping with a parent but is dreading it. Chris wants to convince his friend that with a humorous attitude the experience won't be so bad.

Allow five to ten minutes for the role play. Afterward, discuss questions such as:

- **What did you see happening in this scene?**

- **If you were Chris's friend, would Chris have convinced you that a sense of humor will help get you through your shopping trip?**

- **How did this role play affect or change your understanding of Chris's story?**

Scenario B

Characters: Chris, his mother

Procedure
Ask for volunteers to enact this scene:

Chris wants his mother to keep a low profile while they're shopping together. His mother wants to have a say in everything, since she's paying for the clothes.

As a variation, this role play can involve any adult in a teen's life who interferes too much, and in any situation, not just shopping.

Allow five to ten minutes for the role play. Afterward, discuss questions such as:

- **What did you see happening in this scene?**

- **If you were Chris, would your mother have convinced you that she has a right to approve whatever you want her to buy?**

- **If you were Chris's mother, would Chris have convinced you to keep a low profile?**

5. Writing Activities: Taking It Further

Ask students to complete one or more of the following activities individually, in small groups, or at home. Modify the activities as needed to suit the writing ability of group members. When activities are completed, invite volunteers to read their work to the group. Discuss how teens felt about the purpose and value of the writing.

Activity A

Objective: Group members will describe Chris's humor in their own words.

Pretend you're Chris. Write a letter to a friend describing how you got through a shopping trip with your mother by using your sense of humor.

Activity B

Objective: Group members will describe their own sense of humor.

How would you describe your sense of humor to someone who doesn't know you? Do you use _self-deprecating_ humor—making fun of yourself— as Chris does? Do you ever _exaggerate_ to make something funny? How have relatives, friends, TV, or movies influenced your sense of humor?

Activity C

Objective: Group members will consider Chris's story from a parent's point of view.

Pretend you're a parent of a teenager. Write about taking your son or daughter shopping for clothes. How would you use humor to get through it? If you like, write this in dialogue form between the teen and the parent.

6. In Your Journal: Making It Personal

Encourage group members to reflect on the following topic in their journals:

Chris uses humor to make the best of shopping with his mother. Think of an awkward or embarrassing situation you were in. Describe the situation. Now describe it again, but this time with humor. Did a humorous approach make the situation seem less awkward or embarrassing? If so, how? If not, why not?

TWO TEENS: THE IMPORTANCE OF HUMOR

As necessary, refer to pages 124 and 125 in the anthology to review with your group what humor is and why it's a resilience. Then invite group members to compare how humor works in the lives of the two teen writers in this section. (To help students recall each writer, you might list their first names on the board.) Ask questions such as:

• **Which writer do you think has the harder time finding the funny aspects of his situation? Why do you think so?**

• **Which writer do you think has the better sense of humor? Why do you think so?**

• **Which writer do you think is more likely to continue to use humor throughout his life? Why do you think so?**

• **Which story in this section do you like better? Which teen writer do you admire more? Explain your choices.**

Many of the teen writers in this book demonstrate more than one resilience. If your group has read other stories, you might ask members to discuss how writers in other sections also demonstrate humor.

MORALITY
DOING THE RIGHT THING

Before discussing the stories in this section, ask the group to read the introductory material about morality in their anthology, pages 134 and 135. Allow time for questions and brief discussion. Be sure teens understand the following:

- **Morality** is thinking of others as well as yourself. It's learning what other people need and trying to give it to them.

- The opposite of **morality** is thinking only of yourself, or doing whatever suits you or whatever you can get away with.

- **Morality** is hard because it can mean sacrificing your own best or short-term interests to do what's right for other people.

- **Morality** helps connect you to other people through being useful and caring. **Morality** helps you feel you're a good person.

As teens read each story, encourage them to look for ways the writer demonstrates morality. Also suggest that they reflect on—and possibly jot down ideas about—the questions that follow each story ("Think About It"). Refer them to the introductory section "'Think About It'—and Maybe Write About It," pages 7–8 in the anthology.

A MOTHER TO MY MOTHER'S CHILDREN
by Charlene Johnson

Pages 136–140 in *The Struggle to Be Strong*

PREPARING TO LEAD THE ACTIVITIES

Story Summary

At age twelve, Charlene takes over responsibility for her five brothers and sisters when their mother becomes disabled by drugs. Charlene gets her siblings to and from school, oversees their homework, settles their fights, and does the household chores. She also raises Troy, the youngest, from infancy. At one point, Charlene buckles under the pressure and runs away, thinking a relative has everything under control. When she returns after three weeks, she finds her mother "high as the sky" and the kids gone. (It turns out they were at an aunt's house.) Soon after, Charlene is placed in foster care and the family is split up. Charlene vows to get an education and be a good parent to her own future children.

A Moment of Reflection

To connect with the story's themes, consider from your own perspective the questions group members will address during freewriting: Think of a time when you had to take responsibility for something or someone that wasn't really your responsibility—or shouldn't have been. What was the situation? How did you handle it? How did you feel about it? How did taking on this responsibility affect you? Looking back, would you take on this responsibility again?

How Morality Works in the Story

Seeing Charlene's Morality

When her mother can no longer take care of the family, Charlene, still a child herself, does what needs to be done: she fills in for her mother. In her new role as parent, Charlene learns what her siblings need and tries to give it to them. She even takes care of her mother, although she has caused Charlene and the family great suffering. Sacrificing her education and "a normal teenage life," Charlene also takes on the care of her mother's new baby. Charlene's morality is also seen in her vow not to duplicate her mother's actions—she will be a loving and responsible parent. She offers what she's learned to other teens in similar situations: "I want to say to them—don't look at your troubles in a bad way. Try to think of them as temporary setbacks that have made you a stronger person."

Why Morality Is a Struggle for Charlene

Doing the right thing when one has been wronged—being generous when one has been deprived—is hard for anyone. It's also hard to accept the consequences of someone else's mistakes. When her mother can no longer take care of the family, Charlene does what's right, although it's difficult for her. She struggles with the feeling that she's trapped: "Many teenagers choose to become parents. I didn't have that choice." When her mother has another baby but quickly goes back to drugs, Charlene's hopes of having a "normal teenage life" are dashed. Anger adds to her struggle, and she comes close to abusing Baby Troy. At one point Charlene buckles under the burden and she and her sister run away—but not for long. After three weeks, she returns home and resumes her responsibilities. Despite Charlene's efforts, the family is broken up. Her pain is great, but she continues to do what's right. She promises herself that she will get the education she needs to be self-sufficient and will take care of her own future children.

Useful Concept Words

To assist teens in understanding and discussing this story, you may want to introduce some or all of the following concept words by making them part of discussions and activities. Write them on the board in advance and plan to explain each word when it appears in a suggested discussion question or activity (where the words are shown in italics). Here are the concept words, with definitions and sentences relating them to the story.

obligation: *something one has to do; a duty*
*Charlene believes it's her **obligation** to take charge of her siblings when her mother can't.*

obstacle: *something that stands in the way*
*After her experiences, Charlene feels she has the power to overcome any future **obstacles.***

resentment: *a feeling that one has been treated wrongly or unfairly*
*Charlene feels **resentment** about having to take care of the family.*

responsible: *accountable for the care or welfare of another*
*Charlene becomes **responsible** for the care of her family.*

sacrifice: *to suffer the loss of something*
*Charlene **sacrifices** a normal life to do what's right for her family.*

ACTIVITIES

1. Freewriting: Finding Yourself in the Story

After group members have finished reading the story, ask them to take out writing materials. If you'll be writing also, have handy your own journal and tell students you'll be participating. For a description of freewriting, see pages 14–15.

The following statement and questions are similar to those you considered earlier in "A Moment of Reflection." This time, you may want to write along with your group.

Think of a time when you had to take responsibility for something or someone that wasn't really your responsibility—or shouldn't have been. What was

the situation? How did you handle it? How did you feel about it? How did taking on this responsibility affect you? Looking back, would you take on this responsibility again? Why or why not?

After the freewriting, invite volunteers to share what they wrote. Allow time for brief discussion.

2. Discussion: Understanding Events

To be sure group members have understood the story, ask questions such as:

- Why does Charlene take charge of her brother and sisters? What does she do to take care of the family?

- After her mother gives birth to Baby Troy, why does Charlene think her "mother days" are over? What actually happens?

- When does Charlene begin to dislike being with Baby Troy? What happens the day she can't get him to stop crying?

- Why do Charlene and her sister run away for three weeks? What do they find when they get back?

- Why doesn't Charlene like to visit Baby Troy? Why has her experience with him made her change her mind about having children?

3. Discussion: Understanding Issues

Charlene's Morality

Review with the group what morality is, why it's sometimes hard to come by, and how it can be helpful. Then, referring as necessary to "How Morality Works in the Story" (page 130), ask questions such as:

- Charlene says she had no choice but to become *responsible* for her siblings—that it was her *obligation.* Do you agree that she had no choice? Why or why not?

- According to Charlene, "People say children are products of their environment. Well, I am not." What does she mean?

- Do you think Charlene will keep her promise to herself and not repeat her mother's neglect? Why or why not?

Connecting with the Issues

Suggest that group members silently review what they wrote during freewriting. Then ask questions such as:

- How would you feel if you were Charlene? Would you feel *resentment* toward your mother? Would you be able to look back and see your troubles as "temporary setbacks"? Explain your answer.

- Charlene remarks, "People say children are products of their environment." What does this mean to you? Do you think it's true? Why or why not? Do you think some people grow up to live completely different lives from the ones they knew as children? Explain your thinking.

- What's the difference between taking on too much responsibility and doing the right thing? How can you tell the difference?

- Was there a time in your life when you had to take on too much responsibility? What happened? What did you gain from the experience? What did you lose?

4. Role Plays

For guidelines on role playing, see pages 15–16.

Objective: Group members will identify with the cost of making moral choices.

Scenario A

Characters: Charlene, her mother

Procedure
Ask for volunteers to enact this scene:

Charlene wants her mother to know what she's been feeling and experiencing as "mother" to her brothers and sisters. Her mother wants Charlene to know the problems she's faced in her life.

Allow five to ten minutes for the role play. Afterward, discuss questions such as:

- What did you see happening in this scene?

- If you were Charlene's mother, how would you feel about what Charlene told you? If you were Charlene, how would you feel about what your mother told you?

- How did this role play affect or change your understanding of Charlene's story?

Scenario B

Characters: Charlene, her friend

Procedure
Ask for volunteers to enact this scene:

Charlene's friend wants to convince Charlene that it's not her responsibility to take care of the family and that she should run away. Charlene wants to convince her friend that it is her responsibility and she must stay.

Allow five to ten minutes for the role play. Afterward, discuss questions such as:

- What did you see happening in this scene?

- If you were Charlene's friend, would Charlene have convinced you that caring for her family is her responsibility?

- How did this role play affect or change your understanding of Charlene's story?

5. Writing Activities: Taking It Further

Ask students to complete one or more of the following activities individually, in small groups, or at home. Modify the activities as needed to suit the writing ability of group members. When activities are completed, invite volunteers to read their work to the group. Discuss how teens felt about the purpose and value of the writing.

Activity A

Objective: Group members will describe Charlene's morality in their own words.

Pretend you're Charlene as an adult. Write a letter to your youngest brother, Troy, explaining why you took responsibility for his care and why caring for him made you decide to have children of your own.

Activity B

Objective: Group members will evaluate the effects of Charlene's experiences.

Charlene believes her experiences have made her stronger. She feels she can overcome any *obstacle* that comes her way. What are the positive things Charlene learned? Could her experiences also have a negative impact on her? If so, in what way? If not, why not?

6. In Your Journal: Making It Personal

Encourage group members to reflect on the following topic in their journals:

By doing what she thinks is right, even though she has to *sacrifice* "a normal teenage life," Charlene gains strength and self-confidence. When did you struggle with an *obligation* or responsibility you didn't want? What did you have to sacrifice, or give up? What did you learn or gain from your struggle? Do you think you're a stronger person because of it? Why or why not?

NO ONE SPOKE UP FOR IRMA
by Ana Angélica Pines

Pages 141–146 in *The Struggle to Be Strong*

PREPARING TO LEAD THE ACTIVITIES

Story Summary

Ana has many childhood memories of watching her friend Irma being abused by her mother, Carmen. Carmen "would hit her, throw things at her, and curse her." Ana also remembers that all the neighbors saw the abuse but no one intervened to stop it. Ana was deeply disturbed at the time and considered calling a hotline. Feeling she wouldn't be believed because she was a child, Ana didn't act. Instead, when she couldn't stand watching the abuse any longer, she stopped visiting Irma. Now, whenever Ana looks into Irma's eyes, she sees "reflections of the past." She holds herself responsible because she was silent when she should have spoken up.

A Moment of Reflection

To connect with the story's themes, consider from your own perspective the questions group members will address during freewriting: Think of a time when your conscience told you to speak up about something you knew was wrong. Maybe you saw a child being mistreated, someone committing a crime or doing something unethical, someone being unjustly blamed for something. Did you speak up or keep silent? What was difficult for you about the situation? If you didn't get involved, what held you back? If you spoke up or did something to help, what pushed you to get involved? Looking back at the incident, how do you feel about the choice you made?

How Morality Works in the Story

Seeing Ana's Morality

Everyone who knew Irma, including Ana, saw the abuse she suffered. Some of the neighborhood children—and Ana's own sister—tried to help by speaking up or by doing things for Irma. Ana herself did very little, deciding that no one would listen because she was a child and that, even if social workers came to Irma's house, Irma's mother may only have increased her abuse. Ana's morality emerges as she grows up and begins to question her past behavior. Acknowledging her inaction and avoidance as a child, she now tries to help Irma: "I try to make things appealing to her so she'll want to do better." Ana also acknowledges that those who keep silent in the face of abuse are "to blame—including me."

Why Morality Is a Struggle for Ana

Ana's attempt to answer the moral question about her level of responsibility to Irma is a struggle because she feels guilty for what she didn't do in the past. Whenever she looks into Irma's eyes, she sees the damaging effects of Irma's childhood: "These days Irma always has this blank look on her face—like there's nothing there. It's like looking into space. It's scary. She's so lost and seems to have no sense of direction." As with many moral questions, there are no easy answers. It's true that as a child, Ana could have done very little. It's also true that she deserted Irma when other children didn't. But what did their actions accomplish? Struggling through her confusion, Ana comes to understand that we're responsible for what happens to each other. She can't undo the past, but she knows she must now help Irma as best she can. Her acceptance of personal responsibility for Irma's abuse seems a necessary, if painful, ending to her struggle.

Useful Concept Words

To assist teens in understanding and discussing this story, you may want to introduce some or all of the following concept words by making them part of discussions and activities. Write them on the board in advance and plan to explain each word when it appears in a suggested discussion question or activity (where the words are shown in italics). Here are the concept words, with definitions and sentences relating them to the story.

accountable: *answerable to someone or to some principle*

*Ana holds herself **accountable** for her failure to speak up about Irma's abuse.*

conscience: *the voice inside that tells one the difference between right and wrong*

*Ana's **conscience** tells her that she could have done more to help Irma.*

guilt: *a painful awareness of having done something wrong*

*Ana feels **guilt** about not having spoken up.*

standard: *something that measures or defines value or worth*

*Ana holds herself to high **standards** of behavior.*

witness: *someone with personal knowledge of something*

*Ana is a **witness** to Irma's abuse.*

ACTIVITIES

1. Freewriting: Finding Yourself in the Story

After group members have finished reading the story, ask them to take out writing materials. If you'll be writing also, have handy your own journal and tell students you'll be participating. For a description of freewriting, see pages 14–15.

The following statement and questions are similar to those you considered earlier in "A Moment of Reflection." This time, you may want to write along with your group.

Think of a time when your *conscience* told you to speak up about something you knew was wrong. Maybe you saw a child being mistreated, overheard someone saying mean or cruel things about a classmate, or were a *witness* when someone was blamed for something the person didn't do. Did you speak up or keep silent? What was hard for you about the situation? If you didn't get involved, what held you back? If you spoke up or did something to help, what pushed you to get involved? When you look back at what happened, how do you feel about the choice you made?

After the freewriting, invite volunteers to share what they wrote. Allow time for brief discussion.

NOTE: Avoiding Roadblocks

The kind of abuse described in this story is, unfortunately, not uncommon. Although the intent of this discussion is to examine the difficult moral choices confronting Ana, and not for teens to disclose their own abuse or abuse they've witnessed, those disclosures may happen. Teens in abusive situations may also seek you out individually. Remind your group about the importance of confidentiality, as well as circumstances for which confidentiality must be waived in the interest of protection. If a teen approaches you individually, be sure to review "Handling Sensitive Issues," pages 7–8, including "Know When to Seek Outside Help."

2. Discussion: Understanding Events

To be sure group members have understood the story, ask questions such as:

- **How does Carmen treat Irma? How does she treat Irma's sister, Lydia?**

- **What's one example of Carmen's mistreatment of Irma?**

- Ana says, "Carmen's abuse wasn't always physical, however." What does she mean?

- What happens when two neighborhood children, Peter and Melissa, confront Carmen about the way she treats Irma?

- How does Ana's sister help Irma?

- What happens on Irma's sixteenth birthday?

- How does Irma look and behave now?

- When Ana was a child, why didn't she call a hotline for abused children about Irma?

3. Discussion: Understanding Issues

Ana's Morality

Review with the group what morality is, why it's sometimes hard to come by, and how it can be helpful. Then, referring as necessary to "How Morality Works in the Story" (pages 134–135), ask questions such as:

- At the beginning of the story, what does Ana mean when she says she sees "reflections of the past" in Irma's eyes?

- In trying to explain the way Irma is now, Ana says, "When somebody tells you something often enough, sooner or later you begin to believe it." What does she mean? What does Irma come to believe about herself?

- How do you feel about the way Ana handled the situation with Irma as a child?

- How does Ana explain her failure, as a child, to speak up about Irma's abuse? How do you think her failure to act was influenced by her friends and family?

- Do you think Ana can ever make up for her failure to help Irma? If so, how? If not, why not? Do you think she'll ever stop feeling *guilt*? Why or why not?

Connecting with the Issues

Suggest that group members silently review what they wrote during freewriting. Then ask questions such as:

- Why do you think people are so afraid of getting involved in other people's lives?

- If you were in Ana's shoes, what would you have done about Irma?

- Have you been in a situation similar to Ana's? What did you do, and why?

- How do you decide when to act on your own values and *standards*, rather than on somebody else's?

4. Role Plays

For guidelines on role playing, see pages 15–16.

Objective: Group members will identify with the complexity of holding themselves to high standards and taking moral action.

Scenario A

Characters: Ana as a child, an adult from the neighborhood

Procedure
Ask for volunteers to enact this scene:

Ana wants to call a hotline to get help for Irma. The adult believes the situation is none of Ana's business.

Allow five to ten minutes for the role play. Afterward, discuss questions such as:

- What did you see happening in this scene?

- If you were Ana, how would you feel about what the adult told you?

- How did this role play affect or change your understanding of Ana's story?

Scenario B

Characters: Ana now, Irma now

Procedure
Ask for volunteers to enact this scene:

Ana wants Irma to understand how bad she feels about not speaking up for Irma when they were children. Irma doesn't understand how Ana could see what was going on and not speak up.

Allow five to ten minutes for the role play. Afterward, discuss questions such as:

- **What did you see happening in this scene?**

- **If you were Ana, how would you feel about what Irma says? If you were Irma, how would you feel about what Ana says?**

- **How did this role play affect or change your understanding of Ana's story?**

5. Group Activity

Objective: Teens will consider the complexities of writing guidelines for reporting child abuse.

Procedure
Tell the group that the object of this activity is to explore what's involved in creating guidelines for reporting child abuse. First, brainstorm some issues raised by the task of creating guidelines; for example, the difference between disciplining children and abusing them, the value of family privacy versus the value of child protection. Write all ideas on the board. Next, ask teens to form small groups. Each group is to write a set of simple guidelines for reporting child abuse that could be circulated on neighborhood flyers. When they've finished, compare the various guidelines and how they address some of the issues raised during brainstorming. (You might also share the guidelines of your own school or agency, mentioning any difficulties or conflicts raised.) Finally, discuss what the group learned from the activity. Ask:

- **What's the value of having written guidelines about reporting child abuse?**

- **How did this activity affect or change your understanding of Ana's story?**

6. Writing Activities: Taking It Further

Ask students to complete one or more of the following activities individually, in small groups, or at home. Modify the activities as needed to suit the writing ability of group members. When activities are completed, invite volunteers to read their work to the group. Discuss how teens felt about the purpose and value of the writing.

Activity A

Objective: Group members will describe Ana's morality in their own words.

Pretend you're Ana. Write a letter to your sister, explaining how you admire her behavior toward Irma and how you hold yourself *accountable* for Irma's abuse.

Activity B

Objective: Group members will reflect on the pros and cons of the advice to "mind your own business."

How do you feel when you hear someone say, "Mind your own business"? When is "minding your own business" the wrong thing to do? When is it the right thing?

7. In Your Journal: Making It Personal

Encourage group members to reflect on the following topic in their journals:

Is there something happening now that you want to speak up about, but haven't yet? Describe the situation. What would you say has kept you from getting involved? What would help you speak up? How do you think you'll feel if you decide not to get involved? How do you think you'll feel if you decide to speak up or take action?

I'M A SEVENTEEN-YEAR-OLD THERAPIST
by Quantwilla L. Johnson

Pages 147–149 in *The Struggle to Be Strong*

PREPARING TO LEAD THE ACTIVITIES

Story Summary

When Quantwilla was eight years old, she was in therapy and hated it. She felt that her therapist was prying instead of listening to her and letting her problems come out naturally. Years later, as a teenager, Quantwilla finds that people turn to her for help when they're in trouble. For example, an older friend takes her advice about leaving an abusive boyfriend. Puzzled at first, Quantwilla soon gets used to helping people, begins to like it, and refers to herself as a "therapist." She explains her techniques: establish trust; never pry, pass judgment, or brush off problems; treat others as equals. Quantwilla's future goal is "to become a real therapist and help teenagers with their problems."

A Moment of Reflection

To connect with the story's themes, consider from your own perspective the questions group members will address during freewriting: Think of a time when someone tried to help you with a personal problem, but made things worse instead. For instance, the person may have missed the point, offered poor advice, talked instead of listened, or betrayed your trust by telling others about your problem. How did the experience make you feel? Who has been truly able to help you with a problem? How did the person help? How did that experience make you feel?

How Morality Works in the Story

Seeing Quantwilla's Morality

We see Quantwilla's morality in the way she uses what she knows about giving and receiving help to do the right thing for others. At first, she's puzzled about why people seek her out. Gradually she realizes that she's doing what her therapist failed to do. She's a good listener. She establishes trust. She doesn't pass judgment. She doesn't rush people or become nosy. Instead, she establishes an equal relationship. She takes people's problems seriously and doesn't dismiss their concerns, even if they seem trivial: "The thing I hate most is when you tell friends your problem, and to them it's nothing and they tell you to get over it. I think no matter what the problem is, if it's hurting your friend, don't say, 'Get over it.'" Helping others gives Quantwilla great satisfaction. Her story ends with her sense of moral achievement: "I've been through a lot," she writes, "and I know I can relate."

Why Morality Is a Struggle for Quantwilla

Quantwilla knows what it's like not to get the help one needs; her therapist "would force things" out of her in a way that made her "want to cry." Instead of giving up on therapy or being angry, she learns from the experience and uses it to help others. She knows how to treat the people who confide in her—"the same way I wanted to be treated when I was in therapy." Quantwilla has also been hurt by people who didn't take her problems seriously. "In the past, a lot of people have tried to help me with my problems, but then they disappeared and never came back." Again, she does the opposite: "That's why I want to be there for people who need someone to listen."

Useful Concept Words

To assist teens in understanding and discussing this story, you may want to introduce some or all of the following concept words by making them part of discussions and activities. Write them on the board in advance and plan to explain each word when it appears in a suggested discussion question or activity (where the words are shown in italics). Here are the concept words, with definitions and sentences relating them to the story.

accept: *to receive willingly*
Quantwilla **accepts** *her friends' problems without judgment.*

dismiss: *to send away or discount*
Quantwilla never **dismisses** *her friends' problems.*

empathy: *the ability to understand another person's situation and feelings*
Quantwilla has **empathy** *for her "clients."*

evolve: *to develop or achieve something gradually*
Quantwilla doesn't rush her relationships; rather, she lets them **evolve.**

therapeutic: *having healing powers*
Quantwilla's role as an advisor is **therapeutic** *both for her and for her friends.*

ACTIVITIES

1. Freewriting: Finding Yourself in the Story

After group members have finished reading the story, ask them to take out writing materials. If you'll be writing also, have handy your own journal and tell students you'll be participating. For a description of freewriting, see pages 14–15.

The following statement and questions are similar to those you considered earlier in "A Moment of Reflection." This time, you may want to write along with your group.

Think of a time when someone tried to help you with a personal problem, but made things worse instead. For instance, the person may have missed the point, offered poor advice, talked instead of listened, or betrayed your trust by telling others about your problem. How did the experience make you feel? Who has been truly able to help you with a problem? How did the person help? How did that experience make you feel?

After the freewriting, invite volunteers to share what they wrote. Allow time for brief discussion.

2. Discussion: Understanding Events

To be sure group members have understood the story, ask questions such as:

- **Why did Quantwilla hate her own therapy and swear she'd never become a therapist?**

- **Why does Quantwilla's older friend Jamie come to her for advice? What does she tell Jamie? What does Jamie do?**

- **Why does Quantwilla think people come to her for help?**

- **What are some of Quantwilla's techniques as a "therapist"?**

- **What's her goal for the future?**

3. Discussion: Understanding Issues

Quantwilla's Morality

Review with the group what morality is, why it's sometimes hard to come by, and how it can be helpful. Then, referring as necessary to "How Morality Works in the Story" (page 138), ask questions such as:

- **In the past, Quantwilla says, people tried to help her with her problems but then disappeared or didn't take her seriously. What impact did those experiences have on her?**

- **What response does Quantwilla hate most when she tells a friend a problem? How does she show that she** *accepts* **whatever her friends tell her? What is it about her style that makes her helpful to people?**

- **How does she behave when a friend confides in her? How does she help relationships** *evolve*?

- **Would you call Quantwilla a therapist? Why or why not?**

Connecting with the Issues

Suggest that group members silently review what they wrote during freewriting. Then ask questions such as:

- **Would you feel comfortable opening up to Quantwilla? Why or why not?**

- **Is there a Quantwilla in your life—someone you can talk with about your problems and end up feeling better? What is it about this person that makes him or her easy to talk to?**

- **What's the connection between being a good listener and being a moral person?**

- **Do you feel comfortable or uncomfortable when friends confide in you or ask you for advice? Why? Why is it sometimes hard to hear about another person's problems?**

- **Do you think it's possible for one person to understand fully what another person is going through? Can you have *empathy* for another person if you haven't experienced the same things?**

4. Role Plays

For guidelines on role playing, see pages 15–16.

Objective: Group members will understand that empathizing with another human being—especially one in pain—is a moral act.

Scenario A

Characters: Quantwilla, her friend

Procedure
Ask for volunteers to enact this scene:

Quantwilla's friend is going through a very difficult situation, is depressed, and feels no one—not even Quantwilla—can help her. Quantwilla, using her skills, wants her to open up about her feelings.

Allow five to ten minutes for the role play. Afterward, discuss questions such as:

- **What did you see happening in this scene?**

- **If you were Quantwilla's friend, would Quantwilla have persuaded you to confide in her?**

- **How did this role play affect or change your understanding of Quantwilla's story?**

Scenario B

Characters: Quantwilla, an adult therapist

Procedure
Ask for volunteers to enact this scene (you may want to play the therapist yourself):

The adult therapist thinks Quantwilla is getting in over her head by giving advice and wants to convince her to stop. Quantwilla believes she is helping her friends and wants to convince the therapist that it would be immoral not to respond to friends in need.

Allow five to ten minutes for the role play. Afterward, discuss questions such as:

- **What did you see happening in this scene?**

- **If you were the therapist, would Quantwilla have convinced you that she's right about acting as a therapist to her friends?**

- **How did this role play affect or change your understanding of Quantwilla's story?**

5. Writing Activities: Taking It Further

Ask students to complete one or more of the following activities individually, in small groups, or at home. Modify the activities as needed to suit the writing ability of group members. When activities are completed, invite volunteers to read their work to the group. Discuss how teens felt about the purpose and value of the writing.

Activity A

Objective: Group members will describe Quantwilla's morality in their own words.

Pretend you're Quantwilla. Write a letter to your godmother, Susan, describing how she helped you with your problems and has been your role model as you help others.

Activity B

Objective: Group members will reflect on activities they consider therapeutic.

The people who come to Quantwilla with their problems seem to consider talking to her *therapeutic;* that is, something that helps them heal. What activities are therapeutic for you? Such activities might be talking to certain people, playing sports, meditating or praying, playing a musical instrument, writing, drawing, reading, or working out. Write about what you do when you feel troubled and how the activity helps you.

Activity C

Objective: Group members will describe a personal problem that others failed to understand.

Have you ever had a problem that was important to you, but that others couldn't understand? What was the problem? What did it feel like to be misunderstood or to have your problem *dismissed*? Were you able to make yourself understood eventually? If so, what happened? If not, what do you think stood in the way?

6. In Your Journal: Making It Personal

Encourage group members to reflect on the following topic in their journals:

Quantwilla is able to feel *empathy*—to see things through her friends' eyes. Think of a person you know who has a problem you think is silly or that you can't relate to. What is the person's problem? Why can't you relate to it? Now try putting yourself in this person's shoes. Describe the problem from her or his point of view. When you're done, ask yourself: Has describing the problem from the other person's point of view helped you relate better to it? Why or why not? How might developing empathy for this person be helpful to you?

SOLDIER GIRL
by Max Morán

Pages 150–154 in *The Struggle to Be Strong*

PREPARING TO LEAD THE ACTIVITIES

Story Summary

Max meets Linda, a "pretty girl crying," in a park. They soon become best friends. Max notices that Linda is always tired and often goes to the doctor. Eventually, she tells him that she's HIV-positive as the result of a rape. Rather than abandon her, as Linda expects him to and as her family and other friends have, Max promises to "always be there for her." The two become even closer, although they don't make love; Linda wears Max's clothes and allows him to accompany her to the doctor. Gradually, Max realizes that Linda "had full-blown AIDS." He suffers greatly as she begins to weaken and get sicker. After Linda dies, her parents don't tell Max where she's buried. So he devises a burial ritual of his own—he digs a symbolic grave and buries his Army suit, which Linda loved to wear. Months later he digs in the ground and finds the suit gone.

A Moment of Reflection

To connect with the story's themes, consider from your own perspective the questions group members will address during freewriting: Think of a time when you had to witness the suffering of someone you felt close to. How did you react? What was hardest for you about the situation? Were you able to help the person? Were you ever tempted to turn away or close yourself off emotionally? Looking back, is there anything you would do differently?

How Morality Works in the Story

Seeing Max's Morality

Max's morality becomes evident when Linda tells him she is HIV-positive. She expects him to aban-don her. Instead, Max stays and devotes himself to her. Although her pain is nearly as hard for him to bear as it is for her, Max gives Linda unlimited sympathy and care. Another aspect of Max's morality is his insistence on the beauty in life, despite Linda's suffering and eventual death. His positive outlook sustains his will to remain generous and compassionate.

Why Morality Is a Struggle for Max

When a loved one is dying, it's hard to see the beauty in life. Confronted by Linda's progressing illness, Max struggles not to be bitter: "Sometimes I felt anger and hatred when I thought about a guy taking advantage of such a beautiful person." When he's with her, he sometimes feels he's "dying inside." Yet Max fights back these feelings to create a "beautiful thing" between them. He also continues to feel he can help her, buying her teddy bears and searching for ways to make her smile. Unlike Linda's friends and family, who have turned away from her, Max is her companion to the end.

Useful Concept Words

To assist teens in understanding and discussing this story, you may want to introduce some or all of the following concept words by making them part of discussions and activities. Write them on the board in advance and plan to explain each word when it appears in a suggested discussion question or activity (where the words are shown in italics). Here are the concept words, with definitions and sentences relating them to the story.

affection: *a fond or tender feeling toward another*
Both Max and Linda need each other's **affection.**

bereft: *suffering the loss of a loved one*
Max is **bereft** *after Linda dies.*

closure: a satisfying finish or conclusion

*Max seeks **closure** to his relationship with Linda by burying his Army suit in their favorite place.*

compassion: sympathy; feeling for the suffering of another

*Max has **compassion** for Linda after learning of her illness.*

ACTIVITIES

1. Freewriting: Finding Yourself in the Story

After group members have finished reading the story, ask them to take out writing materials. If you'll be writing also, have handy your own journal and tell students you'll be participating. For a description of freewriting, see pages 14–15.

The following statement and questions are similar to those you considered earlier in "A Moment of Reflection." This time, you may want to write along with your group.

Think of a time when someone you cared about was going through a very difficult time. How did you react? What was hardest for you about the situation? Were you able to help the person? If so, how? If not, why not? Were you ever tempted to turn away and just live your own life? Looking back, what would you do differently?

After the freewriting, invite volunteers to share what they wrote. Allow time for brief discussion.

NOTE: Avoiding Roadblocks

The topic of AIDS may bring up misconceptions about the disease and prejudices against people who have it. For instance, someone may say that Linda could infect Max. Remind students that Max and Linda have a close but platonic relationship. His physical contact with her is limited to touching, and touching doesn't transmit HIV or AIDS. If you encounter negative comments about people with AIDS, handle them as you would such comments about any other group. As necessary, review "Handling Sensitive Issues," pages 7–8.

2. Discussion: Understanding Events

To be sure group members have understood the story, ask questions such as:

- Before he knows what's wrong with her, what makes Max suspect that Linda's sick?

- What is Max's reaction when Linda tells him she is HIV-positive? When he sees that she has "full-blown AIDS"?

- What kinds of things does Max do to help Linda?

- What would Max like to believe happened to the Army suit he buried?

3. Discussion: Understanding Issues

Max's Morality

Review with the group what morality is, why it's sometimes hard to come by, and how it can be helpful. Then, referring as necessary to "How Morality Works in the Story" (page 142), ask questions such as:

- Why do you think Linda's family and friends turn their backs on her?

- Why do you think Max is so supportive of Linda? Why does he stick by her, despite the pain he feels about her illness? What does his concern for her tell you about his sense of what's right?

- What does Max sacrifice by being a friend to Linda? What does he gain?

- Since Max doesn't go to Linda's funeral and doesn't know where she's buried, how does burying his Army suit in their favorite place give him *closure* (a satisfying conclusion) to their relationship? Why is it important to feel closure about an important situation or relationship?

Connecting with the Issues

Suggest that group members silently review what they wrote during freewriting. Then ask questions such as:

- If you were Max, would you have been able to feel *compassion* for Linda? Why or why not?

- Would the fact that Linda had AIDS affect your feelings about her? Explain your answer.

- Was there a time you gave support to someone who was suffering? What was the experience like? Did you ever feel you were getting too involved? Explain.

4. Role Play

For guidelines on role playing, see pages 15–16.

Objective: Group members will identify with the pros and cons of helping someone who is ill.

Characters: Max, his friend

Procedure
Ask for volunteers to enact this scene:

Max's friend, who feels overburdened, wants to stop taking care of a sick relative. Max, based on his experience with Linda, wants to convince his friend to stay and help the relative.

Allow five to ten minutes for the role play. Afterward, discuss questions such as:

- What did you see happening in this scene?

- If you were Max's friend, how would you feel about what Max told you?

- How did this role play affect or change your understanding of Max's story?

5. Writing Activities: Taking It Further

Ask students to complete one or more of the following activities individually, in small groups, or at home. Modify the activities as needed to suit the writing ability of group members. When activities are completed, invite volunteers to read their work to the group. Discuss how teens felt about the purpose and value of the writing.

Activity A

Objective: Group members will describe Max's morality in their own words.

Pretend you're Max. Write a letter to Linda's parents explaining why you stuck by Linda, why her death has left you *bereft,* and why you regret not knowing where she's buried.

Activity B

Objective: Group members will reflect on possible reasons why Max was so compassionate toward Linda.

Why do you think Max had such deep *compassion* for Linda? Why did he feel such *affection* for her? Finish this sentence: "I think Max felt so deeply for Linda because . . ."

Activity C

Objective: Group members will reflect on what Linda contributed to the relationship with Max.

Max describes his deep feelings for Linda. What do you think Linda gives to Max in the relationship?

6. In Your Journal: Making It Personal

Encourage group members to reflect on the following topic in their journals:

Max stood by Linda, even though her suffering was painful for him to bear. Many people wouldn't have been able to do what Max did. Think of a time when you knew someone who was hurt or suffering—such as a classmate who was being treated cruelly or someone who was very sick—and you did little or nothing to help or comfort the person. How do you feel about the situation now? Would you do anything differently? If so, what would you do? If not, why not?

HOW I MADE PEACE WITH THE PAST
by Paula Byrd

Pages 155–159 in *The Struggle to Be Strong*

PREPARING TO LEAD THE ACTIVITIES

Story Summary

Paula is angry with her mother for abandoning her children and for transmitting AIDS to her youngest child. Now that her mother is dying, however, Paula visits her regularly and uses the little time that's left to rebuild their relationship. Her first step is to express her true feelings to her mother: "She had done the one thing no child should ever have to face. She chose her boyfriend over her own children." Paula's mother apologizes and acknowledges her mistakes. Just before she dies, Paula tells her she loves her and forgives her. Paula also vows to make something of herself and to help hold the family together. She advises kids in similar situations to express their feelings to people who have hurt them "so that when they do pass on, you won't feel cheated."

A Moment of Reflection

To connect with the story's themes, consider from your own perspective the questions group members will address during freewriting: Think of a time when you had mixed feelings about an important person in your life—maybe you felt both love and anger. How did you deal with your mixed feelings toward this person? Did you ever tell the person how you felt? If so, was it easier to express your positive feelings or your negative feelings? If not, how do you feel now about not letting the person know how you felt?

How Morality Works in the Story

Seeing Paula's Morality

We see Paula's morality emerge as she rebuilds her relationship with her dying mother. Paula had been terribly angry and bitter about her mother's abandonment of her children and about her transmitting AIDS to her youngest child. But after her mother goes into the hospital Paula realizes, "I had to learn to forgive her mistakes and accept what happened to her and my sister." Paula's understanding propels her actions. She visits her mother in the hospital regularly. Guided by decency and compassion, she finds the right combination of words to help her mother find peace, and yet to be fair to herself by expressing her true feelings. Before her mother dies, Paula also expresses her love and forgiveness, pledging to make something of herself and to keep the family together. In essence, she says, *I want you to know that the damage you have done can and will be mended.* Paula's words seem designed to lift the burden of her mother's guilt and to grant her final forgiveness.

Why Morality Is a Struggle for Paula

Paula is justifiably angry and bitter that her mother rejected her children and transmitted AIDS to her youngest child. At the same time, Paula loves and needs her mother. With her father already dead of "AIDS and drugs," Paula is terrified of being without any parent at all. Her struggle is to sort out her confusion, find her way through the intense clash of feelings inside her, and figure out what's right to do. That Paula finds a balance between her positive and negative feelings—and is able to tell her mother how she feels—is testimony to her great moral strength.

Useful Concept Words

To assist teens in understanding and discussing this story, you may want to introduce some or all of the following concept words by making them part of discussions and activities. Write them on the board in advance and plan to explain each word when it appears in a suggested discussion question or activity (where the words are shown in italics). Here are the concept words, with definitions and sentences relating them to the story.

ambivalent: *having conflicting feelings or thoughts*
Paula feels **ambivalent** *toward her mother, loving her and being angry at the same time.*

integrity: *strength or firmness of character; honesty*
Paula has the **integrity** *to try to repair her relationship with her dying mother.*

peace: *inner contentment or serenity*
By expressing both her anger and her love and forgiveness, Paula brings **peace** *to herself and her mother.*

resolve: *to bring to a successful conclusion*
Paula is able to **resolve** *her conflicting feelings toward her mother.*

validate: *to prove the truth of something*
Paula's feelings about the past are **validated** *when her mother apologizes to her.*

ACTIVITIES

1. Freewriting: Finding Yourself in the Story

After group members have finished reading the story, ask them to take out writing materials. If you'll be writing also, have handy your own journal and tell students you'll be participating. For a description of freewriting, see pages 14–15.

The following statement and questions are similar to those you considered earlier in "A Moment of Reflection." This time, you may want to write along with your group.

Think of a time when you had mixed feelings about an important person in your life—maybe you felt both love and anger. How did you deal with your mixed feelings toward this person? Did you ever tell the person how you felt? If so, was it easier to express your positive feelings or your negative feelings? Why? If you didn't tell the person how you felt, how do you feel about that now?

After the freewriting, invite volunteers to share what they wrote. Allow time for brief discussion.

2. Discussion: Understanding Events

To be sure group members have understood the story, ask questions such as:

- **Why is Paula's mother in the hospital?**

- **Why is Paula angry with her mother?**

- **What does Paula decide she needs to do before her mother dies?**

- **When Paula expresses her feelings to her mother, what's the effect on their relationship?**

- **What does Paula tell her mother about her plans for the future?**

- **What's Paula's advice to other kids who are going through what she's "overcome"?**

3. Discussion: Understanding Issues

Paula's Morality

Review with the group what morality is, why it's sometimes hard to come by, and how it can be helpful. Then, referring as necessary to "How Morality Works in the Story" (page 145), ask questions such as:

- **Why does Paula decide that she has to express both her anger *and* her love and forgiveness before her mother dies?**

- **Do you think Paula was right or wrong in expressing her true feelings to her dying mother? Why?**

- **If Paula had not expressed her feelings to her mother, how would her life be different today? Why do you think so?**

- **Paula calls her story "How I Made Peace with the Past." What does she mean by making *peace* with the past? How is making peace different from forgetting the past?**

- **Why does Paula advise other kids to express their feelings to people who have hurt them, "even if the person hates the truth"? Do you think she's right? Why or why not?**

Connecting with the Issues

Suggest that group members silently review what they wrote during freewriting. Then ask questions such as:

- People often find it hard to express angry feelings. Why is it especially hard to express those feelings to a person who's suffering, as Paula's mother is?

- If you were in Paula's situation, would you have told your mother how you felt about the past? Would you have forgiven her? Why or why not?

- Have you ever done what Paula did—express your true feelings to someone who hurt you? How did the experience affect you and your relationship with the person?

- Is there someone in your life to whom you wish you could express your true feelings? What do you think is keeping you from doing this?

4. Role Plays

For guidelines on role playing, see pages 15–16.

Objective: Group members will practice expressing true feelings without alienating the other person.

Scenario A

Characters: Paula, her mother

Procedure
Ask for volunteers to enact these two versions of the scene:

1. Paula visits her mother in the hospital, but she has decided not to express her true feelings. She and her mother have a short conversation about unimportant matters, during which they avoid talking about the past.

2. Paula visits her mother in the hospital, having decided to express her true feelings. She and her mother talk about the past and about Paula's anger and bitterness.

Allow about five minutes for each version. Afterward, discuss questions such as:

- What did you see happening in each of the scenes?

- How would you compare the scenes? How were they similar? How were they different?

- How did this role play affect or change your understanding of Paula's story?

Scenario B

Characters: Paula, her friend

Procedure
Ask for volunteers to enact this scene:

Paula's friend is very angry with a parent but is afraid if these feelings are expressed, the parent will be bitter and rejecting. Paula wants her friend to understand how to express honest feelings without losing the relationship.

Allow five to ten minutes for the role play. Afterward, discuss questions such as:

- What did you see happening in this scene?

- If you were Paula's friend, would Paula have convinced you to talk honestly with your parent?

- How did this role play affect or change your understanding of Paula's story?

5. Writing Activities: Taking It Further

Ask students to complete one or more of the following activities individually, in small groups, or at home. Modify the activities as needed to suit the writing ability of group members. When activities are completed, invite volunteers to read their work to the group. Discuss how teens felt about the purpose and value of the writing.

Activity A

Objective: Group members will describe Paula's morality in their own words.

Pretend you're Paula. Write a letter to a friend, explaining how you *resolved* and healed your relationship with your mother and how your life has been affected by what you did.

Activity B

Objective: Group members will reflect on Paula's advice to express our true feelings to people who have hurt us.

Paula says, "A lot of times you might feel that what happened to you is all right. You may feel that you shouldn't say anything, because the person who committed the acts has suffered enough. Even if that's true, though, it's also important to let the person know it wasn't all right and they hurt you." What do you think she means? Have you faced a similar situation with someone in your life? Do you agree or disagree with Paula's advice? Why?

Activity C

Objective: Group members will reflect on the meaning of Paula's poem.

Reread Paula's poem and write a paragraph about what it means to you.

6. In Your Journal: Making It Personal

Encourage group members to reflect on the following topic in their journals:

Paula is rightfully angry, but she has the *integrity* to work through the anger and to forgive and love her mother. Think about someone close to you toward whom you feel *ambivalent* or have mixed feelings— maybe both love and anger. How did your mixed feelings begin? How do you think the other person would describe your relationship? Would you say that both of you need to express your feelings? Do both of you need to be right? Do both of you need to be loved? What steps could you take to *validate* your own feelings and *resolve* your relationship with this person? What effects would this have on you, the other person, and your relationship?

FIVE TEENS: THE IMPORTANCE OF MORALITY

As necessary, refer to pages 134 and 135 in the anthology to review with your group what morality is and why it's a resilience. Then invite group members to compare how morality works in the lives of the five teen writers in this section. (To help students recall each writer, you might list their first names on the board.) Ask questions such as:

- **Which writer do you think has the hardest time deciding what's right and then doing it? Why do you think so?**

- **Which writer do you think shows the most courage in sacrificing his or her own interests to do what's right for another person? Why do you think so?**

- **Which writer do you think changes the most because of her or his acts of morality? Why do you think so?**

- **Which story in this section do you like best? Which teen writer do you admire most? Explain your choices.**

Many of the teen writers in this book demonstrate more than one resilience. If your group has read other stories, you might ask members to discuss how writers in other sections also demonstrate morality.

DISCUSSION GROUP EVALUATION

What did you think of the discussion group experience? Your feedback is important! Your honest—and anonymous—responses will help future groups. Please complete and return this evaluation form. Thank you for your time.

1. Circle the number that best describes how you would rate each of the following.

1 = excellent   2 = good   3 = average   4 = fair   5 = poor

1 2 3 4 5   The group experience as a whole

1 2 3 4 5   The leader's ability to guide the group

1 2 3 4 5   The leader's warmth and concern

1 2 3 4 5   The leader's respect for every group member

1 2 3 4 5   The value of the group for teens

1 2 3 4 5   The value of the group for me personally

1 2 3 4 5   The general level of comfort and safety for sharing feelings

1 2 3 4 5   The level of comfort and safety I felt

1 2 3 4 5   The respect I felt for the other group members

1 2 3 4 5   The respect that other group members showed toward me

2. Which topics were most interesting and helpful for you?

3. I would/wouldn't recommend this group to a friend because:

4. Additional comments:

From *A Leader's Guide to The Struggle to Be Strong* by Sybil Wolin, Al Desetta, and Keith Hefner, copyright © 2000 by Youth Communication and Project Resilience. Free Spirit Publishing Inc., Minneapolis, MN; 800/735-7323 *(www.freespirit.com)*. This page may be photocopied for individual, classroom, or group work only.

ABOUT YOUTH COMMUNICATION

Youth Communication is a nonprofit youth development program, located in New York City, whose mission is to teach writing, journalism, and leadership skills. The teenagers trained by Youth Communication, most of whom are New York City public high school students, become writers for two teen-written magazines, *New Youth Connections,* a general interest youth magazine, and *Foster Care Youth United,* a magazine by and for young people in foster care. The stories in *The Struggle to Be Strong* were originally published in these two magazines.

Youth Communication was created in 1980 in response to a nationwide study which found that the high school press was characterized by censorship, mediocrity, and racial exclusion. Keith Hefner cofounded the program and has directed it ever since.

Each year, more than one hundred young people participate in Youth Communication's school-year and summer journalism workshops. They come from every corner of New York City, and the vast majority are African-American, Latino, or Asian teens. The teen staff members work under the direction of several full-time adult editors in Youth Communication's Manhattan newsroom.

Teachers, counselors, social workers, and other adults circulate the magazines to young people in their classes, after-school youth programs, and agencies. They distribute 70,000 copies of *New Youth Connections* each month during the school year, and 10,000 bimonthly copies of *Foster Care Youth United.* Teachers frequently tell the Youth Communication staff that teens in their classes—including students who are ordinarily resistant to reading—clamor for these publications. For the teen writers, the opportunity to reach their peers with important self-help information, and with accurate portrayals of their lives, motivates them to create powerful stories.

Running a strong youth development program, while simultaneously producing quality teen magazines, requires a balance between a process that is sensitive to the complicated lives and emotions of the teen participants and one that is intellectually rigorous. That balance is sustained in the writing/teaching/editing relationship, which is the core of Youth Communication's program.

The teaching and editorial process begins with discussions between the adult editors and the teen staff, during which they seek to discover the stories that are both most important to each teen writer and potentially most appealing to the magazines' readers.

Once topics have been chosen, students begin the process of crafting their stories. For a personal story, that means revisiting events from the past to understand their significance for the future. For a commentary, it means developing a logical and persuasive argument. For a reported story, it means gathering information through research and interviews. Students look inward and outward as they try to make sense of their experiences and the world around them, and to find the points of intersection between personal and social concerns. That process can take a few weeks, or a few months. Stories frequently go through four, five, or more drafts as students work on them under the guidance of editors in the same way that any professional writer does.

Many of the students who walk through Youth Communication's doors have uneven skills as a result of poor education, living under extremely stressful conditions, or coming from homes where English is a second language. Yet, to complete their stories, students must successfully perform a wide range of activities, including writing and rewriting, reading, discussion, reflection, research, interviewing, and typing. They must work as members of a team, and they must accept a great deal of individual responsibility. They learn to read subway maps, verify facts, and cope with rejection. They engage in explorations of truthfulness and fairness. They meet deadlines. They must develop the boldness to believe that they have something important to say, and the humility to recognize that saying it well is not a process of instant gratification, but usually requires a long, hard struggle through many discussions and much rewriting.

It would be impossible to teach these skills and dispositions as separate, disconnected topics such as grammar, ethics, or assertiveness training. However, the staff has found that students make rapid progress when they are learning skills in the context of an inquiry that is personally significant to them, and which they think will benefit their peers.

Writers usually participate in the program for one semester, though some stay much longer. Years later, many of them report that working at Youth Communication was a turning point in their lives—that it helped them acquire the confidence and skills they needed for success in their subsequent education and careers. Scores of Youth Communication's graduates have overcome tremendous obstacles to become journalists, writers, and novelists. Hundreds more are working in law, teaching, business, and other careers.

RESOURCES FROM YOUTH COMMUNICATION

Breaking Away: Teens Write About Leaving Foster Care, edited by Al Desetta and Tom Brown. Youth Communication, 1999.

Getting Help: Teens Write About Therapy, Peer Support, and Self-Help, edited by Tom Brown and Al Desetta. Youth Communication, 1999.

Growing Up Girl: Young Women Write About Their Lives, edited by Andrea Estepa. Youth Communication, 1999.

The Heart Knows Something Different: Teenage Voices from the Foster Care System, edited by Al Desetta. Persea Books, 1996. Foreword by Jonathan Kozol.

Out With It: Gay and Straight Teens Write About Homosexuality, edited by Philip Kay, Andrea Estepa, and Al Desetta. Youth Communication, 1996. (Includes teacher's guide.)

Starting With "I": Personal Essays by Teenagers, edited by Andrea Estepa and Philip Kay. Persea Books, 1997. Foreword by Edwidge Danticat.

A Teacher's Guide to Starting With "I," by Andrea Estepa. Youth Communication, 1997.

Things Get Hectic: Teens Write About the Violence That Surrounds Them, edited by Philip Kay, Andrea Estepa, and Al Desetta. Simon and Schuster, 1998. Foreword by Geoffrey Canada.

Available by subscription:

New Youth Connections, a general interest teen magazine.

Foster Care Youth United, a magazine written by and for young people in foster care.

For ordering information, contact:

Youth Communication
224 West 29th Street, 2nd Floor
New York, NY 10001
Telephone: (212) 279-0708
Fax: (212) 279-8856
Email: info@Youthcomm.org
Web site: *www.Youthcomm.org*

ABOUT PROJECT RESILIENCE

Project Resilience was founded by Sybil Wolin and Steven Wolin. Their mission is to advance a balanced view of the effects of hardship on youth, one that includes the pain and damage that hardship can cause and the strength that can be forged under pressure. They conduct research, write educational materials, and provide training for use in education, treatment, and prevention settings.

The Wolins began their work in 1989 by interviewing 25 adults who had grown up in families disrupted by divorce, poverty, mental illness, violence, neglect, or alcohol or substance abuse. All were nonetheless leading satisfying, constructive lives. The core question asked of this group was: "How did you do it?" Studying their answers, the Wolins were struck most by the behaviors these adults described—what they had done in childhood, adolescence, and adulthood to protect themselves and remain healthy despite the challenges they faced. The Wolins grouped those behaviors into seven categories they called resiliencies—strengths that are forged in a struggle with hardship. The seven were insight, independence, relationships, initiative, creativity, humor, and morality.

Since that initial study, Sybil and Steven Wolin have written and lectured widely on resilience. They have conducted more than 250 workshops across the United States, Canada, Europe, and South America. They have also trained trainers and provided consultation and support to school systems, youth development programs, and government and private agencies serving children, youth, and families. Much of that work, including the framework for *The Struggle to Be Strong* and this leader's guide, has been based on the seven resiliencies and the Wolins' understanding of how these seven strengths limit the harm that hardship can cause.

Prior to 1989, Sybil and Steven Wolin worked separately. Though they still maintain individual careers, their professional lives converged when they developed, via different experiences, the same interest in resilience. At the time, Steven, a psychiatrist in private practice and Director of Family Therapy Training at the George Washington University Medical School, was studying alcoholism in families. The original impetus for his work was to discover why alcoholism runs in families, but along the way, he became more curious about children of alcoholics who did *not* repeat their parents' drinking problems than about those who did. At the same time, working as an advocate, Sybil was prompted to explore how families met the challenge of having a disabled child and what enabled so many of the parents she saw to hold on to their joy in life despite their anxieties and pain.

The Wolins' similar interest in strengths in the face of adversity resulted in the establishment of Project Resilience. They are presently codirectors of the organization.

RESOURCES FROM PROJECT RESILIENCE

Wolin, S.J., et al. "Three Spiritual Perspectives on Resilience: Buddhism, Christianity, and Judaism," in *Spiritual Resources in Family Therapy,* edited by Froma Walsh (New York: Guilford Press, 1999).

Wolin, S., & Wolin, S.J. "The Challenge Model: Working with the Strengths of Children of Substance Abusing Parents," *Child and Adolescent Psychiatric Clinics of North America* 5, no. 1 (1996).

Wolin, S., & Wolin, S.J. "Morality in COA's: Revisiting the Syndrome of Over-Responsibility," in *Children of Alcoholics: Selected Readings,* edited by S. Abbott (Rockville, MD: National Association of Children of Alcoholics—NACoA, 1995).

Wolin, S., & Wolin, S.J. *The Resilient Self: How Survivors of Troubled Families Rise Above Adversity* (New York: Villard Books, 1993).

Wolin, S., & Wolin, S.J. "Survivor's Pride: Building Resilience in Youth at Risk"; "Voices from the Front: James's Story"; "Voices from the Front: Tanika's Story"—videos (Verona, WI: Attainment Co., 1994).

Project Resilience offers training, consultation, and educational materials for clinicians, educators, prevention specialists, and youth workers using *The Struggle to Be Strong.* For more information or to place an order, contact Project Resilience at:

Project Resilience
5410 Connecticut Avenue NW
Washington, DC 20015
Telephone: (202) 966-8171
Fax: (202) 966-7587
Email: sybil@projectresilience.com
Web site: *www.projectresilience.com*

FOR FURTHER READING

See also "Resources from Youth Communication," page 151, and "Resources from Project Resilience," pages 152–153.

The following resources discuss and describe resilience in ways that are especially helpful for people new to the field:

Benson, P.L., J. Galbraith, and P. Espeland. *What Teens Need to Succeed: Proven, Practical Ways to Shape Your Own Future* (Minneapolis: Free Spirit Publishing, 1998).

DeSalvo, L. *Writing as a Way of Healing: How Telling Our Stories Transforms Our Lives* (San Francisco: Harper, 1999).

Henderson, N., B. Benard, and N. Sharp-Light, eds. *Resiliency in Action* (Gorham, ME: Resiliency in Action, 1999).

McLaughlin, M.W., M.A. Irby, and J. Langman. *Urban Sanctuaries: Neighborhood Organizations in the Lives and Futures of Inner-City Youth* (San Francisco: Jossey-Bass, 1994).

Seligman, M.E.P., K. Reivich, L. Jaycox, and J. Gillham. *The Optimistic Child* (Boston: Houghton Mifflin, 1995).

The concept of resilience presented in *The Struggle to Be Strong* builds on a great deal of prior research and theory building. See the following resources:

Anthony, E.J., and B.J. Cohler, eds. *The Invulnerable Child* (New York: Guilford Press, 1987).

Beardslee, W.R., and D. Podorefsky. "Resilient Adolescents Whose Parents Have Affective and Other Psychiatric Disorders: Importance of Self-Understanding and Relationships," *American Journal of Psychiatry* 145, no. 1 (January 1988), 63–69.

Benard, B. *Fostering Resiliency in Kids: Protective Factors in the Family, School, and Community* (Portland, OR: Western Regional Center for Drug-Free Schools and Communities, Far West Laboratory, 1991).

Benard, B. "How to Be a Turnaround Teacher," *Reaching Today's Youth, The Community Circle of Caring Journal* 2, no. 3 (spring 1998), 31–35.

Benard, B. *Turning the Corner: From Risk to Resiliency* (Portland, OR: Western Regional Center for Drug-Free Schools and Communities, Far West Laboratory, 1993).

Coles, R. *The Moral Life of Children* (Boston: Houghton Mifflin, 1986).

Dugan, T.F., and R. Coles, eds. *The Child in Our Times: Studies in the Development of Resiliency* (New York: Brunner/Mazel, 1991).

Garmezy, N., and M. Rutter, eds. *Stress, Coping and Development in Children* (New York: McGraw-Hill, 1983).

Goleman, D. *Emotional Intelligence: Why It Can Matter More than IQ* (New York: Bantam Books, 1995).

Haggerty, R., L. Sherrod, N. Garmezy, and M. Rutter, eds. *Stress, Risk, and Resilience in Children and Adolescents: Processes, Mechanisms, and Interventions* (New York: Cambridge University Press, 1994).

Higgins, G.O. *Resilient Adults: Overcoming a Cruel Past* (San Francisco: Jossey-Bass, 1994).

Jessor, R. "Successful Adolescent Development Among Youth in High-Risk Settings," *American Psychologist* 48, no. 2 (February 1993), 117–126.

Lifton, R.J. *The Protean Self: Human Resilience in an Age of Transformation* (Chicago: University of Chicago Press, 1993).

Linquanti, R. *Using Community-Wide Collaboration to Foster Resiliency in Kids: A Conceptual Framework* (Portland, OR: Western Regional Center for Drug-Free Schools and Communities, Far West Laboratory, Northwest Regional Educational Laboratory, 1992).

Masten, A.S. "Resilience in Development: Implications of the Study of Successful Adaptation for Developmental Psychopathology," in *The Emergence of a Discipline,* edited by D. Cicchetti (Hillsdale, NJ: Lawrence Erlbaum, 1989).

Masten, A.S. "Successful Adaptation Despite Risk and Adversity," in *Educational Resilience in Inner-City America: Challenges and Prospects,* edited by M.C. Wang and E.W. Gordon (Hillsdale, NJ: Lawrence Erlbaum, 1994).

Pennebaker, J.W. "Confession, Inhibition, and Disease," in *Advances in Experimental Social Psychology,* Vol. 22, edited by L. Berkowitz (New York: Academic Press, 1989).

Pennebaker, J.W. *Opening Up: The Healing Power of Confiding in Others* (New York: Morrow, 1990).

Pennebaker, J.W. "Writing About Emotional Experiences as a Therapeutic Process," *Psychological Science* 8, no. 3 (1997), 162–66.

Pennebaker, J.W. "Writing Your Wrongs," *American Health* 10, no. 1 (1991), 64–67.

Rutter, M. *Fifteen Thousand Hours: Secondary Schools and Their Effects on Children* (Cambridge, MA: Harvard University Press, 1984).

Rutter, M. "Stress, Coping and Development: Some Issues and Some Questions," in *Stress, Coping and Development in Children,* edited by N. Garmezy and M. Rutter (New York: McGraw-Hill, 1983).

Saleebey, D. *The Strengths Perspective in Social Work Practice* (New York: Longman, 1992).

Seligman, M.E.P. *Learned Optimism* (New York: Pocket Books, 1990).

Wang, M.C., and E.W. Gordon, eds. *Educational Resilience in Inner-City America: Challenges and Prospects* (Hillsdale, NJ: Lawrence Erlbaum, 1994).

Werner, E.E., and R.S. Smith. *Overcoming the Odds* (Ithaca, NY: Cornell University Press, 1992).

Werner, E.E., and R.S. Smith. *Vulnerable But Invincible: A Longitudinal Study of Resilient Children and Youth* (New York: McGraw-Hill, 1982; New York: Adams, Banister, Cox, 1989).

INDEX

A

Abandonment, 24–27, 79–82
Abuse
  breaking the cycle of, 36–39
  mandatory reporting of, 8
  responding to, 94–96, 110–113,
    134–137
Accept, definition of, 139
Accountable, definition of, 135
Acknowledge, definition of, 33
Activities, group. *See* Group sessions
Addiction. *See* Alcohol abuse;
    Drug abuse
Affection, definition of, 142
Affirm, definition of, 84
Aggravate, definition of, 94
AIDS, 142–144, 145–148
Alcohol abuse, 36–39
"All Talk and No Action"
  concept words, 69
  discussing story events, 69
  discussing story issues, 69–70
  freewriting activity, 69
  journal writing, 71
  reflecting on personal
    perspectives, 68
  role plays, 70
  seeing Elizabeth's relationships, 68
  story summary, 68
  understanding Elizabeth's struggles,
    68–69
  writing activities, 70–71
Ambiguous, definition of, 40
Ambivalent, definition of, 146
Anger
  controlling, 32–35
  getting rid of, 83–86, 117–119,
    145–148
Anonymous, definition of, 69
Anorexia. *See* Eating disorders
"Answer Was Me, The"
  avoiding discussion roadblocks, 37
  concept words, 36–37
  discussing story events, 37–38
  discussing story issues, 38
  freewriting activity, 37
  journal writing, 39
  reflecting on personal
    perspectives, 36
  role plays, 38
  seeing Eliott's insight, 36
  story summary, 36
  understanding Eliott's struggles, 36
  writing activities, 39
Anticipate, definition of, 33

Anxieties, overcoming, 100–103,
    104–107
Appearance, worrying about, 50–53,
    122–124
Aspire, definition of, 101
Associate, definition of, 41
Assume, definition of, 73
Authentic, definition of, 118
Awkward, definition of, 90

B

Backfire, definition of, 123
Balance, definition of, 51
Beautiful, being, 28–31, 46–49, 50–53
"Beauty Is More Than Skin Deep"
  avoiding discussion roadblocks, 29
  concept words, 28–29
  discussing story events, 29
  discussing story issues, 29–30
  freewriting activity, 29
  journal writing, 31
  reflecting on personal
    perspectives, 28
  role plays, 30
  seeing Danielle's insight, 28
  story summary, 28
  understanding Danielle's
    struggles, 28
  writing activities, 30–31
Benard, Bonnie, 8
Bereft, definition of, 142
Black, being, 40–43, 63–66
Black pride, 63–66
Bond, definition of, 75
"Bonding Through Cooking"
  concept words, 75–76
  discussing story events, 76
  discussing story issues, 76–77
  freewriting activity, 76
  group activities, 77
  journal writing, 78
  reflecting on personal
    perspectives, 75
  role plays, 77
  seeing Aurora's relationships, 75
  story summary, 75
  understanding Aurora's struggles, 75
  writing activities, 77–78
Boyfriends, 68–71
Bulimia. *See* Eating disorders
Burden, definition of, 51

C

Charisma, definition of, 91
Closure, definition of, 143
Clothes, shopping for, 125–128

Cloud, definition of, 47
College, attending, 97–99
"College Can Be Hell"
  concept words, 97–98
  discussing story events, 98
  discussing story issues, 98–99
  freewriting activity, 98
  journal writing, 99
  reflecting on personal
    perspectives, 97
  role plays, 99
  seeing Tamecka's initiative, 97
  story summary, 97
  understanding Tamecka's
    struggles, 97
  writing activities, 99
"Color Me Different"
  avoiding discussion roadblocks, 41
  concept words, 40–41
  discussing story events, 41
  discussing story issues, 41–42
  freewriting activity, 41
  group activities, 42
  journal writing, 43
  reflecting on personal
    perspectives, 40
  role plays, 42
  seeing Jamal's insight, 40
  story summary, 40
  understanding Jamal's struggles, 40
  writing activities, 42–43
Coming out, 58–62
Commitment, definition of, 37
Compassion
  definition of, 143
  showing, 142–144
Compensate, definition of, 55, 114
Competent, definition of, 98
Compliments, dealing with, 28–31
Comply, definition of, 126
Conceal, definition of, 59
Conceited, definition of, 28
Concept words, 13
Confidentiality, maintaining
  challenges of, 7
  importance of, 7
  and mandatory reporting
    requirements, 8
Conflicts, resolving, 32–35
Conform, definition of, 51, 55
Confront, definition of, 25
Conscience
  definition of, 135
  listening to one's, 134–137
Consequences, definition of, 114

"Controlling My Temper"
  avoiding discussion roadblocks, 33
  concept words, 32–33
  discussing story events, 33
  discussing story issues, 34
  freewriting activity, 33
  journal writing, 35
  reflecting on personal
    perspectives, 32
  role plays, 34–35
  seeing Christopher's insight, 32
  story summary, 32
  understanding Christopher's
    struggles, 32
  writing activities, 35
Cooking, bonding through, 75–78
Counseling, 83–86, 138–141
Courage, 142–144
Craving, definition of, 94
Creativity
  behaviors associated with, 3
  challenges and benefits of, 109
  definition of, 109
  making comparisons among
    writers, 120
  stories about, 109–120
Criticism, responding to, 28–31,
  110–113
Cycle, definition of, 25
Cycles, breaking destructive, 24–27

D

Dating, 63–66, 68–71, 90–93
Daydreaming, 114–116
Death, coping with, 142–144
Deception, 46–49
Defer, definition of, 47
Deny, definition of, 25
Dependent, definition of, 76
Depression, 50–53
DeSalvo, Louise, 12
Despair, definition of, 111
Devastated, definition of, 80
Dilemma, definition of, 126
Discussion Group Evaluation form, 149
Disguise, definition of, 118
Dismiss, definition of, 139
Disrespect, definition of, 33
Distance, definition of, 64
Diversion, definition of, 37
Divided, definition of, 69
Dreams, 24–27, 46–49
Drug abuse
  by parents, 130–133
  quitting, 94–96
  resisting peer pressure, 54–57

E

Eating disorders, 50–53
Embarrassment, using humor to cope
  with, 125–128

Empathy
  definition of, 139
  feeling, 138–141
Endurance, definition of, 111
Evaluate, definition of, 64
Evaluation form, 149
Evolve, definition of, 139
Exaggerate, definition of, 126
Excessive, definition of, 114–115
Experiment, definition of, 91
Exploit, definition of, 47
Express, definition of, 118

F

Fantasizing, 114–116
Fantasy, definition of, 115
Fat, feeling, 50–53
Fears, overcoming, 100–103
Feedback, on group sessions, 11, 149
Feelings, expressing, 110–113, 145–148
Flirting, 90–93
Focus, definition of, 105
Forgive, definition of, 84
Forgiveness, 36–39, 83–86, 145–148
Foster care system, 79–82
Foster Care Youth United, 1, 150
Foster child, being a
  and going to college, 97–99
  making friends, 72–74, 75–78, 79–82
  and succeeding in high school,
    104–107
Foster parents, 75–78, 104–107
Freak, definition of, 123
Freewriting
  procedure for, 14
  reading teens' freewriting, 14–15
  rules for, 14
  value of, 14, 15
Friendships
  counseling friends, 138–141
  developing, 68–71, 72–74, 75–78
  having realistic expectations for,
    79–82
  with people who are dying, 142–144

G

Gay, being, 58–62
Girlfriends, 90–93
Grief, 142–144
Group evaluation form, 149
Group homes, 79–82
Group leadership
  acknowledging teens' central
    issues, 6–7
  conveying respect
    importance of, 8
    showing interest in what teens
      think, 8
    tips for, 9
    waiting for teens to talk, 8–9
    withholding judgment, 9

establishing group guidelines
  for confidentiality, 7
  obtaining agreement, 7
  for sensitive issues, 7–8
  setting general guidelines, 7
  value of, 7
exploring sensitive issues at a safe
  distance, 6
importance of caring adults, 6
talking about strengths
  and acknowledging painful
    feelings, 9
  emphasizing opportunities, 10
  expressing confidence, 9
  tips for, 10
  using names of resiliencies, 9–10
using the stories as a bridge for
  communication, 6–7
Group sessions
  accommodating specific needs, 11
  directing sessions
    encouraging identification with
      the writer, 18
    going with the flow, 17, 18
    making personal preparations, 17
    moving to new activities, 18
    steps for, 17–18
  getting feedback on, 11, 149
  holding introductory meetings
    clarifying logistics, 19
    discussing group guidelines, 19
    explaining the leader's role, 19
    introducing the anthology, 19
    introducing the concept of
      resilience, 19–20
  leading activities
    avoiding discussion roadblocks, 15
    discussing story events, 15
    discussing story issues, 15
    freewriting, 14–15
    group activities, 17
    journal writing, 17
    role plays, 15–16
    writing activities, 17
  preparing to lead activities
    building a vocabulary of
      resilience, 13
    considering discussion questions
      from a personal perspective, 13
    reviewing the story's main
      points, 13
    seeing the writer's resilience, 13
    selecting activities, 13–14
    understanding the writer's
      struggles, 13
  supplies for sessions, 11
  typical sequence for, 11
  value of including writing, 12
Guilt
  dealing with, 134–137
  definition of, 135

H

Habits, breaking, 94–96
Hair, dyeing, 122–124
High school, succeeding in, 104–107
HIV, 142–144, 145–148
Homophobic, definition of, 59
Homosexuality, 58–62
Honesty, 24–27, 28–31
Hope, definition of, 111
Hostile, definition of, 84
"How I Graduated"
  concept words, 105
  discussing story events, 105
  discussing story issues, 105–106
  freewriting activity, 105
  journal writing, 107
  reflecting on personal
     perspectives, 104
  role plays, 106
  seeing Angi's initiative, 104
  story summary, 104
  understanding Angi's struggles, 104
  writing activities, 106–107
"How I Made Peace with the Past"
  concept words, 145–146
  discussing story events, 146
  discussing story issues, 146–147
  freewriting activity, 146
  journal writing, 148
  reflecting on personal
     perspectives, 145
  role plays, 147
  seeing Paula's morality, 145
  story summary, 145
  understanding Paula's struggles, 145
  writing activities, 147–148
"How to Survive Shopping with Mom"
  concept words, 125–126
  discussing story events, 126
  discussing story issues, 126
  freewriting activity, 126
  journal writing, 128
  reflecting on personal
     perspectives, 125
  role plays, 127
  seeing Chris's humor, 125
  story summary, 125
  understanding Chris's struggles, 125
  writing activities, 127
"How Writing Helps Me"
  concept words, 110–111
  discussing story events, 111
  discussing story issues, 111
  freewriting activity, 111
  group activities, 112
  journal writing, 113
  reflecting on personal
     perspectives, 110
  role plays, 112
  seeing Terry-Ann's creativity, 110
  story summary, 110
  understanding Terry-Ann's
     struggles, 110
  writing activities, 112–113
Humility, definition of, 29
Humor
  behaviors associated with, 3
  challenges and benefits of, 121
  definition of, 121
  making comparisons among
     writers, 128
  stories about, 121–128
Hypocrite, definition of, 123

I

Idealize, definition of, 80
Identity, personal, 24–27, 40–43,
  46–49, 58–62
"I Don't Know What the Word Mommy
  Means"
  avoiding discussion roadblocks, 25
  concept words, 25
  discussing story events, 25
  discussing story issues, 25–26
  freewriting activity, 25
  journal writing, 27
  reflecting on personal
     perspectives, 24
  role plays, 26
  seeing Younique's insight, 24
  story summary, 24
  understanding Younique's
     struggles, 24
  writing activities, 27
Imagining, 114–116, 125–128
"I'm a Seventeen-Year-Old Therapist"
  concept words, 138–139
  discussing story events, 139
  discussing story issues, 139–140
  freewriting activity, 139
  journal writing, 141
  reflecting on personal
     perspectives, 138
  role plays, 140
  seeing Quantwilla's morality, 138
  story summary, 138
  understanding Quantwilla's
     struggles, 138
  writing activities, 140–141
"I'm Black, He's Puerto Rican . . .
  So What?"
  avoiding discussion roadblocks, 65
  concept words, 64
  discussing story events, 64–65
  discussing story issues, 65
  freewriting activity, 64
  journal writing, 66
  reflecting on personal
     perspectives, 63
  role plays, 65–66
  seeing Artiqua's independence, 63
  story summary, 63
  understanding Artiqua's struggles,
     63–64
  writing activities, 66
Impression, definition of, 73
Impulse, definition of, 126
Independence
  behaviors associated with, 3
  challenges and benefits of, 45
  definition of, 45
  making comparisons among
     writers, 66
  stories about, 45–66
Initiative
  behaviors associated with, 3
  challenges and benefits of, 89
  definition of, 89
  making comparisons among
     writers, 107
  stories about, 89–107
"Inner voices," negative, 104–107
Insight
  behaviors associated with, 3
  challenges and benefits of, 23
  definition of, 23
  making comparisons among
     writers, 43
  stories about, 23–43
Integrity
  definition of, 55, 146
  maintaining, 54–57
Intimate, definition of, 69
Introspective, definition of, 37
Invade, definition of, 73
Isolated, definition of, 80
"It Takes Work to Flirt"
  concept words, 90–91
  discussing story events, 91
  discussing story issues, 91
  freewriting activity, 91
  group activities, 92
  journal writing, 93
  reflecting on personal
     perspectives, 90
  role plays, 92
  seeing Danny's initiative, 90
  story summary, 90
  understanding Danny's struggles, 90
  writing activities, 92–93
"I Was a Beauty School Sucker"
  avoiding discussion roadblocks, 47
  concept words, 46–47
  discussing story events, 47
  discussing story issues, 47–48
  freewriting activity, 47
  group activities, 48–49
  journal writing, 49
  reflecting on personal
     perspectives, 46
  role plays, 48
  seeing Tonya's independence, 46
  story summary, 46

understanding Tonya's struggles, 46
writing activities, 49

J
Jealousy, 97–99, 104–107
Journal writing, 17

L
Label, definition of, 73
Leading groups. *See* Group leadership;
  Group sessions
"Learning to Forgive"
  avoiding discussion roadblocks, 84
  concept words, 84
  discussing story events, 85
  discussing story issues, 85
  freewriting activity, 84
  journal writing, 86
  reflecting on personal
    perspectives, 83
  role plays, 85–86
  seeing Christopher's relation-
    ships, 83
  story summary, 83
  understanding Christopher's
    struggles, 84
  writing activities, 86
Liberate, definition of, 59
Life experiences, difficult
  as the central issues in teens'
    lives, 6–7
  reframing, 4
Listener, being a good, 138–141
"Losing My Friends to Weed"
  avoiding discussion roadblocks, 55
  concept words, 54–55
  discussing story events, 55–56
  discussing story issues, 56
  freewriting activity, 55
  journal writing, 57
  reflecting on personal
    perspectives, 54
  role plays, 56–57
  seeing Jamel's independence, 54
  story summary, 54
  understanding Jamel's struggles, 54
  writing activities, 57
Love
  for a dying friend, 142–144
  expressing, 145–148
  having realistic expectations for,
    79–82
"Love Too Strong, A"
  avoiding discussion roadblocks, 80
  concept words, 80
  discussing story events, 80–81
  discussing story issues, 81
  freewriting activity, 80
  journal writing, 82
  reflecting on personal
    perspectives, 79
  role plays, 81–82

seeing Tamecka's relationships, 79
story summary, 79
understanding Tamecka's
  struggles, 79–80
writing activities, 82
Loyalty, definition of, 64

M
Mandatory reporters, 8
Marijuana, 54–57, 94–96
Mood swings, responding to, 117–119
Morality
  behaviors associated with, 3
  challenges and benefits of, 129
  definition of, 129
  making comparisons among
    writers, 148
  stories about, 129–148
Mothering, 130–133
"Mother to My Mother's Children, A"
  concept words, 131
  discussing story events, 131
  discussing story issues, 131–132
  freewriting activity, 131
  journal writing, 133
  reflecting on personal
    perspectives, 130
  role plays, 132
  seeing Charlene's morality, 130
  story summary, 130
  understanding Charlene's
    struggles, 130
  writing activities, 132–133
Mutual, definition of, 69
"My Hair Is Blue—But I'm Not
  a Freak!"
  concept words, 122–123
  discussing story events, 123
  discussing story issues, 123–124
  freewriting activity, 123
  journal writing, 124
  reflecting on personal
    perspectives, 122
  role plays, 124
  seeing Lenny's humor, 122
  story summary, 122
  understanding Lenny's struggles, 122
  writing activities, 124
"My Struggle with Weed"
  avoiding discussion roadblocks, 95
  concept words, 94–95
  discussing story events, 95
  discussing story issues, 95–96
  freewriting activity, 95
  journal writing, 96
  reflecting on personal
    perspectives, 94
  role plays, 96
  seeing Craig's initiative, 94
  story summary, 94
  understanding Craig's struggles, 94
  writing activities, 96

"My Weight Is No Burden"
  avoiding discussion roadblocks, 51
  concept words, 51
  discussing story events, 52
  discussing story issues, 52
  freewriting activity, 51
  journal writing, 53
  reflecting on personal
    perspectives, 50
  role plays, 52
  seeing Charlene's independence, 50
  story summary, 50
  understanding Charlene's struggles,
    50–51
  writing activities, 53

N
Needy, definition of, 80
Neglect, 24–27
New Youth Connections, 1, 150
"No One Spoke Up for Irma"
  avoiding discussion roadblocks, 135
  concept words, 135
  discussing story events, 135–136
  discussing story issues, 136
  freewriting activity, 135
  group activities, 137
  journal writing, 137
  reflecting on personal
    perspectives, 134
  role plays, 136–137
  seeing Ana's morality, 134
  story summary, 134
  understanding Ana's struggles,
    134–135
  writing activities, 137
Novice, definition of, 76

O
Obligation, definition of, 131
Obstacle, definition of, 131
Optimism, communicating, 4
Ostracize, definition of, 55
"Out, Without a Doubt"
  avoiding discussion roadblocks, 59
  concept words, 59
  discussing story events, 59–60
  discussing story issues, 60
  freewriting activity, 59
  group activities, 61
  journal writing, 62
  reflecting on personal
    perspectives, 58
  role plays, 60–61
  seeing Craig's independence, 58
  story summary, 58
  understanding Craig's struggles,
    58–59
  writing activities, 61
Overcome, definition of, 101

P

Pain, acknowledging, 9
Paranoid, definition of, 95
Parent-child relationships
    dealing with abandonment, 24–27
    learning to forgive, 83–86, 145–148
    parenting siblings, 130–133
Parenting, irresponsible, 24–27,
        130–133
Peace, definition of, 146
Peer pressure, resisting, 54–57
Performance anxiety, definition of, 101
Persevere, definition of, 105
Perspective, definition of, 51
Platonic, definition of, 69
Poetry, writing and reading, 100–103
"Poetry Brought Out the Performer
        in Me"
    concept words, 100–101
    discussing story events, 101
    discussing story issues, 101–102
    freewriting activity, 101
    group activities, 102
    journal writing, 103
    reflecting on personal
        perspectives, 100
    role plays, 102
    seeing Shaniqua's initiative, 100
    story summary, 100
    understanding Shaniqua's
        struggles, 100
    writing activities, 102–103
Pot, 54–57, 94–96
Prejudice
    definition of, 64
    racial, 63–66
Principles, definition of, 55
Privacy. See Confidentiality,
        maintaining
Problems, facing, 24–27, 36–39, 97–99
Project Resilience
    how to contact, 153
    information about, 1, 152
    resources available from, 152–153
Provocative, definition of, 73

R

Race, stereotypes about, 40–43, 63–66
Reality, definition of, 115
Reflect, definition of, 33
Reframing, 4
Refuge, definition of, 105
Relationships
    behaviors associated with, 3
    challenges and benefits of, 67
    definition of, 67
    making comparisons among
        writers, 87
    stories about, 67–87
Release, definition of, 111

Reporting requirements, mandatory, 8
Resentment, definition of, 131
Resilience
    definition of, 1, 2
    as a paradox, 3–4
    and reality, 4–5
    as a strengths-based way to help
        teens, 2, 4
    vs. dramatic success, 4–5
Resiliencies
    as behaviors, 2–3
    reframing life experiences in terms
        of, 4
    using the names of, 9–10
    See also specific resiliencies
Resolve, definition of, 146
Respect, conveying
    importance of, 8
    showing interest in what teens
        think, 8
    tips for, 9
    waiting for teens to talk, 8–9
    withholding judgment, 9
Responsibility, accepting, 130–133,
        134–137
Responsible, definition of, 131
Restore, definition of, 118
Reveal, definition of, 59
Ridicule, definition of, 123
Risk, definition of, 84
Role plays
    discussing, 16
    establishing guidelines, 16
    follow-up activities, 16
    instructions for, 16
    objectives of, 15
    participation in, 15
    preparing teens for, 15–16
Roommates, getting along with, 72–74

S

Sacrifice, definition of, 55, 131
Self-acceptance
    definition of, 51
    learning, 58–62
Self-appraisal, 28–31
Self-assured, definition of, 47
Self-conscious
    being, 122–124
    definition of, 123
Self-deception, 46–49
Self-defeating, definition of, 105
Self-deprecating, definition of, 126
Self-doubt, definition of, 98
Self-forgiveness, 36–39
Self-image, definition of, 105
Self-improvement, 90–93
Self-pity
    definition of, 37, 98
    overcoming, 97–99
Self-respect, definition of, 37

Self-sufficient
    becoming, 75–78
    definition of, 76
Sensitive issues, handling
    keeping control of the discussion, 7
    knowing when to get help, 8
    maintaining a safe arena, 8
    mandatory reporting requirements, 8
    setting boundaries, 7
    tips for, 8
Sessions, group. See Group sessions
"She's My Sister (Not Foster)"
    concept words, 73
    discussing story events, 73
    discussing story issues, 73–74
    freewriting activity, 73
    journal writing, 74
    reflecting on personal
        perspectives, 72
    role plays, 74
    seeing Tamara's relationships, 72
    story summary, 72
    understanding Tamara's struggles,
        72–73
    writing activities, 74
Shopping, with one's mother, 125–128
Shyness, overcoming, 90–93, 100–103
Siblings, being mother to, 130–133
"Soldier Girl"
    avoiding discussion roadblocks, 143
    concept words, 142–143
    discussing story events, 143
    discussing story issues, 143–144
    freewriting activity, 143
    journal writing, 144
    reflecting on personal
        perspectives, 142
    role plays, 144
    seeing Max's morality, 142
    story summary, 142
    understanding Max's struggles, 142
    writing activities, 144
Speaking up, 134–137
Standard, definition of, 135
Steadfast, definition of, 64
Stereotype, definition of, 41
Stereotypes
    of gays, 58–62
    racial, 40–43, 63–66
    responding to, 40–43, 58–62
Stigma, definition of, 98
Strengths
    focusing on, 2, 4
    talking about
        and acknowledging painful
            feelings, 9
        emphasizing opportunities, 10
        expressing confidence, 9
        tips for, 10
        using names of resiliencies, 9–10
Stress, relieving, 117–119

Stuck-up, being, 28–31
Substitute, definition of, 80
Success
    importance of recognizing, 5
    vs. resilience, 4–5
Suffering, responding to, 142–144
Suicide, 50–53
"Superkids," 4
Supplies, for sessions, 11
Sustain, definition of, 84

T

Teasing, responding to, 122–124
Temper, controlling, 32–35
Therapeutic, definition of, 139
Therapy, 83–86, 138–141
Thin, being, 50–53
Tolerance, definition of, 41
Transform, definition of, 118
"Turnaround relationships," 8

U

Unfairness, responding to, 32–35,
    40–43

V

Validate, definition of, 146
Values, definition of, 29
Vanity
    definition of, 47
    resisting appeals to, 46–49
Vulnerable, definition of, 76, 91

W

Walking, as a way to relieve stress,
    117–119
"Walking Out the Anger"
    concept words, 117–118
    discussing story events, 118
    discussing story issues, 118
    freewriting activity, 118
    journal writing, 119
    reflecting on personal
        perspectives, 117
    role plays, 119
    seeing Tamara's creativity, 117
    story summary, 117
    understanding Tamara's
        struggles, 117
    writing activities, 119
Weed, 54–57, 94–96
Weight, worrying about, 50–53
"Why I Live in a Fantasy World"
    concept words, 114–115
    discussing story events, 115
    discussing story issues, 115
    freewriting activity, 115
    journal writing, 116
    reflecting on personal
        perspectives, 114
    role plays, 116
    seeing Cassandra's creativity, 114
    story summary, 114

    understanding Cassandra's
        struggles, 114
    writing activities, 116
Willpower, definition of, 95
Witness, definition of, 135
Writing
    encouraging clear expression, 17
    journal writing, 17
    linking events and emotions, 12
    to make sense of chaotic feelings, 12
    as a source of strength, 110–113
    for teens with varying abilities and
        interests, 12
    as a tool for encouraging
        reflection, 12
    using a variety of activities, 17
    as a way to relieve stress, 117–119
    See also Freewriting
Writing as a Way of Healing, 12

Y

Youth Communication organization
    how to contact, 151
    information about, 1, 150–151
    resources available from, 151

ABOUT THE AUTHORS

Sybil Wolin, Ph.D., is a developmental psychologist who has taught high school English, adult education, and special education. She has been an advocate for children with special needs and has worked with their parents to develop their own advocacy skills. Her writing has been published in many magazines and journals, including *Principal, Learning, Pediatric Clinics of North America, Resilience in Action,* and *Reaching Today's Youth.*

Al Desetta, M.A., began working for Youth Communication in 1985 and has served as editor of the organization's three youth-written publications: *Spofford Voices,* a poetry journal written by inmates at the Spofford Juvenile Detention Center in New York City; *New Youth Connections (NYC);* and *Foster Care Youth United (FCYU).* Under his direction as founding editor, *FCYU,* a bimonthly publication, has grown to a circulation of about 10,000 in 46 states. During the 1990–91 academic year, Desetta was a Charles H. Revson Fellow on the Future of the City of New York at Columbia University.

Keith Hefner is the executive director of Youth Communication, a program he cofounded in 1980. He was a Revson Fellow at Columbia University during the 1986–87 academic year. He is the recipient of a MacArthur Fellowship for his work in youth development, and the Luther P. Jackson Award for Excellence in Journalism Education from the New York Association of Black Journalists.

Other Great Books from Free Spirit

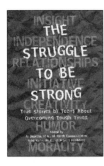

The Struggle to Be Strong
True Stories by Teens About Overcoming Tough Times
edited by Al Desetta, M.A., of Youth Communication, and Sybil Wolin, Ph.D., of Project Resilience
In 30 first-person accounts, teens tell how they have overcome major life obstacles. As teens read this book, they'll learn about seven resiliencies—insight, independence, relationships, initiative, creativity, humor, and morality—that everyone needs to overcome tough times. For ages 13 & up.
$14.95; 192 pp.; softcover; illus.; 6" x 9"

Leader's Guide
by Sybil Wolin, Ph.D., of Project Resilience, and Al Desetta, M.A., and Keith Hefner of Youth Communication
For teachers, social workers, case workers, clinicians, prevention specialists, counselors, and other adults who work with youth in grades 7–12.
$21.95; 180 pp.; softcover; 8½" x 11"

Fighting Invisible Tigers
A Stress Management Guide for Teens
Revised & Updated
by Earl Hipp
Proven, practical advice for teens on coping with stress, being assertive, building relationships, taking risks, making decisions, dealing with fears, and more. For ages 11 & up.
$12.95; 160 pp.; softcover; illus.; 6" x 9"

Leader's Guide
12 Sessions on Stress Management and Lifeskills Development
by Connie C. Schmitz, Ph.D., with Earl Hipp
For grades 6–12.
$19.95; 136 pp.; softcover; 8½" x 11"

Worth the Risk
True Stories About Risk Takers Plus How You Can Be One, Too
by Arlene Erlbach
In an era when risk taking is most often associated with dangerous behavior or poor choices, this uplifting book points out the benefits of taking a chance. Includes 20 first-person stories about young risk takers plus step-by-step advice on how to take risks, set goals, and more. For ages 10–15.
$12.95; 136 pp.; softcover; B&W photos; 6" x 9"

Succeed Every Day
Daily Readings for Teens
by Pamela Espeland
Each reading begins with an inspiring quotation related to a particular developmental asset. A brief essay offers questions to consider, tips to try, advice, examples, and/or anecdotes. A positive affirmation suggests an action, a decision, or more food for thought. For ages 11 & up.
$10.95; 400 pp.; softcover; 4¼" x 6¼"

Making Every Day Count
Daily Readings for Young People on Solving Problems, Setting Goals, & Feeling Good About Yourself
by Pamela Espeland and Elizabeth Verdick
Each entry in this book of daily readings includes a thought-provoking quotation, a brief essay, and a positive "I"-statement that relates the entry to the reader's own life. For ages 11 & up.
$9.95; 392 pp.; softcover; 4¼" x 6¼"

Making the Most of Today
Daily Readings for Young People on Self-Awareness, Creativity, & Self-Esteem
by Pamela Espeland and Rosemary Wallner
Quotes from figures including Eeyore, Mariah Carey, and Dr. Martin Luther King Jr. guide you through a year of positive thinking, problem solving, and practical lifeskills—the keys to making the most of every day. For ages 11 & up.
$9.95; 392 pp.; softcover; 4¼" x 6¼"

Can You Relate?
Real-World Advice for Teens on Guys, Girls, Growing Up, and Getting Along
by Annie Fox, M.Ed.
(also known as Hey Terra!)
Online, the author is "Terra"— a wise person who's been around long enough to know plenty, but not so long that she's forgotten what it's like to be a teen. This book brings Terra out of cyberspace and onto the printed page. Based on hundreds of emails Annie has received, it gives readers the scoop on what matters most to teens: their feelings, looks, and decisions; boyfriends and girlfriends; sex and sexuality; and much more. For ages 13 & up.
$15.95; 256 pp.; softcover; illus.; 7¼" x 9¼"

When A Friend Dies

A Book for Teens About Grieving and Healing

by Marilyn E. Gootman, Ed.D.

Marilyn Gootman offers genuine understanding and gentle advice for any grieving teen. She knows what teenagers go through when another teen dies; she has seen her own children suffer from the death of a friend. She has written this book out of compassion, love, and a genuine desire to help young people cope and heal. For ages 11 & up.

$9.95; 120 pp.; softcover; 5" x 7"

When Nothing Matters Anymore

A Survival Guide for Depressed Teens

by Bev Cobain, R.N.,C.

Written for teens with depression—and those who feel despondent, dejected, or alone—this powerful book offers help, hope, and potentially life-saving facts and advice. Includes true stories from teens who have dealt with depression, survival tips, resources, and more. For ages 13 & up.

$13.95; 176 pp.; softcover; illus.; 6" x 9"

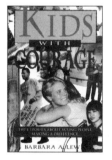

Kids with Courage

True Stories About Young People Making a Difference

by Barbara A. Lewis

Eighteen remarkable kids speak out, fight back, come to the rescue, and stand up for their beliefs, proving that anyone, at any age, can make a difference in the world. For ages 11 & up.

$11.95; 184 pp.; softcover; B&W photos; 6" x 9"

HIGHS!

Over 150 Ways to Feel Really, REALLY Good...Without Alcohol or Other Drugs

by Alex J. Packer, Ph.D.

This book describes safe, creative ways to find peace, pleasure, excitement, and insight. Because most teens are stressed out, the author starts with serenity highs: breathing and meditation. Then he describes highs related to sports and exercise, food, the senses, nature, creativity, family, friends, and more. For ages 13 & up.

$14.95; 264 pp.; softcover; 7¼" x 9¼"

Teen Angst? Naaah . . .

A Quasi-Autobiography

by Ned Vizzini

With humor, wit, and refreshing honesty, Ned leads the reader on a hilarious ride through his own '90s adolescence. This book is for anyone who wants to laugh out loud while enjoying a really good read. For ages 13 & up.

$12.95; 240 pp.; softcover; illus.; 6" x 8"

Gutsy Girls

Young Women Who Dare

by Tina Schwager, P.T.A., A.T.,C., and Michele Schuerger

In exciting, inspiring first-person stories, 25 intrepid young women tell of their daring feats—from extreme sports to ground-breaking, history-making achievements. They will motivate young readers (girls *and* boys) to strive for their personal best. For ages 11 & up.

$14.95; 272 pp.; softcover; B&W photos; 6" x 9"

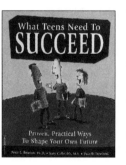

What Teens Need to Succeed

Proven, Practical Ways to Shape Your Own Future

by Peter L. Benson, Ph.D., Judy Galbraith, M.A., and Pamela Espeland

Based on a national survey, this book describes 40 developmental "assets" all teens need to succeed in life, then gives hundreds of suggestions teens can use to build assets at home, at school, in the community, in the congregation, with friends, and with youth organizations. For ages 11 & up.

$14.95; 368 pp.; softcover; illus.; 7¼" x 9¼"

Write Where You Are

How to Use Writing to Make Sense of Your Life

by Caryn Mirriam-Goldberg, Ph.D.

This insightful book helps teens articulate and understand their hopes and fears, lives and possibilities through writing. Not just another writing skills book, it invites teens to make sense of their lives through writing—and shows them how. Recommended for young writers, English teachers, and writing instructors. For ages 12 & up.

$14.95; 168 pp.; softcover; illus.; 7¼" x 9"

What Do You Really Want?
How to Set a Goal and Go for It!
A Guide for Teens
by Beverly K. Bachel
This upbeat and inspiring book is a step-by-step guide to goal setting, written especially for teens. Each chapter includes fun, creative exercises, practical tips, words of wisdom from famous "goal-getters," real-life examples from teens, and success stories. For ages 11 & up.
$12.95; 152 pp.; softcover; illus.; 6" x 9"

Taking Charge of My Mind & Body
A Girls' Guide to Outsmarting Alcohol, Drug, Smoking, and Eating Problems
by Gladys Folkers, M.A., and Jeanne Engelmann
First-person stories, current research, and clear advice empowers and encourages girls and young women to make responsible decisions about how to treat their minds and bodies. For ages 11–18.
$13.95; 208 pp.; softcover; illus.; 6" x 9"

Writing Down the Days
365 Creative Journaling Ideas for Young People
Revised & Updated
by Lorraine M. Dahlstrom, M.A.
This revised and updated edition of a Free Spirit classic includes a whole year's worth of fresh, inventive creative writing assignments, all linked to the calendar year. Also includes tips for teachers, a note to parents, extra encouragement for young writers, and a list of resources. For ages 12 & up.
$14.95; 176 pp.; softcover; illus.; 6" x 9"

Talk with Teens About Feelings, Family, Relationships, and the Future
50 Guided Discussions for School and Counseling Groups
by Jean Sunde Peterson, Ph.D.
Fifty guided discussions help students share their feelings and concerns, understand mood swings, anger, and sadness, make career choices, and much more. For grades 7–12.
$23.95; 216 pp.; softcover; 8½" x 11"

What Do You Stand For?
A Kid's Guide to Building Character
by Barbara A. Lewis
Young people need guidance from caring adults to build strong, positive character traits—but they can also build their own. This inspiring book invites them to explore and practice honesty, kindness, empathy, integrity, tolerance, patience, respect, and more. For ages 11 & up.
$19.95; 284 pp.; softcover; B&W photos and illus.; 8½" x 11"

Talk with Teens About Self and Stress
50 Guided Discussions for School and Counseling Groups
by Jean Sunde Peterson, Ph.D.
Fifty guided discussions help students share their feelings and concerns, gain self-awareness and self-esteem, make better decisions, anticipate and solve problems, cope with stress, and more. Includes 20 reproducible handout masters. For grades 7–12.
$21.95; 192 pp.; softcover; 8½" x 11"

To place an order or to request a free catalog of SELF–HELP FOR KIDS® and SELF–HELP FOR TEENS® materials, please write, call, email, or visit our Web site:

Free Spirit Publishing Inc.
217 Fifth Avenue North • Suite 200 • Minneapolis, MN 55401-1299
toll-free 800.735.7323 • local 612.338.2068 • fax 612.337.5050
help4kids@freespirit.com • www.freespirit.com

Visit us on the Web!
www.freespirit.com

Stop by anytime to find our Parents' Choice Approved catalog with fast, easy, secure 24-hour online ordering; "Ask Our Authors," where visitors ask questions—and authors give answers—on topics important to children, teens, parents, teachers, and others who care about kids; links to other Web sites we know and recommend; fun stuff for everyone, including quick tips and strategies from our books; and much more! Plus our site is completely searchable so you can find what you need in a hurry. Stop in and let us know what you think!

Just point and click!

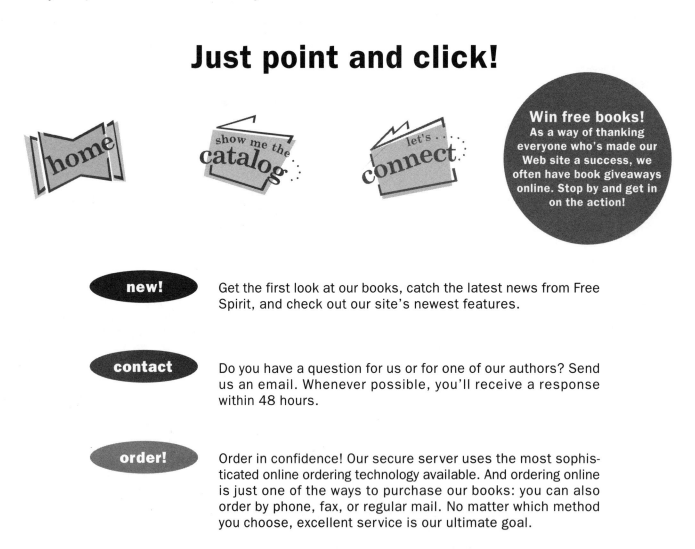

home

show me the
catalog

let's . . .
connect

Win free books!
As a way of thanking everyone who's made our Web site a success, we often have book giveaways online. Stop by and get in on the action!

new! Get the first look at our books, catch the latest news from Free Spirit, and check out our site's newest features.

contact Do you have a question for us or for one of our authors? Send us an email. Whenever possible, you'll receive a response within 48 hours.

order! Order in confidence! Our secure server uses the most sophisticated online ordering technology available. And ordering online is just one of the ways to purchase our books: you can also order by phone, fax, or regular mail. No matter which method you choose, excellent service is our ultimate goal.

1.800.735.7323 • fax 612.337.5050 • help4kids@freespirit.com